Advance Praise

"Vogts and Groshek offer fascinating insights into the polarized media ecosystem of rural America, an under-researched area that is meticulously addressed in this innovative book. It empirically provides an understanding of the way many rural Americans in Kansas distrustfully view media, and the impact of social networks on them, especially their beliefs in misinformation itself. The authors cleverly attempt to go beyond the standard discussion of misinformation, offering a more nuanced view with their origination of the "Misinformation Finds Them" concept. It is a must read for any citizen or scholar interested in better understanding the contemporary media environment of rural America."

—Ahmed al-Rawi
Associate Professor
Simon Fraser University

"A timely, unflinching investigation into how misinformation quietly radicalizes rural America. *Misinformation Finds Them* doesn't just expose echo chambers. It humanizes them. Vogts and Groshek's essential read challenges stereotypes, connects hybrid media, bonding social capital, news finds me perception, and other media theories to real lives, and urges us to rethink how truth, identity, and democracy intersect in USA's heartland."

—Homero Gil de Zúñiga
Distinguished Professor
University of Salamanca and Pennsylvania State University

Misinformation Finds Them

Mitchell S. McKinney and Karrin Vasby Anderson
General Editors

VOL. 54

Todd R. Vogts and Jacob Groshek

Misinformation Finds Them

Hybrid Media and Radicalization in Rural America

PETER LANG

New York · Berlin · Bruxelles · Chennai · Lausanne · Oxford

Bibliographic information published by the Deutsche Nationalbibliothek.
The German National Library lists this publication in the German National Bibliography; detailed bibliographic data is available on the Internet at http://dnb.d-nb.de.

Library of Congress Cataloging-in-Publication Data
LCCN: 2025047219.

Cover image: "Trump 2024" Roadside Sign (Source: Todd R. Vogts, Ph.D.)

An electronic version of this book is freely available, courtesy of libraries collaborating with Knowledge Unlatched (KU). KU is a pioneering initiative aimed at making high-quality books Open Access for the public benefit. The Open Access ISBN for this book is 9783034355919. For more details and access to the OA version, visit www.knowledgeunlatched.org.

ISSN 1525-9730
ISBN 978-3-0343-5590-2 (Print)
ISBN 978-3-0343-5591-9 (E-PDF)
ISBN 978-3-0343-5592-6 (E-Pub)
DOI 10.3726/b21945

Open Access: This work is licensed under a Creative Commons Attribution CC-BY 4.0 license. To view a copy of this license, visit https://creativecommons.org/licenses/by/4.0/

© 2026 Todd R. Vogts and Jacob Groshek

Published by Peter Lang Publishing Inc., New York, USA

info@peterlang.com

This publication has been peer reviewed.

www.peterlang.com

Table of Contents

List of Figures ix
List of Tables xi

Introduction   More Radical Than You Think 1

Chapter 1   Regarding Rural America 7
Chapter 2   Rounding up Rural Characters 23
Chapter 3   Constantly Consuming News 41
Chapter 4   Unearthing Rural Roots of Media Distrust 59
Chapter 5   Misinformation Taints Media Diets 69
Chapter 6   Religious Beliefs Plant Political Views 83
Chapter 7   Partisanship Cultivates Radical Political Engagement 95
Chapter 8   Pathways Forward When "Misinformation Finds Them" 109

Bibliography 125
Appendix 1   Sample Survey Questions 165
Appendix 2   Sample Interview Questions 183
Index 187

Figures

Figure 2.1.	"Vote Trump" roadside sign	24
Figure 2.2.	"Fuck Biden" flag	25
Figure 2.3.	"Take my hand not my life" anti-abortion billboard	26
Figure 3.1a.	Total of 1.93 million social media mentions of "Trump" by Kansans in 2024	45
Figure 3.1b.	Total of 798,000 social media mentions of "Biden" by Kansans in 2024	45
Figure 3.1c.	Total of 515,000 social media mentions of "Harris" by Kansans in 2024	46
Figure 3.2a.	Total social media mentions of "Fox News" or "Wall Street Journal" or "Breitbart" by Kansans in 2024	55
Figure 3.2b.	Total social media mentions of "BBC" or "NPR" or "CNN" by Kansans in 2024	55
Figure 5.1.	Total social media mentions of "misinformation" or "disinformation" or "fake news" by Kansans in 2024	74
Figure 6.1.	Total social media mentions of "faith" or "religion" or "Christian" by Kansans in 2024	86
Figure 7.1.	"Trump 2024" roadside sign	105
Figure 8.1.	"Ask For A Paper Ballot" roadside sign	116

Tables

Table 4.1. Survey Respondents' Top Four Most Reliable Cable News Outlets 66
Table 5.1. Total Social Media Mentions of "misinformation" or "disinformation" or "fake news" by Kansans in 2024 77

Introduction—More Radical Than You Think

This project began long before the 2024 campaign was underway, and, like most observers looking down the tracks, we had almost no idea what to expect and all that would unfold. What we did know was that simple explanations regarding misinformation and polarization were insufficient and the nature of discourse—even within the academy—was shifting under our feet and in the world around us. In our view, there seemed to be more advocacy than ever before, and an accompanying retreat into media theorizing that recalled the hypodermic needle model and other powerful media effects models that had largely been disproven but were potent shorthand ways to explain the behavior of citizens in the face of misinformation—especially in the case of conservatives voters in more rural areas.

Ironically enough, this same population was less studied and, as a result, more weighted in surveys but simultaneously positioned as a crucial block of actors adopting more "radical" views in an increasingly polarized and divided nation. Here it is important to note that we began this project with the understanding of "radicalization" as the process of expanding parameters on political discussion and viewpoints that are generally unmoored to, and independent of, political elites and journalists in an undoing of what Bennett (1990) famously described as the indexing hypothesis. Thus, while we do not consider radicalization normatively, we were challenged to ask ourselves how we could better understand these phenomena and just what polarization has to do with misinformation, hybrid media, and radicalization, particularly in rural America. This book doesn't answer all those questions, but we believe it shines light on assumptions and in the process hopefully diffuses the root of some debate, rather than pouring gasoline on a fire.

Again, in contemporary politics, the term "radical" simply refers to ideas, movements, or policies that seek significant, fundamental, and often structural change in society, rather than incremental reforms. The term can apply across the political spectrum, from left to right, depending on the context, and there has objectively been a wide range of radical politics in recent years. From the storming of the Capitol on January 6, 2021 to the widespread protests later that year seeking systemic racial justice and the downstream diversity, equity, and inclusion (DEI) initiatives to individuals who refused the COVID-19 vaccines in the face of government and employer mandates to drastic reshaping of laws surrounding reproductive and gender identity issues, America has been awash in radicalization.

Radicalism is not inherently negative or positive, indeed, it depends on perspective, historical context, and the outcomes it produces. Bötticher (2017) argued that concepts of radicalism and extremism within a political context "both refer to socio-political forces that exist at the edges of liberal-democratic societies" (p. 76), and, although they are distinct, they are similar in terms of willingness to use violence and aggressive confrontation to achieve political goals derived from strong moral beliefs. Carter (2018) conducted a study looking at numerous definitions for radicalism and extremism. The research determined the two concepts are closely aligned. Different tines of the same pitchfork, if you will. Consequently, Carter (2018) developed a minimal definition for extremism and radicalism: "an ideology that encompasses authoritarianism, anti-democracy and exclusionary and/or holistic nationalism" (p. 174). Likewise, Frounfelker et al. (2021) discussed the overlap and synonymous depiction of these terms by highlighting the Radicalism Intention Scale (RIS), which is a subscale of the Activism and Radicalism Intention Scales (ARIS) developed by Moskalenko and McCauley (2009). Schmid (2013) proposed the following definition of radicalization:

> an individual or collective (group) process whereby, usually in a situation of political polarisation, normal practices of dialogue, compromise and tolerance between political actors and groups with diverging interests are abandoned by one or both sides in a conflict dyad in favour of a growing commitment to engage in confrontational tactics of conflict-waging. These can include either (i) the use of (non-violent) pressure and coercion, (ii) various forms of political violence other than terrorism or (iii) acts of violent extremism in the form of terrorism and war crimes. The process is, on the side of rebel factions, generally accompanied by an ideological socialization away from mainstream or status quo-oriented positions towards more radical or extremist positions involving a dichotomous world view and the acceptance of an alternative focal point of political mobilization outside the dominant political order as the existing system is no longer recognized as appropriate or legitimate. (p. 18)

For the purposes of this book, we adopted this definition for the concept of being radical.

Based on such ideas, some radical movements have driven social progress such as the civil rights movement, while others have led to authoritarianism or political violence. While the outcome is not yet known, we can nonetheless drill down into instances of radical political behavior, its sources, and the ongoing social negotiation of democratic processes and norms. Doing so positions this research to look beyond what might typically be considered reactionary politics. According to Parker and Barreto (2013), reactionary politics attracts "people who fear change of any kind—especially if it threatens to undermine their way of life" (p. 6). Such movements drag political parties to extreme ideological positions (MacKay & LaRoche, 2018; Parker & Lavine, 2024). Through this extremism, radicalism emerges. As Capelos et al. (2021) argued, reactionism and radicalism "share disaffection with the present but their realities collide as they gaze in opposite directions: the reactionary orientation towards the restoration of an idealised past, and the radical orientation towards the establishment of a different, imagined future" (p. 186). Though President Donald Trump claims he wants to "make America great again" and thus implying a reactionary perspective (Parker & Lavine, 2024), the adoption of legal viewpoints amenable to the likes of the unitary executive theory and torture as an interrogation method paint a much more radical picture (Hajjar, 2020). President Trump and members of this administration of have done this and violence has been committed in Trump's name, which is why we adopted the aforementioned definition of "radical" for this book and our characterizations of what is happening in the United States political system.

An illustrative example of a politically radical perspective is evident in a social media post made by a tenured professor from a leading state university, whose name was omitted intentionally in the spirit of the "right to be forgotten" (e.g., Auxier, 2020; European Commission, 2018), to an audience of over 1,400 followers after the 2024 presidential election was called:

I am gutted. After Kamala Harris took an early lead in North Carolina, I thought she was going to win big. She ended up losing all seven swing states. I have read some of the election analyses about what Democrats did wrong and how the Trump campaign was savvy enough to try to appeal to the Gen Z male. I think this election is an indictment of the American voters. There are simply not enough of them willing to vote for a Black female for president.

This statement creates disinformation. It challenges the legitimacy of the electoral outcome by attributing the loss to systemic biases among the electorate, suggesting that deep-seated racism and sexism influenced the results. Such a perspective calls for a fundamental reassessment of societal attitudes and structures, aligning with radical critiques that seek profound change.

Following the social media post shared above, conventional wisdom now suggests that a significant driver of radical beliefs and actions in the modern era is misinformation and disinformation spread through social media. In a simple, linear manner, it is presumed that online platforms amplify extreme viewpoints by creating echo chambers where users are exposed primarily to information that aligns with their existing beliefs. Algorithms prioritize sensational content, often promoting conspiracy theories and falsehoods that fuel political outrage. Additionally, online celebrity status augments the impact of biased and polarizing posts (R. Lewis, 2020).

In response to radical perspectives within academia, legislative measures have been proposed to regulate the expression of certain viewpoints. For instance, Kansas House Bill 2105 (HB 2105) prohibits postsecondary educational institutions from requiring diversity, equity, and inclusion (DEI) statements from applicants for admission or employment. The bill also restricts mandatory DEI training and the consideration of DEI criteria in hiring and admissions decisions. However, it explicitly protects academic freedom, allowing faculty to engage in scholarly activities related to DEI topics without restriction.

The enactment of HB 2105 reflects a tension between radical academic perspectives that advocate for significant societal change and legislative efforts to maintain certain educational standards or prevent perceived ideological imposition. This dynamic illustrates the complex interplay between radicalism in public discourse and the regulatory frameworks that seek to balance free expression with institutional neutrality. As both authors' home institutions are based in Kansas, we have witnessed firsthand the uneven implementation of HB 2105 to impose vastly divergent ideologies without debate or transparency.

Radical perspectives often challenge prevailing societal norms and advocate for substantial change. At the same time, social media-fueled misinformation has arguably contributed to real-world radical actions, as seen in events like the January 6 attack on the U.S. Capitol. Legislative responses, such as Kansas HB 2105, highlight the ongoing debate over the role of radical perspectives in public institutions and the extent to which they should influence policies and practices. In an era where digital platforms shape political discourse, the intersection of radicalism, misinformation, and governance remains a pressing issue, and to address it, we posit the Misinformation Finds Them (MFT) perception.

MFT sprouts out of the News-Finds-Me (NFM) perception (Gil de Zúñiga et al., 2017), a phenomenon where individuals believe they do not need to actively seek news because they assume that important information will reach them through their social circles or digital feeds. The MFT perception suggests that rural residents are not only exposed to misinformation simply by participating in their usual media and social ecosystems but—more importantly—that they consider the threat of misinformation real while having a greater impact on others, but not necessarily themselves. Here, because their primary news sources tend to be partisan and because their social circles often reinforce rather than challenge these sources, misinformation is absorbed and internalized with little scrutiny. The problem is compounded by the very nature of social capital and media use—particularly bonding social capital and the third-person effect—which strengthens trust within homogenous groups while fostering skepticism toward outside perspectives, and overestimating the impact of media on others unlike the homogenous group (Arachchi & Managi, 2021; Heath & Lowrey, 2021; Putnam, 2001).

Therefore, this book presents an opportunity to better understand those processes as they exist in rural, red-state America without condescension and without judgment. In the wake of the 2024 election, holding and sharing radical views is now mainstream. To harness that energy in the furtherance of bringing the nation together through better understanding would be truly radical.

CHAPTER 1

Regarding Rural America

Shots rang out. People in the crowd screamed. Former President Donald J. Trump clutched at his right ear as he ducked behind the lectern. Secret Service agents rushed onto the stage to shield his body with their own. As the agents ushered him off stage, former President Trump pushed through his protectors and raised a fist in defiance as blood ran down his face, creating an iconic image of the assassination attempt that took place on July 13, 2024, at a political rally in Butler, Pennsylvania (National Press Office, 2024).

The FBI identified the shooter as 20-year-old Thomas Matthew Crooks of Bethel Park, Pennsylvania (Borter et al., 2024), who was a registered Republican and used a legally purchased AR-style-5.56 caliber rifle (Reid et al., 2024). Members of the Secret Service shot and killed Crooks almost immediately after he fired several shots. Though he missed his intended target, others were struck. Corey Comperatore, a 50-year-old Pennsylvania native and volunteer firefighter, died protecting his family during the mele. He dove onto them to shield them from the bullets. Two others were injured—57-year-old David Dutch and 74-year-old James Copenhaver.

As is human nature, the incident inspired a variety of chatter about who was involved, why it happened, and what it all meant. Before the dust had even settled in Pennsylvania, misinformation about the assassination attempt began to flood the internet, especially on social media. Without backing their claims with facts, some suggested the Chinese government or Antifa orchestrated the attempt on President Trump's life (Jingnan et al., 2024). Others argued it was a false flag operation directed by President Trump himself (Klepper & Swenson, 2024). Others still accused President Joe Biden of ordering the attack. According to reporting by CBS News, Rep. Mike Collins (R-GA) was one such person. On his personal X account, the platform formerly known as Twitter, he posted: "Joe Biden sent the orders" (Ingram & Bladt, 2024, para. 7). Not to be left out, conspiracy theorist Alex Jones sent an email blast to push claims that the shooting was a "deep state" assassination attempt (Dickey, 2024). Such talking points persisted in the news cycle even as President Trump announced 39-year-old U.S. Sen. J. D. Vance from Ohio as his running mate on July 15; President Biden dropped out of the race on July 21, 2024, and endorsed Vice President Kamala Harris for president; and on August 6 Vice President Harris selected 60-year-old Minnesota Gov. Tim Walz as her running mate (Miller et al., 2024; Watson, 2024; Yilek et al., 2024).

Regardless of what else was in the news, the fact that President Trump survived by mere centimeters delivered a powerful message to his followers—he was chosen by God to win the U.S. Presidency in 2024. Newsmax anchors Bianca de la Garza and Larry Elder expressed their beliefs that President Trump "survived due to divine intervention," and during a July 15, 2024, broadcast on Fox News, host Kayleigh McEnany said, "It's a miracle. Providence comes to mind, you know. He clearly had Christ protecting him in that moment" (as cited in Olmsted, 2024, para. 7–8). According to reporting by Politico, pastors at megachurches told their congregants that President Trump was saved because of his stance on Israel (Fertig & Rivard, 2024). Countless politicians, religious figures, and online influencers joined this chorus. Some suggested President Trump "wears the Armor of God" and that God is using President Trump for His purposes, meaning he was protected from his would-be assassin thanks to "the grace of God" and the "protective hand" of "divine intervention" (Gilbert, 2024; Hobbs, 2024; Joseph, 2024; Ramirez & McCarthy, 2024). It fueled the belief among his supporters that President Trump "is a messiah figure, anointed by God to save a troubled nation" (Harwell et al., 2024, para. 1).

President Trump adopted these views. He tapped into ideas of Christian Nationalism. According to Amanda Tyler, executive director of the Baptist Joint Committee for Religious Liberty, during an interview with NPR, Christian Nationalism is "an ideology and a movement that tries to merge American and Christian identities, and 'relies heavily on this mythological telling of American history and American present as being a, quote-unquote Christian nation, as being a country that has been singled out by God for God's special providence and God's special design in the world'" (DeRose, 2024, para. 20). It comes as no surprise, then, that at his first political rally following the assassination attempt, President Trump said he "took a bullet for Democracy" (Leary, 2024). Despite this, he also inspired historic anti-democratic actions just a few years earlier.

Discourse and Democracy: Fomenting an Insurrection

On Jan. 6, 2021, protesters gathered outside the United States Capitol to dispute the results of the 2020 election. They hoped to disrupt and prevent the certification of the results to prevent the transfer of power from former President Trump to President Joe Biden so President Trump would remain in office. After all, from their view, the election had been stolen (Whitehurst, 2022).

Armed with bear spray, police batons, baseball bats, guns, and more (Dreisbach & Mak, 2021), an estimated 10,000 people were in attendance. Waves of energy ripple through the assembled masses before the crowd surged forward and crashed into "The People's House." Windows shattered. The protest evolved into a riot as individuals crawled through the openings, resulting in 2,000 individuals breaching the halls of democracy (Rubin et al., 2022). Capitol Police officers attempted to quell the insurrection. One officer fired a gun. The bullet struck and killed 35-year-old Air Force veteran Ashli Babbitt who presumably traveled from Southern California to hear President Trump speak (Healy, 2021), and another protester was trampled to death. Within 36 hours, five people died and more than 200 people were injured.

The events of Jan. 6, 2021, marked a dark moment in U.S. history. The date is now infamous, along with the likes of Sept. 11, 2001, and Dec. 7, 1941. However, foreign actors or terrorists did not perpetrate this attack on America. It came from within as a mob of President Trump's supporters transformed into a powder keg. The reality-television-star-turned-politician then ignited the simmering unrest during a noon speech at the White House on Jan. 6, 2021, when he said to his followers, "We will never give up. We will never concede [...] We're going to the Capitol. We're going to try and give them [Republicans] the kind of pride and boldness that they need to take back our country" (Lonsdorf et al., 2022).

Though the spark that led to the eruption of violence occurred that day, political rhetoric promulgated by elected officials and news outlets stacked a layer of polarizing and divisive kindling. Years of election fraud lies spewed by President Trump fanned the flames. At the foundational level, though, inaccurate, and untrustworthy information created the layer of tinder where embers of radicalism smoldered.

Misinformation started the fire.

Misinformation and the Media: Fostering Polarization

Misinformation isn't new, of course. It has existed since people learned to communicate. People lie. Like it or not, it's human nature. Faulty information springs up for a variety of reasons. One might lie to protect someone else's feelings or save themselves from consequences of their actions in an attempt at self-preservation. Perhaps people want to make sense of the world, so they concoct explanations to put themselves at ease. Such is the essence of conspiracy theories. Maybe the objective is humor or to spotlight the absurdity of people's actions. In such an instance, it becomes satire. Sometimes it is an intentional creation of false information devised to gain a political or other type of advantage over another person or group of people. Then it's referred to as disinformation (White, 2022). In other cases, people share incorrect information without realizing it is wrong. This is the technical definition of misinformation, which serves as a larger umbrella term for inaccurate and faulty information (White, 2022). Regardless of the reason behind it, fretting over the fact it exists distracts from the real concerns of where it pops up, how it spreads, how it impacts society, and what can be done to combat it.

To begin exploring such ideas, it's important to consider how people learn about the world and become socialized as they consume information and develop beliefs and attitudes that construct their ideologies. Communication is the culprit, specifically the media. In the past, people chose from a limited number of options. Now, they can belly up to a variable smorgasbord of media options thanks to technology and the internet, such as via social media (Gaultney et al., 2022). Combine these newer options with the traditional mediums of print, radio, and television, and the resulting hybrid media systems creates fertile ground for democracy-endangering polarization and division to grow (e.g., Darr et al., 2018, 2021; Padgett et al., 2019).

That is how the insurrection of the U.S. Capitol occurred. The media reported the inflammatory rhetoric and misinformation originating from politicians. Such coverage served as a siren call that spurred people to action. After all, the media wields powerful influence, especially when it comes to cultivating particular political ideologies. For example, the reporting of such ideas by the media is how assassination attempt conspiracy theories and views that President Trump is ordained by God entered the mainstream consciousness.

Media consumption has been shown to impact political activity and belief (Johnson & Kaye, 2013). This proves to be especially true thanks to the wide range of media options available. Individuals engage with a variety of media daily, including news (Pipal et al., 2022) and entertainment (Sienkiewicz & Marx, 2022). This allows individuals to consume only information that aligns with their previously held beliefs and opinions, which creates an echo chamber or filter bubble (Nechushtai & Lewis, 2019; Torres-Lugo et al., 2020). Conventional wisdom suggests this type of consumption contributes to polarization and the entrenchment of political views (Iyengar et al., 2019), and party-aligned sources exist, such as Fox News for Republicans or MSNBC for Democrats (Druckman et al., 2019).

Partisan media provide fertile ground for misinformation to spread, fueling polarization and incivility. Social media make it even easier for this false and unreliable information to reach the masses (Gaultney et al., 2022), but misinformation travels via all media channels. One goal of this communication is to achieve political goals or promote commercial interests through false or misleading statements designed to be believed by audiences and disseminators alike (de Ridder, 2021). Another goal is to evoke an emotional and visceral response (Han & Federico, 2018), and both liberal and conservative media do this. One side just does it better.

Research shows conservative media create more emotional responses by leveraging outrage (Sobieraj & Berry, 2011). Conservatives "have their own cable news network and their own TV personalities. They can turn to nearly any station on the AM dial to hear their views confirmed" (Frank, 2004, p. 142). A prime example of this is conservative talk radio. Names like Sean Hannity and Rush Limbaugh may come to mind when thinking about right-wing radio. However, the history of conservative media goes back further (Hemmer, 2016). These roots burrow into the heart of rural America, growing out of plains of the Midwest. For example, in the 1920s and 1930s, Kansas "was home to a quack doctor of national celebrity, Dr. John Brinkley of Milford, who claimed to cure impotence by surgically transplanting bits of goat testicle to humans. Brinkley was also a pioneer in radio, obtaining a license in 1923 for a clear-channel station on which he broadcast word of his miraculous cure across the entire country" (Frank, 2004, p. 196). In 1929, Americans voted Brinkley's station as the most popular in the country.

The prevalence of misinformation and partisan media outlets fertilizes a distrust of news and journalism. "Fake news" became the rallying cry of then-candidate Donald Trump in the run-up to the 2016 election, and this rhetoric served the goal of casting doubt on media coverage that Trump believed to be unfavorable to him or incompatible with his ideas and opinions. His supporters bought into this line of thinking, perhaps because conservatives felt the American dream was slipping from their grasps due to the collapse of institutions such as marriage and the church (Carney, 2019). The reason people accept and share misinformation and "fake news" is the subject of many academic research projects and books (e.g., Brummette et al., 2018; Finneman & Thomas, 2018; Greifeneder et al., 2021; Vu & Saldaña, 2021). This is for good reason. Misinformation breeds polarization, and polarization damages democracy.

At a time when as many as two-thirds of Americans can't name all three branches of government (Annenberg Public Policy Center, 2019, 2021, 2023, 2024), it isn't hard to imagine the polarization and misinformation causing the complete collapse of democracy. It's already hanging on by a thread. After all, nearly 20% of Americans surveyed believed a 5–4 decision by the Supreme Court of the United States is either sent to Congress or back to the federal court of appeals for a decision (Annenberg Public Policy Center, 2020, 2023, 2024), one in 20 American adults can name all five First Amendment freedoms (Annenberg Public Policy Center, 2023, 2024), and three-quarters of the American population don't trust the federal government (Pew Research Center, 2021a).

Clearly, polarization divides the country (Darr et al., 2018, 2021; Padgett et al., 2019). It's why, as of January 2024, more than 1,200 people had been charged in the insurrection at the Capitol. The perpetrators believed President Trump's conspiratorial and baseless assertions that 2020 elections were stolen. This is a falsehood that became known as the "big lie" and harkens back to Adolf Hitler and Nazi Germany (Block, 2021). Yet, despite clear evidence that the election was not stolen or rife with fraud, those charged in the insurrection represent every U.S. state (NPR Staff, 2021).

Of course, certain parts of the country were represented more than others. Using region designations from the U.S. Census Bureau (2010a), the numbers show that more than 530 people from the South were charged in the insurrection. Florida checked in with the most, having more than 120 insurrectionists. Texas came in second with more than 95.

The region with the second-most insurrectionists was the Midwest. More than 250 people from this area participated in the riots at the Capitol. The majority came from Ohio, which had more than 65 individuals charged. Illinois followed with more than 40.

As for the remaining regions of the country, more than 240 people came from the Northeast, and nearly 200 came from the West, including 41-year-old Aaron James Mileur from Alaska and 34-year-old Nicholas Ochs from Hawaii. Each of these individuals were the lone representatives for their states. Considering they win the prize for greatest distances traveled, their belief in the "big lie" and President Trump should be evident.

Also, in the case of Ochs, his devotion to his ideology is permanently inscribed on his flesh. According to reports, a tattoo on his right forearm reads "Proud Boy." He was one of more than 170 people who were charged in the insurrection and had ties to far-right extremist groups such as The Proud Boys or the Oath Keepers. Additionally, Ochs was a retired Marine. More than 190 others charged for crimes occurring during the insurrection also had military or law enforcement ties.

It would be nice to suggest these individuals are outliers. However, Republicans remained aligned with the sentiment of Trump's claims. Polls showed that nearly 70% of Republicans didn't believe President Joe Biden was legitimately elected

(Greenberg, 2022). Conservatives in general seemed to agree with this line of thinking.

Red and Rural: Aligning Political Beliefs and Media Consumption

Conservatives live in all parts of the country, but two regions of the United States are dominated by this political alignment. According to election statistics, the South and the Midwest are reliably red in terms of electoral politics as Republican presidential candidates regularly win these areas (Woolley & Peters, n.d.). With such political ideologies, it makes sense that those charged in the insurrection at the Capitol predominately came from these areas.

It's also worth noting that these two regions have the largest rural populations in the county. On average, the 31.47% of Southerners and 29.74% of Midwesterners live in rural communities, while 27.03% of the entire U.S. population are considered rural (U.S. Census Bureau, 2023). These rural Americans largely live and work in agrarian communities and exist as an important voting block within democratic politics as was evident in the 2016 election of President Donald Trump and the controversy surrounding the outcome of the 2020 election.

Research by Johnson and Scala (2020) showed that rural voters demonstrated social and political views different from urban voters, providing Republican candidates with a strong foothold in these areas. However, difference between beliefs of rural and urban Republicans are minimal, and the same is true for rural and urban Democrats (Lin & Lunz Trujillo, 2024). Such findings speak to the idea of place. This concept contributes to social identity formation (Jacobs & Munis, 2023; Lyons & Utych, 2023; Scala et al., 2015). One's social identity, then, serves as a foundation for political beliefs. Through experimental validation, Hershewe and Smith (2025) showed that rural identity reinforces Republican alignment, but Democrats tend to shy away from their rural identity when they are prompted to think about partisan issues.

One contributing factor in this is place resentment. Such a phenomenon focuses on how people react when they feel they are being overlooked (Cramer, 2016; Lunz Trujillo & Crowley, 2022). According to Munis (2022), place resentment develops when a group of people believe "their status in society as members of a symbolic geographical community has been unjustly and deliberately diminished by those wielding the levers of power" (p. 1060). The result is an "us versus them" tribalism (Brown et al., 2021; Mettler & Brown, 2022), which leads to more polarization and division (e.g., Lin & Lunz Trujillo, 2023). It can be argued, then, that the rural identifier is useful when investigating subjects related to politics. Lunz Trujillo (2024) found "that people identify as rural are similar psychologically and politically, regardless of their current location" (p. 2236), which is why a voter being from a rural or urban area continues to be a significant data point (Scala & Johnson, 2017). In fact, identifying as rural proves to be particularly important in terms of political proclivities because "rural issue attitudes tend to be partisan attitudes" (Lin & Lunz Trujillo, 2024, p. 676). Yet despite its demonstrated importance to electoral outcomes, current research largely ignores this swath of the United States population.

In addition to feeling overlooked (Currid-Halkett, 2023), individuals living in rural parts of the country also experience a lack of local news. According to the U.S. Census Bureau (2023), there are 3,140 counties in the United States. Of these, 204 counties have no local news outlets, such as newspapers, digital news sites, or public broadcasting, and 1,559 have only one local news outlet (Abernathy, 2023). These are news deserts. They lack access to local and reliable news and information. The Midwest and South regions are home to the majority of them. In fact, only a combined 54 counties don't have a news outlet in the Northeast and West regions, and only a combined 240 counties have one news outlet in those same areas. This means rural Americans face a drought of local news.

National outlets fill this void. Serving a steady diet of politically partisan content lacking nutrients that serve the public good, these media companies sow democracy-damaging polarization. This polarization takes root due to the erosion of reliable information brought on by confirmation bias that constructs filter bubbles and echo chambers (Flaxman et al., 2016; Lee et al., 2021; Nechushtai & Lewis, 2019; Pearson & Knobloch-Westerwick, 2019). Through this, misinformation flourishes, infecting the media ecosystem.

Therefore, it's no wonder that Americans don't trust the media, especially if the news doesn't align with their political, religious, or other closely held beliefs. Of course, trust also can erode if individuals feel a given institution or organization has failed them in some way (S. Lewis, 2020) or if they don't feel like they exist as part of the in-crowd (Usher, 2019). As Wuthnow (2019) suggested, those who feel left behind develop more antipathy and seek alternatives to the establishment. Seemingly, such sentiments align with political beliefs, especially when it comes to trust in news.

Gottfried (2021) highlighted that even though 83% of United States adults trust political news to some extent when it is coming from mainstream sources, only 24% of Republicans have "a great deal" of trust compared to 53% of Democrats. Such data paints a concerning portrait of the state of journalism, and it gets worse when considering the media more broadly than only political news. According to research, more than 50% of Americans have little to no confidence in the news media nor confidence in the public-interest motives of journalists, and this lack of news trust becomes more pronounced when divided along political lines as 60% of Republicans believe the media intends to mislead the public, which causes inaccuracies in news reports (Gottfried et al., 2020).

Understanding news trust and the media ecosystem is crucial for democracy. After all, democracy functions within the public sphere, which is the area of social life where public opinion is formed (Habermas et al., 1974). It is within this space where members of society discuss important matters of public concern (Habermas, 1991). These discussions highlight how democracy functions (Habermas, 1994). Of course, Fraser (1990) rightly points out that a more nuanced conceptualization of the public sphere within an existing democratic society compared to that of Habermas is needed by being more inclusive and acknowledging "a multiplicity of publics is preferable to a single public sphere" (p. 77), which is particularly important in the contemporary media environment. After all, the media facilitate communicative acts of dialogic exchange through information dissemination (Habermas, 1994; Fraser, 1990) and by determining what news is reported in what ways (Kent & Davis, 2006; McCombs & Shaw, 1972; Shoemaker et al., 2009; Whitney & Becker, 1982). When people are informed and able to talk with each other, social capital can be built (Siisiainen, 2003). Putnam (2001) referred to social capital as a web of mutual trust and cooperation among members of a community or society. Gastil and Keith (2005) built upon this to suggest the term concerned democracy-sustaining social networks.

A byproduct of social capital development is increased civic engagement. This idea can be understood as demonstrating a conscious awareness of and knowledge about political news and actions taking place both locally and nationally within an understanding of the civic process (Bobkowski & Miller, 2016). Community media feed into this by ensuring people receive the information they need (Bressers et al., 2015; Carey, 2020). Being civically engaged goes beyond voting or adopting a mindset of volunteerism (Gibson, 2006). It requires actions that "citizens take in order to pursue common concerns and address problems in the communities they belong to" (Skoric et al., 2016, p. 1822).

When social capital and civic engagement are high, democracy thrives, but the opposite is equally true. Regardless of the positive or negative nature, journalistic products serve as the field in which democratic seeds germinate or remain dormant. This is due to the intrinsic linkage between journalism and democracy forged through the rights of a free press explicitly defined in the First Amendment of the United States Constitution. The entire process can be knocked off course, though, if mis- and disinformation seeps into news coverage or flood other media spaces, endangering democracy (Morgan, 2018). Community media are particularly well-suited to counter such falsehoods to ensure development of social capital and civic engagement (Bressers et al., 2015; Leupold et al., 2018; Muscat, 2018; Thompson, 2021), but individuals are exposed to far more information than that which comes from the local press. Eventually, people get frustrated and seek ways to make sense of all the information flying around them. If a politician that citizens agree with suggests a given news outlet is or is not reliable, they may use that recommendation to shape their own behaviors.

The outcome of this hybrid media process often leaves red-state Americans being labeled as rural and "radical"—which drives a wedge in American democracy.

Woke and Indoctrinated? Political Influence in Higher Education

Less than one week before the November election, a tenured professor of journalism at a taxpayer-funded university, whose name was omitted intentionally in the spirit of the "right to be forgotten" (e.g., Auxier, 2020; European Commission, 2018), publicly posted the following statement to an audience of over 1,400 followers on social media: "Just a reminder that if you vote for Trump you vote for a rapist. And convicted felon."

This factually unproven statement to persuade eligible voters was made by someone who is not only on the state payroll but also training future journalism and media professionals in concepts such as objectivity and fairness raises critical important questions about the boundaries of academic freedom, the responsibilities of educators, and the evolving role of higher education in a deeply polarized society. The post, which included a link to a *Business Insider* article detailing former President Donald Trump's legal issues, such as the jury's finding of sexual abuse in the E. Jean Carroll case (Business Insider, 2023), is more than a personal political expression. For critics, it symbolizes a troubling shift in higher education, one where ideological advocacy increasingly appears to eclipse the university's mission of fostering intellectual exploration.

While defenders of such statements may argue that professors have a right to voice their opinions under the principles of academic freedom, which has clearly come under attack since Trump took office in 2025, others contend that the highly charged nature of these comments risks alienating students, undermining the intellectual rigor of academic discourse, and reducing trust in educational institutions. When faculty members use their positions to promote overtly partisan views, it is worth considering how this affects their role as educators and the environments they are tasked with creating. This singular example reflects a much larger debate about the influence of political ideologies in academia and whether the modern university is fulfilling its role as a space for balanced and critical thought.

University professors hold considerable influence both within and beyond the classroom. Their authority extends beyond the syllabus, as they shape students' intellectual development, expose them to new ideas, and often act as role models for academic and ethical engagement. This influence grows exponentially when professors leverage social media platforms, professional networks, or public commentary to voice their opinions. For students, especially those navigating formative stages of their intellectual and social identities, these public pronouncements can have significant impacts.

However, when professors publicly share overtly partisan or polarizing political opinions, such as equating support for a political candidate with moral failure, they risk creating an academic environment where dissenting perspectives feel unwelcome. This phenomenon is not hypothetical. Numerous studies document the ideological leanings of faculty in American higher education. Gross and Simmons (2014) found that only about 10% of professors identified as conservative, and disciplines such as sociology and literature often exhibit even greater ideological imbalance. A study by the *National Association of Scholars* reported a striking 12-to-1 ratio of liberal to conservative faculty in certain fields (Langbert, 2018). While political diversity in academia is not inherently necessary for intellectual rigor, the lack of it raises concerns about whether students are being exposed to a sufficiently wide range of perspectives.

For conservative students, this environment can feel stifling. Research by Abramowitz and Webster (2016) highlights the growing polarization of American society, where political identity often serves as a proxy for deeper cultural divides. Conservative students frequently report feelings of isolation, self-censorship, or even fear of academic retribution if they express dissenting views. This phenomenon, often referred to as the "chilling effect," erodes the foundational principles of open inquiry and critical debate that universities are meant to uphold.

The concerns surrounding ideological imbalance in academia are not new, but they have become more acute in recent years as higher education increasingly mirrors the broader polarization of American society. Universities, traditionally seen as bastions of progressive thought, are often viewed by critics as breeding grounds for ideological indoctrination. This perception has gained traction amid high-profile incidents where professors have publicly ridiculed or dismissed conservative viewpoints. These incidents fuel the narrative that universities prioritize activism over education and advocacy over intellectual exploration.

Examples of this dynamic abound. In 2020, a professor at a prominent university was widely criticized for mocking a conservative student group's event on social media, characterizing their beliefs as "antithetical to human progress." Such public denouncements do not occur in a vacuum. Conservative students often report that these incidents make them reluctant to engage in classroom discussions or challenge prevailing narratives. A 2020 survey conducted by Brooks et al. found that over half of conservative students on liberal-majority campuses admitted to self-censoring their political views to avoid social or academic backlash. The result is a narrowing of intellectual diversity and a diminished capacity for critical engagement with opposing ideas.

On the other side of the political spectrum, advocates for more politically engaged faculty argue that academia has an obligation to address pressing societal issues, precisely *because* of the expertise demonstrated by their scholarship that may have demonstrable real-world applications. Climate change, systemic racism, gender inequality, and other topics often intersect with political ideologies, making it difficult to entirely separate scholarly inquiry from political engagement. Professors who advocate for specific causes might view their activism as a necessary extension of their scholarship and a requisite justification for abandoning objectivity or tolerance of diverse viewpoints both inside and outside of their classrooms. However, this approach risks activism that can, at minimum, give the appearance of indoctrination while at the same time failing to protect the intellectual autonomy and academic freedom of students and colleagues by creating a spiral of silence (Noelle-Neumann, 1974) whereby individuals that feel their opinions are in the minority do not speak up for fear of reprisal.

Academic freedom is one of the cornerstones of higher education, protecting educators' rights to research, teach, and express ideas without interference. It allows faculty members to challenge societal norms, explore controversial topics, and advance critical thinking. However, with this freedom comes an equally significant responsibility: the obligation to foster environments where diverse perspectives are valued, and intellectual rigor is maintained.

Fish (1994) famously argued that there is no such thing as completely free speech, especially in academia, where the context and responsibilities of communication matter. Professors occupy a unique space where their words carry weight not just as individuals but as representatives of their institutions. When faculty members publicly espouse polarizing opinions, particularly in spaces that may be visible to their current or former students, they risk compromising the perception of neutrality essential to their roles as educators. Neutrality does not mean avoiding controversy, but it does require creating an intellectual space where students feel free to explore ideas without fear of reprisal or judgment.

To position this tension further into the framework of the Misinformation Finds Them perspective, another tenured professor of communication at a taxpayer-funded university (also with their name omitted) shared this statement to an audience of more than 2,300 followers several months *after* Trump was in office:

"Listening to guys at the auto repair shop debate politics and media effects, while I sit here as a tenured media effects scholar at one of the top programs in the world, and have published papers in this area, while saying nothing, sure is entertaining." When encouraged in the comments, the professor continued, "It also underscored that people who get their news from FOX have their worldviews warped and receive tons of false information or news that is distorted. Also, when confronted with accurate information that counters their narrative, they just dismiss it out of hand. They cannot be dissuaded and it's really hard to do because they have some information completely correct, so they cannot believe the parts that are inaccurate."

In short, this award-winning scholar whose expertise includes media portrayals of African Americans as well as a range of diverse social impacts, encapsulates not only an ideological worldview that could either alienate or galvanize students and colleagues, but also demonstrates the perceived risk of MFT that even as a world-leading expert is not equipped to challenge among the public community.

At minimum, this helps to demonstrate that the balance between academic freedom and responsibility is not easily achieved. As Furedi (2004) points out, the purpose of academia is not to indoctrinate but to cultivate independent thinkers capable of engaging with complex, competing ideas. When professors allow their personal political beliefs to dominate their public and professional personas, they risk undermining this mission. The challenge, then, lies in ensuring that academic freedom remains a tool for inquiry rather than advocacy. The consequences of ideological polarization in higher education extend beyond the confines of the classroom. Universities play a critical role in shaping civic engagement, fostering social capital, and preparing students to participate in democratic processes. When students feel excluded or alienated due to their political beliefs, their ability to engage meaningfully in these processes diminishes. Furthermore, the public's perception of universities as partisan institutions contributes to a broader erosion of trust in higher education, and this can be weaponized by political opponents.

A 2019 report by Pew Research Center found that trust in higher education has declined significantly among Republicans, with 59% believing that colleges negatively impact the country. This skepticism is often fueled by high-profile examples of perceived bias, such as the professors' statements quoted previously and numerous anecdotes of ideological clashes on college campuses that feed political narratives highlighted by Vivian (2023). For many, such incidents reinforce the belief that universities have abandoned their role as neutral spaces for learning and inquiry and instead are becoming arenas for political advocacy. This erosion of trust has far-reaching implications, particularly as the professor quoted here is charged with training future media professionals concepts that include fairness, balance, and objectivity. Higher education has historically served as a cornerstone of democratic society, providing a space for individuals to encounter new ideas, challenge their assumptions, and develop the skills necessary for informed citizenship. When universities lose their credibility as impartial institutions, their ability to fulfill this role is compromised and there are wide-ranging downstream effects for trust in media organizations.

The professor's statement at the heart of this discussion exemplifies a larger debate about the role of political expression in higher education as it relates to disinformation in this election because the statement that Trump is a rapist has never been proven, insofar as he has never been convicted of rape, and as such is disinformation itself. While faculty members have the right to voice their opinions, the manner and context in which these opinions are shared carry significant implications for the perceived neutrality and integrity of academic institutions—particularly if those statements are not factually true.

Beliefs and Democracy: Investigating Misinformation

Farmers and ranchers throughout rural America spend countless hours in farm trucks, tractors, and other implements of the farming trade. Whether driving through pastures to check cattle or through fields to plant and harvest crops, these individuals need to pass the time. One way to do so is to listen to music or the radio, and in the rural parts of the country, conservative talk radio is readily available to fill that entertainment void. All it takes is a twist of the dial. Because of this, partisan misinformation spreads. The farmers and ranchers talk about what they heard at the CO-OP and share their ideas via social media. When they receive affirmation, it emboldens them and deepens polarization, and then the process repeats with great amplification and fervor.

The implications of this are obvious. Misinformation has permeated the hybrid media ecosystem and polarized American politics, which has already begun to chip away at the foundations of democracy by preventing fair and informed debate. The result thus far has led to an erosion of truth in reporting that divides, rather than unifies, the citizenry. This is most evident in rural America where access to reliable news is spotty at best. For the sake of democracy, the flow of misinformation must be stopped to fix society's division and polarization.

But how?

The first step in answering that question is to understand how misinformation seeps into communities and explain why people believe and propagate it. This is particularly pertinent in rural America, which has become sharply divided from its coastal and urban areas. The most effective way to understand why people believe and spread misinformation is simple. We just need to ask them.

By interviewing rural Americans to understand their lived experiences and perspectives, this book makes sense of polarized American politics by exploring the pathways to news these individuals travel, their trust of the media, and their views of and interactions with misinformation. Combined with survey responses and millions of social media data points, a broader and more nuanced picture of how rural and urban Americans use and are impacted by the hybrid media ecosystem they exist within comes into focus.

By unpacking these complex questions through an exploration of attitudes and beliefs prevalent in the red-state heartland of rural America, it becomes clear that partisan and biased media outlets fuel a growing distrust of media and political systems. Investigating a microcosm of rural American reveals the insidiousness of the problem and highlights individuals' thirst for reliable news. To that end, this investigation zeros in on rural Kansans as representatives of rural America.

Though Kansas is not unique in having political division and polarization, it serves as an example of how media sources cultivate the opinions and beliefs of audiences. Being situated in the middle of the country as part of the Midwest and removed from the cultural considerations of coastal areas, Kansas epitomizes rural America. Considering the state and how its citizens' politics are influenced through their media consumption and exposure to misinformation can shed light on why seemingly rational people succumb to falsehoods and conspiracy theories that influence their politics in manners that are harmful to their ways of life. As Frank (2004) argued, this means reconciling contradictory beliefs in "the small towns they profess to love and the market forces that are slowing grinding those small towns back into the red-state dust" (p. 248).

Understanding how misinformation is cultivated and impacts individuals provides valuable insights and best practices, not just for the red or blue states but for the function and soul of American democracy. Perhaps polarization and misinformation grow out of the fields in America's heartland. Maybe the problem isn't the news consumers, though. Maybe the problem is the media they're not only consuming but also co-creating.

CHAPTER 2

Rounding up Rural Characters

The sun beat down from above while the wind blast hot air and clouds of dust across the field. It was July 2013, and wheat harvest was well-underway in northwestern Kansas. A farmhand, a local schoolteacher looking to earn a little extra money during the summer months, pulled a grain cart across the stubble in a 1981 4640 John Deer tractor to meet the combines loaded with wheat. Snot ran down his face, and his eyes constantly leaked, mixing with the torrents of sweat and causing the dust swirling in the cab to stick to his skin. Even though there was no air conditioning, the tractor cab's windows were closed in an attempt to keep the dirt out and save him from his allergies.

To help pass the time, he listened to music on his MP3 player. When its battery died, he was left with few options. He didn't have a smartphone loaded with tunes, so he turned to the radio. The built-in radio had quit working some years back, but there was a portable, battery-operated stereo strapped into the cab. He snapped it on and twisted the dial around. He was greeted with country music and the voices of conservative talk radio hosts like Rush Limbaugh, and not much else. Not being a fan of country music, he settled for talk radio.

Conservative talk radio is readily accessible. What's interesting about talk radio is that though there have been both conservative and liberal talk radio, conservative talk radio succeeded, and liberal talk radio has, essentially, died. Of course, now with podcasts, one might argue that liberal commentators have a platform of their own.

Regardless, such a scenario isn't surprising or unique. For many rural citizens, access to media outlets can be limited. However, conservative talk radio and other forms of media are often within easy reach. With rural areas often being conservative, this works well, at least in terms of those media outlets finding a welcoming audience.

CHAPTER 2

Take, for example, the State of Kansas.

As a place where Democrats have won the presidential election only five times compared to 26 Republican victories between 1900 and 2020 (Ballotpedia, n.d.; Woolley & Peters, n.d.), Kansas appears to be staunchly conservative. It is considered a red state, which means it is a Republican or conservative region politically speaking (Wenzel, 2020; Wuthnow, 2012). Of course, the state's conservatism can be seen in anecdotal visuals as well. One simply must drive around the state to see the evidence.

Home to the geographic center of the contiguous United States, Kansas is the 15th largest state in terms of land area (U.S. Census Bureau, 2010b) and is home to the geographic center of the 48 contiguous or conterminous United States (Geological Survey, 1964). Additionally, Kansas has 105 counties, which is the fifth most in the United States (U.S. Census Bureau, 2021b). Interstate 70 cuts across the state, going from Missouri in the east to Colorado to the west. Near the middle of Kansas is Salina where the highway connects with Interstate 135.

Figure 2.1. "Vote Trump" roadside sign.
Source: Todd R. Vogts, Ph.D.

This photo provides an example of political messages erected along roadways in rural Kansas. This sign was photographed on July 2, 2022, outside of Salina, Kansas.

This takes travelers south to Wichita, the most populated city in the state (State Library of Kansas, n.d.). Traveling east to west of Interstate 70, the rolling range of lush grasslands that make up the Flint Hills greet visitors. The landscape then begins to flatten out, giving way to expansive pastures where livestock roam and acres of farm ground filled with wheat, corn, soybeans, and more, depending upon the season.

About three miles east of Salina, one pasture hosts a highly visible example of the state's conservative leanings. Erected on telephone poles, a sign consisting of massive, wooden letters painted red proclaims, "Vote Trump." Below the "O" and the "T" of "Vote" is the shape of the United States painted red. Inside the shape and adorned with a white cross, white lettering spells out the following message: "God Bless America."

Other forms of political and religious expression pervade the landscape as well. In Minneapolis, Kansas—a small town north of Salina and home to Rock City, which is a hillside park filled with naturally formed spherical boulders

Figure 2.2. "Fuck Biden" flag.
Source: Todd R. Vogts, Ph.D.

This photo provides an example of vitriolic political messages that can sometimes be seen around rural Kansas. This flag was photographed on July 25, 2022, in Minneapolis, Kansas.

(Schoewe et al., 1937) — a flag proudly proclaiming "Fuck Biden" waves in the Kansas breeze as vehicles travel one of the town's main throughfares. This flag juts out from a tree and hangs next to an American flag. A white, wooden cross leans against the house in the background.

Further west, roadside signs proclaiming political and patriotic affiliations are common as well. These include Trump signs, messages of patriotism complete with American flags, and deeply rooted religious beliefs. For example, along Interstate 70 a series of six signs promote various churches near the town of Quinter, which has a population of approximately 950 residents (U.S. Census Bureau, 2021a). Directly blending politics and religion are anti-abortion signs that express sentiments such as "Protect Life" or "My Mom Chose Life" and are accompanied by images of babies.

The issue of abortion took center stage in Kansas during the 2022 primary midterm elections. Conservatives placed an amendment to the state's constitution

Figure 2.3. "Take my hand not my life" anti-abortion billboard.

Source: Todd R. Vogts, Ph.D.

This photo provides an example of anti-abortion signs that can often be seen along the highways and byways in rural Kansas. This sign was photographed on March 9, 2023, outside of Hutchinson, Kansas.

on the ballot in response to the 2019 decision by the Kansas Supreme Court that struck down a state law banning second-trimester abortion procedures (Smith, 2021). This amendment initiative gained attention after the Supreme Court of the United States overturned Roe v. Wade on June 24, 2022 ("Dobbs v. Jackson Women's Health Organization," 2022), which ended federal protections for abortions. The Kansas ballot decision, called the Value Them Both Amendment, sought to give the state legislature the power to regulate abortions within the state (Value Them Both, n.d.). This ballot measure served as the first test for abortion rights in a post-Roe world (Gowen, 2022; Smith, 2022). In the run-up to the Aug. 2, 2022, elections where the amendment's fate would be decided, signs filled yards. The anti-abortion side's Value Them Both Coalition, the organization behind the amendment, implemented purple signs showing the silhouette of a mother and a baby holding one another that combined to create the outline of a heart positioned next to large, bold text that read, "Vote Yes!" On the abortion rights side, signs with messages such as "Respect Women. Vote No." and "Hands off our rights" could be seen.

Anecdotally, the "Vote Yes!" signs seemed to outnumber the "Vote No" signs in rural and small-town Kansas. Therefore, it made sense that political pundits believed the amendment would pass. Still, local and national media and abortion rights supporters watched the case closely, vaulting the vote to national prominence. To the surprise of many, the amendment was defeated, preserving abortion rights within the state (Kusisto & Barrett, 2022; Smith & Glueck, 2022). What's more, it fell in a landslide by a 20-point margin (Smith & Becker, 2022). This overwhelming victory for abortion rights in a red state seemed to give supporters hope that access to this form of healthcare can be preserved in other parts of the country as well (Ollstein, 2022).

Therefore, this positions Kansas as an interesting case place to study a variety of political, communication, and media questions. Kansas is not new to being the national spotlight for these types of reasons. For example, the state is home to the Topeka-based Westboro Baptist Church (WBC). This religious organization is known for protesting at the funerals of American military personnel, and the protesters often hold signs that contain messages such as "Thank God for Dead Soldiers," "Thank God for IEDs," "God Blew Up the Troops," and "Fag Vets," which also showed stick figures in the middle of a sexual act.[1] WBC leader Fred

---

[1] On February 10, 2006, while working as a student journalist in Hutchinson, Kansas, Todd R. Vogts, Ph.D., covered the funeral of Corporal Peter Daniel Wagler. He was killed Jan. 23, 2006, by an improvised explosive device, or IED, that detonated near his M1A2 Abrams Tank during a patrol in Baghdad where he served the United States Army during Operation

CHAPTER 2

Phelps maintained that the messages promoted by the church were protected forms of speech thanks to the First Amendment of the United State Constitution (Brouwer & Hess, 2007). After being sued by the family of a deceased Marine, the Supreme Court of the United States agreed with Phelps since the speech dealt with sociopolitical issues such as the war in Iraq and government policy, which are matters of public concern (Bruner & Balter-Reitz, 2013; "Snyder v. Phelps," 2011).

Additionally, Kansas played an important role in the history of civil rights. The state's capital city's school system served as the backdrop in the push to desegregate education through "Brown v. Board of Education of Topeka" (1954) that overturned the "separate but equal" doctrine of "Plessy v. Ferguson" (1896). Of course, to play that role means the schools were segregated based on race at that time. Such racial divisions paint Kansas as decidedly not progressive, but there are historical figures that counter that narrative. For example, abolitionist John Brown garnered national notoriety for his efforts to end slavery, and Kansas was his battleground as he embarked on a violent guerilla war with proponents of slavery (Post, 2009). The Civil War eventually settled the issue, but the juxtaposition of John Brown shedding blood to end slavery and Oliver Brown suing to end segregation presents a complex, perhaps even confusing, portrait of the state.

Such confusion continues today when looking back at history. For example, in 1896 the famous newspaper editor of The Emporia Gazette, William Allen White, voiced concerns about the direction Kansas was going. His editorial "What's the Matter with Kansas?" criticized Populist presidential candidate William Jennings Bryan's plans for the country, which included farm programs, graduated income tax, and a paper currency (Frank, 2004). Then in the 2016 presidential election, Kansas went for populist Donald Trump, who used discourse to create cognitive biases that cultivated support of his falsehoods that painted a scene of political elites who were out of touch with the "common" people (Homolar & Scholz, 2019; Steele & Homolar, 2019).

Of course, this apparent identity crisis for the State of Kansas isn't new. Frank (2004) looked at why the state exists as a conservative stronghold, even though many of the Republican policies seem to hurt, rather than help, Kansans. Bartels (2006) argued it is due to economic issues. Wuthnow (2019) suggested the general distrust of typical politicians and the government in general stems from perceived threats to the social fabric of rural, small-town America. Other than a few metropolitan areas in the state, Kansas consists of rural, small towns. Part of being largely rural is relying on farming as a key economic activity. For its part, Kansas

---

Iraqi Freedom. The Westboro Baptist Church protested outside the church where the funeral took place.

is third in the country for the amount of farmland it contains, is the number one producer of both wheat and sorghum, and ranks third in cattle production and beef processing (U.S. Energy Information Administration, 2022). As such, farm subsidies and other policies put forth by Democrats in the legislature would be perfectly suited for Kansas, but the state's farmers don't vote for people on that side of the political aisle, going against their own self-interest (Frank, 2004). Undoubtedly, the reasons for this are complex. It is not purely about income levels or social issues (Gelman et al., 2007). The leading rationale is a sense of pride and self-reliance embedded within the culture of farming (Wuthnow, 2015).

Additionally, religion also plays an important role in red-states (Wuthnow, 2012). According to Pew Research Center (2014), 76% of Kansas adults identify as Christians with 79% saying religion is important in their life and 72% saying they attend religious services at least once or twice a month. With farming playing such a large role in Kansas, it seems logical that a considerable number of farmers are also religious. Therefore, the reason for aligning with the Republican Party and conservativism could be attributed to religious beliefs.

Rural Roots: Understanding the People

No matter their political or religious beliefs, the people of Kansas are often viewed as hardworking and industrious folks who would give the shirts of their backs to help a person in need (Frank, 2004; Nemerever & Rogers, 2021). Hard work is the norm in the world of farming, and farming is a key economic activity in the largely rural state. Afterall, Kansas is third in the country in the amount of farmland, is the number one producer of both wheat and sorghum, and ranks third in cattle production and beef processing (U.S. Energy Information Administration, 2022).

If that doesn't scream, "rural," then maybe this will. In Kansas, there are approximately 2.7 million residents (U.S. Census Bureau, 2021a), and according to Department of Agriculture (2022), there are 6.5 million head of cattle in the state. Quite literally, cattle outnumber people in Kansas. This isn't a recent development, though. Crockett (2016) humorously pointed this out nearly a decade ago, but it still speaks to the focus on farming and ranching, not to mention the difficult work of keeping that many cattle in line.

Outside of farming, healthcare, education, and manufacturing also play important roles in the economy, just as they do in many parts of the country. Small-town, rural news outlets capture the history of these communities and provide foundational information about what is happening even as they face evolving economic hardships and business-model disruptions (Finneman et al.,

2024). Still, polarization and division persist thanks to unreliable news, rumors, and outright falsehoods. The question is: why? To understand how misinformation is cultivated and impacts individuals, we must understand the pathways to news of individuals living and working in rural communities that lead to the belief in and spreading of misinformation and conspiracy theories. To gain such insights, we zeroed in on rural Kansans as avatars for rural Midwesterners.

To achieve this goal, a three-pronged approach was used: social media data collection, an online survey, and interviews. The interviews served as the primary way to collect more depth and context. The social media data collection and survey implementation brought in supportive and supplemental data that helped shed light on how individuals use and are impacted by the news in ways that allow political division and polarization to flourish, which damages social capital and democracy.

Get Acquainted: Meeting the Rural Residents

The social media data came from public profiles. The Meltwater platform was used to collect the posts from a wide variety of publicly available pages and accounts on platforms including Facebook and TikTok, but the vast majority of social media content came from X (formerly Twitter). Anyone wishing to collect this public data can easily do so just by subscribing to Meltwater, though many other techniques and similar data vendors exist.

The survey was a questionnaire consisting of "a collection of written queries grouped together in a single document" (Hesse, 2017, p. 1717), was administered online using the Qualtrics surveying platform, though the option of a physical copy of the survey with paid return postage was available. No one took advantage of this option. Utilizing a survey was advantageous for several reasons. It allowed for data collection from a wide array of respondents with relative ease and was not confined to geographic boundaries formed by the necessity of traveling to gather information (Wimmer & Dominick, 2014). This meant the survey was administered without supervision, which eliminated the potential for interviewer bias that can arise in a face-to-face setting (Berger, 2020). A sample of the survey questions used can be found in Appendix 1.

Survey participants were recruited via a multi-pronged approach. One method consisted of working with Kansas Farm Bureau. The organization, which is a nonprofit advocacy entity, has a presence in all 105 Kansas counties and operates under the mission "to strengthen agriculture and the lives of Kansans through advocacy, education and service" (Kansas Farm Bureau, n.d.). Every Tuesday and Friday the organization sends an electronic newsletter to 13,000 of its members. A brief recruitment message was included in each issue of the newsletter between Dec. 16, 2022, and Jan. 6, 2023. To incentivize participation, respondents had the opportunity to enter a drawing for one of two $50 Amazon gift cards if they completed the survey by Jan. 15, 2023. Similarly, a recruitment message also was published in the email newsletter of the Kansas Sampler Foundation, which is a nonprofit organization whose mission "is to preserve and sustain rural culture by educating Kansans about Kansas and networking and supporting rural communities" (Kansas Sampler Foundation, 2019). The newsletter, called "We Kan! Tidbits," goes to 2,400 subscribers. As was the case with the Farm Bureau population, respondents had the opportunity to enter a drawing for one of two $50 Amazon gift cards if they completed the survey by Jan. 31, 2023.

Additionally, as another way to recruit respondents, the survey was distributed to students, faculty, and staff at both Sterling College in Sterling, Kansas, and Kansas State University in Manhattan, Kansas. Tapping into this population allowed research to make contact with a wide variety of individuals, and their association with an educational institution means they likely are from various parts of Kansas, not from a single area. In the case of Sterling College, the Vice President for Academic Affairs emailed the recruitment message to all faculty, staff, and students, which equated to 700 individuals. To incentivize participation, respondents had the opportunity to enter a drawing for one of two $50 Amazon gift cards if they completed the survey by Feb. 17, 2023. In terms of Kansas State University, the recruitment message was published in the "K-State Today" email newsletter on two separate occasions, going to all student, faculty, and staff email addresses. Each time the newsletter is published, 6,500 faculty and staff email addresses receive it, and approximately 18,900 student email addresses receive it. To incentivize participation from this recruitment effort as well, respondents had the opportunity to enter a drawing for one of two $50 Amazon gift cards if they completed the survey by March 12, 2023.

A sample size of 267 survey respondents was achieved. After data cleaning, 255 respondents participated in the survey and effectively contributed data. *(n=255)*. Based upon established sample size calculations, this resulted in a confidence level of 95% with a 6% margin of error (Gill et al., 2010; Welch & Comer, 1988). This marks the existing sample as reliable if not perfectly generalizable. This calculation was based on a total population of 914,980 rural Kansas residents, according to numbers reported in 2021 (Economic Research Service, 2022). Of these survey respondents, 87.1% *(n=222)* indicated they have roots in rural counties, while 12.9% *(n=33)* claimed urban counties, which are based on rural definitions from

Economic Research Service (2007) that suggested only five Kansas counties are considered urban.

The average age of the participants was 43.16 years old with a median age of 42.00 years old *(SD=17.73)*. For comparison, the average age of Kansas residents is 36.9 (U.S. Census Bureau, 2022a). Females made up 62.4% of respondents, and 36.1% were males. The remaining participants indicated they identified as a different gender or preferred not to say. According to U.S. Census Bureau (2022b), 49.9% of Kansas residents are female. Of the respondents, 91.0% were white, which also aligns with the U.S. Census Bureau (2022b) data that indicated 86.0% of the Kansas population is white.

Additionally, 60.4% of the respondents indicated they were married, and 70.2% reported the highest level of education they have completed was a bachelor's degree or higher. Relatedly, 6.3% have earned an associate's degree, 16.9% have completed some college coursework, 1.2% have earned a technical certificate, and 4.7% have earned only a high school diploma or an equivalent. According to U.S. Census Bureau (2022b), only 34.4% of Kansans have earned a bachelor's degree or more.

Respondents were also asked about their religious beliefs and general income levels. Christianity was reported to be the dominant belief system with 77.7% of the participants claiming that religion. Also, a majority of the respondents indicated they make between $50,000.00 and $139,999.00 per year. This aligns with the state generally, which has a median household income of $64,521.00 (U.S. Census Bureau, 2022b).

In terms of political alignment, 38.0% of the participants reported they aligned with the Republican Party and 29.0% with the Democratic Party. A combined total of 28.7% said they were either Independent or Unaffiliated, while Libertarians and other parties made up 4.3%. Such numbers are in line with overall registration numbers in the state as 45% of registered voters in 2020 were Republican and 26% were Democratic (Kansas Secretary of State, 2023).

As far as the interviews go, participants were recruited through two methods. In some cases, participants were recruited using direct contact in the form of phone calls and emails to individuals known to the researchers that fit the ideal parameters of the study, which is living and working in rural Kansas. In other cases, individuals volunteered to be interviewed by completing a separate form that indicated their willingness to be part of the next phase of the research. This form, created using Google Forms, was made available at the end of the previously discussed survey. By using a separate form, the risk of survey respondents becoming identifiable was minimized as the two sets of data were kept apart. Upon agreeing to be interviewed, respondents signed off on the necessary informed consent documentation as stipulated by the Institutional Review Board (IRB). Then, via a time and method agreed upon by the researcher and the respondent, the interview questions were asked, and observations were gathered. A sample of the survey questions used can be found in Appendix 2.

A total of 35 individuals volunteered to be interview participants, and 25 of them were interviewed. They represented various demographic aspects of Kansas. Seven of the interviewees were female, and the remaining 18 were male. They ranged in age from 21 to 76, averaging 47.28 years old. Of the 25, 12 worked in agriculture-related fields, such as farming and ranching or agriculture-focused financial industries. The remaining respondents worked in areas such as education, manufacturing, and the service industry. With roots from across the state, they represented four of the five conservation district areas that divide Kansas (Kansas Department of Agriculture, 2023), with the exception being the region in the northeast corner of Kansas. Because the volunteers came from across the State of Kansas, this served as a purposeful sample. This means the site of the study and the types of participants were intentionally chosen in order to inform the central research question or phenomenon at the core of the study (Creswell & Poth, 2018; Palinkas et al., 2015; Robinson, 2014).

Interview participants were asked a series of questions during a 30-to-90-minute session or series of sessions that were recorded using video and/or audio recording devices. The recordings were used to develop transcripts of the interviews that were coded and analyzed. In total, the interviews resulted in 37.22 hours of recorded conversations and 267,497 transcribed words to be analyzed. This makes the combined transcripts longer than *Ulysses* by James Joyce, which contains 265,222 words.

The coding and analyzing of the transcripts used the method of thematic analysis (TA). Thematic analysis, according to Terry and Hayfield (2021), "is a flexible analytical method that enables the researcher to construct themes—meaning-based patterns—to report their interpretation of a qualitative data set" (p. 3), and it is used in a variety of settings (e.g., Connaughton et al., 2017; Norander & Galanes, 2014). This method aligns with constructionist lens (Braun & Clarke, 2006, 2021; Kiger & Varpio, 2020; Terry & Hayfield, 2021).

Furthermore, TA provides an accessible form of analysis that relies upon an iterative and reflexive process of investigating the discourses or words used (Nowell et al., 2017), and it exists beneath the larger textual analysis umbrella (Brennen, 2016; Fairclough, 2010; Morphew & Hartley, 2006). Specifically, this research adopted the reflexive TA approach designed by Braun and Clarke (2006).

CHAPTER 2

This style of TA utilizes a six-step process for conducting the research (Braun & Clarke, 2021; Kiger & Varpio, 2020; Maguire & Delahunt, 2017; Terry & Hayfield, 2021), which this research used as its roadmap.

Through the analysis, several commonalities came to light. For instance, the majority of the people interviewed *(n=15)* aligned with conservative politics and reported they were registered as Republicans. This equates to 60% of the volunteers, which aligns with Kansas typically being depicted as a conservative state when discussing electoral politics. Four of the interviewees indicated they were Democrats, four said they were unaffiliated, one described themselves as independent, and one aligned with the Libertarian Party. This relates to the survey respondents, which also skewed toward the Republican Party. Similarly, 24 respondents indicated a strong alignment with religion, specifically Christianity. Likewise, 77.7% of the survey participants also claimed Christianity as their religious belief. This aligns with prior research highlighting the importance of religion in rural areas (e.g., Wuthnow, 2012).

The identities of all the interviewed participants were protected. They were identified by an assigned alias, title, general organizational affiliation, and other demographic information as applicable. For the purposes of this work, it is helpful to "get to know" the characters who shared their thoughts about consuming the news and how misinformation is cultivated in rural America. To that end, allow us to introduce you to our cast of characters:

1. Abraham

A 52-year-old male, Abraham lives in central Kansas where he works in the agriculture industry. The highest level of education he has achieved is his high school diploma. He identified himself as a Christian. Also, he reported being a Republican and that he doesn't vote regularly. He does volunteer in his community, though.

2. Barney

A 34-year-old male, Barney calls central Kansas home, and he works in the finance industry. The highest level of education he has achieved is a bachelor's degree. He identified himself as a Christian. In terms of politics, he reported being unaffiliated with any particular political party. He does vote regularly, but only in the general elections due to his party registration. He volunteers with numerous organizations in his community.

3. Bart

A 37-year-old male, Bart lives in central Kansas where he works in education. The highest level of education he has achieved is a master's degree. He identified himself as a Christian. Politically speaking, he reported being unaffiliated with any particular political party, but he does vote regularly in all elections. He is involved with his community only through his professional capacity.

4. Chalmers

A 59-year-old male, Chalmers resides in central Kansas where he works in education. The highest level of education he has achieved is a doctoral degree. He identified himself as a Christian and a Republican. He does vote regularly in all elections, but he indicated he always votes a straight ticket for the Republican candidates. He volunteers with various organizations in his community.

5. Clancy

A 37-year-old male, Clancy lives in central Kansas where he works in the manufacturing industry. The highest level of education he has achieved is a bachelor's degree. He identified himself as a Christian. He reported being aligned with the Republican Party. He votes frequently but not in every election. When he does cast a ballot, he always votes a straight ticket for the Republican candidates. He doesn't volunteer much in his community, but he does attend public events to show his support.

6. Cletus

A 37-year-old male, Cletus is planted in central Kansas where he works in the agriculture industry. The highest level of education he has achieved is a bachelor's degree. He identified himself as a Christian. In terms of his politics, he reported being Republican who votes in all elections, but he does not vote for Republicans only. He is heavily involved with his community and industry, volunteering for numerous boards.

7. Doris

A 47-year-old female, Doris's roots are in north central Kansas. She works in education, and the highest level of education she has achieved is a doctoral degree.

CHAPTER 2

She identified herself as a Christian and a Democrat. She does vote regularly in all elections, and she volunteers in her community.

8. Eddie

A 43-year-old male, Eddie lives in southeast Kansas where he works in the agriculture industry. The highest level of education he has achieved is a bachelor's degree. He identified himself as a Christian. In terms of his politics, he reported being Republican who votes in all elections, but he does not vote for Republicans only. He is heavily involved with his community and industry, volunteering for numerous boards.

9. Edna

A 44-year-old female, Edna calls central Kansas home. She works in education, and the highest level of education she has achieved is a bachelor's degree. She identified herself as not having any religious affiliation. As far as politics go, she indicated she is a Democrat. She does vote regularly in all elections, and she volunteers with various organizations in her community.

10. Helen

A 21-year-old female, Helen resides in central Kansas where she is a student. The highest level of education she has achieved is a high school diploma. She identified herself as a Christian. Politically, she indicated she is a Republican. She does vote regularly in all elections, but the number of ballots she has cast is limited by her age. She does volunteer work with her church.

11. Herman

A 39-year-old male, Herman lives in central Kansas where he works in the construction industry. The highest level of education he has achieved is a bachelor's degree. He identified himself as a Christian. In terms of his politics, he said he was a Republican. He does vote regularly in all elections, but he indicated he always votes a straight ticket for the Republican candidates. His volunteerism is confined to activities with his church.

12. Jasper

A 76-year-old male, Jasper calls central Kansas home. He works in the agriculture industry. The highest level of education he has achieved is a doctoral degree. He identified himself as a Christian. Also, he reported being a Republican who votes regularly and in all elections. He said he used to do more volunteer work when he was younger.

13. Kent

A 39-year-old male, Kent lives in west central Kansas where he works in the agriculture industry. The highest level of education he has achieved is a bachelor's degree. He identified himself as a Christian. Also, he indicated he is a Republican. He votes regularly in all election, and he she he always votes a straight ticket for the Republican candidates. He is heavily involved in his community.

14. Marvin

A 75-year-old male, Marvin's roots are planted in southeast Kansas. He works in the agriculture industry. The highest level of education he has achieved is a Master of Fine Arts degree. He identified himself as a Christian and a Democrat. He does vote regularly in all elections, but he indicated he always votes a straight ticket for the Democratic Party candidates in national elections. He volunteers with various organizations in his community.

15. Maude

A 31-year-old female, Maude resides in north central Kansas. She works in the agriculture industry. The highest level of education she has achieved is a doctoral degree. She identified as a Christian. In terms of politics, she reported being unaffiliated with any particular political party. She does vote regularly in all elections, and she volunteers with numerous organizations in her community.

16. Moe

A 35-year-old male, Moe lives in central Kansas where he works in the service industry. The highest level of education he has achieved is a bachelor's degree. He identified himself as a Christian. Politically speaking, he reported being unaffiliated with any particular political party. He does not vote regularly or volunteer in his community.

17. Monroe

A 50-year-old male, Monroe calls central Kansas home. He works in education. The highest level of education he has achieved is a doctoral degree. He identified himself as a Christian and a Libertarian. He does not vote regularly or volunteer in his community.

18. Montgomery

A 40-year-old male, Montgomery makes his home in central Kansas. He works in education. The highest level of education he has achieved is a doctoral degree. He identified himself as a Christian. As far as politics go, he considers himself an Independent. He votes regularly, but he said he rarely casts ballots for Democrats because usually Republicans are the only people on the ticket. He is involved with his community, primarily through his professional capacity.

19. Murphy

A 46-year-old male, Murphy lives in south central Kansas where he works in the agriculture industry. The highest level of education he has achieved is a bachelor's degree. He identified himself as a Christian. In terms of his politics, he reported being Republican who votes in all elections, especially local elections since they have the biggest impact on this daily life. He also volunteers for various local and state organizations.

20. Ned

A 69-year-old male, Ned calls north central Kansas home. He works in the agriculture industry. The highest level of education he has achieved is his high school diploma. He identified himself as a Christian. Politically speaking, he reported being Republican who votes in all elections. Also, he is heavily involved in his community.

21. Nelson

A 55-year-old male, Nelson lives in central Kansas. He works in the manufacturing industry. The highest level of education he has achieved is his high school diploma. He identified himself as a Christian and a Republican who votes in all elections. His volunteerism is limited to supporting his grandchildren's athletic teams.

22. Patty

A 64-year-old female, Patty resides in southeast Kansas. She works in the agriculture industry. The highest level of education she has achieved is her high school diploma. She identified as a Christian. In terms of politics, she reported being a Republican. She does vote regularly in all elections, but she said she always votes a straight ticket for the Republican candidates. She is heavily involved in her community, volunteering with numerous organizations.

23. Quimby

A 73-year-old male, Quimby lives in west central Kansas. He works in the agriculture industry. The highest level of education he has achieved is a high school diploma. He identified himself as a Christian and a Democrat who votes in all elections, though he rarely votes for Democrats. He volunteers extensively in his community.

24. Sarah

A 37-year-old female, Sarah makes her home in central Kansas. She works in education. The highest level of education she has achieved is a bachelor's degree. She identified as a Christian. In terms of politics, she reported being a Republican. She does not vote regularly due to feeling uninformed. Her volunteerism centers on her church activities.

25. Sherri

A 42-year-old female, Sherri lives in north central Kansas. She works in marketing. The highest level of education she has achieved is a bachelor's degree. She identified as a Christian. She reported being a Republican who votes regularly in all elections, and she volunteers with several community organizations.

Reaping Responses: Cultivating Data Points

The use of a multi-pronged, mixed-method approach to research is common within communication and media studies of this nature. Numerous scholars leverage the various pieces of data collected via quantitative and qualitative methods in order to develop a clearer answer to their overall research questions (e.g., Creswell, 2014; Mertens, 2010; Pang & Ng, 2017; Westlund & Ekström, 2021). More specific to this study, the combination of social media posts, surveys, and interviews also work well together. For example, Beck (2014) used quantitative surveys supplemented with interviews to provide more depth as part of a study to better understand servant leadership within community programs. Similarly, Smethers et al. (2017) used interviews and focus groups to gain insights into the production process of a hyperlocal news outlet before following up with a 45-item questionnaire to community members as a way to understand how the residents perceived the news outlet. Additionally, Olsen and Solvoll (2018) combined 20 interviews with newspaper managers and a national survey with 1,586 responses to investigate the potential value proposition of news website paywalls as they related to local news outlets and audiences.

The collected data helped to shed insight on how individuals who live and work in rural Kansas consume, use, and are impacted by the news, which aided in understanding the spread of misinformation and helped to harvest knowledge about news habits as they relate to small-town, rural news consumers. In fact, certain categorical themes related to rural news habits and misinformation spread emerged from the data. These themes include the following: Rural Residents Constantly Consume News, Roots of Media Distrust Planted by National Outlets, Disinformation Taints Media Diets, Religion Fertilizes Political Beliefs and Community Connections, and Partisanship Plows Rows for Political Engagement.

By unpacking these themes, one thing becomes quite clear: misinformation finds these individuals, leading them to be more radical in their beliefs.

CHAPTER 3

Constantly Consuming News

To many Americans, a neighbor is someone who lives close by. Perhaps even in the house next door. However, in rural America, the closest neighbor might be several miles away across a landscape dotted with livestock and fields of row crops. As a youth growing up in a farming community and living in the countryside, something as simple as meeting up with a neighborhood friend during the summer to build a fort or go fishing required long walks or riding one's bicycle through the loose sands of the unpaved roads. The nearest town was more than four miles away, so going to the community swimming pool wasn't an option, unless an adult was able to drive. Watching television wasn't an option either. The rabbit ears jutting up from the back of the black-and-white console only picked up a handful of channels, and during the day the programming consisted of game shows and soap operas. Besides, the home's air conditioning consisted of open windows and ceiling fans, so being outside was the best option. Fun and entertainment had to be created, but as people moved off the family farm and into town, the connections between rural families became strained and tenuous.

After all, family farms are on the decline as new generations of farmers find themselves pushed out by large, corporate enterprises (Ferguson, 2021; Union of Concerned Scientists, 2021). This can lead to harmful social isolation, especially when the distance between neighbors expands (Schaller & Waldman, 2024). Still, not being close to another human being doesn't mean a person is disconnected from the world.

Thanks to online and digital technologies, individuals find themselves awash in options for news, information, and entertainment. This can make it difficult to focus on one medium or outlet and to know where to get the most reliable content. Of course, this isn't a modern phenomenon. In 1964, media theorist Marshall McLuhan pointed out that society "lives in a world of information overload" (McLuhan, 2003, p. 52). What one pays attention to is considered to be context-dependent based upon what the individual is thinking, feeling, and experiencing (Stephens, 2013). Crary (2001) suggested, "Attention as a process of selection necessarily meant that perception was an activity of exclusion, of rendering parts of a perceptual field unperceived" (pp. 24–25). Therefore, keeping issues of attention in mind as they relate to media serves an important purpose. The news and information ecosystem is fragmented (Searles & Smith, 2016), so understanding how people find and use news helps shed light on how the belief in and spreading of misinformation and conspiracy theories occurs.

News Navigation: Pinpointing Pathways to Information

According to Newman et al. (2021), 66% of Americans got news via online channels in 2021, while 52% used television and 16% used print as their sources for news. Similarly, Shearer (2021) also reported that 52% of Americans preferred digital platforms for their news but found 35% prefer television. Furthermore, 84% of United States adults get their news on digital devices, compared to 67% for television, 50% for radio, and 34% for print publications (Matsa & Naseer, 2021). The dominance of digital platforms, which include social media, should come as no surprise. Such tools provide users with the ability to tailor their news exposure to fit within ideological, interest-driven, or any other type of categorization (Batsell, 2015; Briggs, 2020).

Within an online environment, information presentation is more dynamic than in static mediums such as print or television. Users are accustomed to a level of interactivity (Allam, 2019; Belair-Gagnon et al., 2017; Briggs, 2007). For example, links to other pieces of content are an important way people use a news outlet's website (Collier et al., 2021) and being able to comment on a story provides users a way to interact with the news (Liu & McLeod, 2021). Of course, that presumes an individual is actively seeking news and information. In some cases, a person can "bump into" news online. Wieland and Kleinen-von Königslöw (2020) referred to this as "incidental news exposure," which is when an individual unintentionally comes across news and subsequently consumes it to the point that knowledge is gained. This inadvertent news exposure can cause the consumer to develop an inflated sense of being informed (Song et al., 2020). As Dahlgren (2018) suggested, perceived knowledge impacts participation in public discourse, especially online.

Similarly, Gil de Zúñiga et al. (2017) developed the News-Finds-Me (NFM) Perception and Effect. They defined this "as the extent to which individuals believe they can indirectly stay informed about public affairs—despite not actively following the news—through general Internet use, information received from peers, and connections within online social networks" (p. 107). Under this framework, people don't have to seek out the news because if they need to know something, that information will end up finding its way to them. That isn't to say people avoid the news as Toff et al. (2023) discussed. Rather, individuals under the NFM Perception want to stay informed but don't believe they to actively pursue the information reported by news outlets (Gil de Zúñiga & Cheng, 2021). This works because numerous other mediums not considered "mainstream" provide pathways to news as well.

Shearer (2021) highlighted that 22% of United States adults get news from podcasts either often or sometimes. Newsletters also provide an entry point to news consumption (Henneman et al., 2015; Newman, 2020; Tornoe, 2017). Still, as has been highlighted, television still exists as an important way for individuals to get news (Newman et al., 2021), and radio use has remained steady for more than a decade (Pew Research Center, 2021b).

Therefore, individuals access news, information, entertainment, and other forms of media content in a variety of ways. There must be a path down which people can travel that gives them the content they want and need. This brings in the idea of Communication Infrastructure Theory (CIT) because the media tell the story of a community to its citizens by working with them. As Paul (2015) noted, "CIT emphasizes interpersonal networks and communities. CIT gives attention to how messages are received and interpreted in different ways depending on these interpersonal and community communication and influence networks" (p. 712). As the architects of the theory, Kim and Ball-Rokeach (2006a) defined CIT as "a theoretical framework that differentiates local communities in terms of whether they have communication resources that can be activated to construct community, thereby enabling collective action for common purpose" (p. 174), which happens within a Storytelling Network (STN).

The core of CIT is the STN, which fosters neighborhood belonging and collective efficacy (Kim & Ball-Rokeach, 2006b). With belonging and efficacy comes trust, which is crucial for community. Since journalism plays an important role in community (Bressers et al., 2015; Smethers et al., 2017; Smethers et al., 2021) and the STN, trust in journalism becomes vital. Largely, community news outlets provide a form of camaraderie, which Nygren (2019) highlighted as "the social role of local media" (p. 53) that brings people together and builds relationships due to coverage of shared experiences. Leupold et al. (2018) referred to this as social cohesion. As Usher (2018) suggested, "Trust in journalism is a critical element of social cohesion: trust enables news media to set the public agenda, influences media effects, and is ultimately the factor that links journalists and audiences together" (p. 565).

Despite this, political partisanship and division erode the binding relationships with a community, especially when community newspapers close and create a STN gap. "Declining access to quality local news is harmful to voter behavior and responsive governance, leading to more corruption and lower voter turnout. In the absence of quality local news options, Americans may rely on partisanship and national news to inform their political decisions" (Darr et al., 2018, p. 1009). Furthermore, communities and regions without reliable, local news coverage become news deserts (Abernathy, 2018a), which Baran and Davis (2021) suggested creates "an information deficit" (p. 313). This is problematic because "people with the least access to local news are often the most vulnerable—the poorest, least educated and most isolated" (Abernathy, 2018a, p. 8).

Daily Drove: Always Absorbing Information

Based on the interviews conducted for this study, it is clear that news consumption plays an important role in the everyday lives of the individuals interviewed for this study. All but one person reported consuming news daily, and most respondents indicated they do so multiple times per day or even hourly. A 75-year-old male who owns cropland and pastures, who was assigned the alias of Marvin, described his consumption this way: "I'm addicted to the subscription level of *The New York Times*."

On a scale of one to five with one being "never" and five being "hourly," 37.1% of the survey respondents indicated they consume news and information from any and all media outlets an average amount of time. Using this as the dividing line, 35.8% reported they consume news and information less often, and 27.0% reported they consume news more often. For both "never" and "hourly," 4.2% used these designations to describe their consumption habits, making the extremes equal. Though there was no statistical significance between the responses of rural *(M = 2.90, SD = 0.93)* and urban *(M = 3.00, SD = 1.02)* participants *(t(235) = -0.36, p = 0.72, equal variances assumed)*, this finding aligns with what the interview and social media data showed.

Specifically, the last year, Kansans alone publicly mentioned "Trump" 1.93 million times on social media (excluding private Facebook and Instagram posts), where they also mentioned "Biden" 798,000 times, and "Harris" another 515,000 times. In sum, this amounts to a total of an impressive 3.24 million posts that directly mention the presumptive and eventual presidential candidates—which represents more than the total population of the state.

CONSTANTLY CONSUMING NEWS

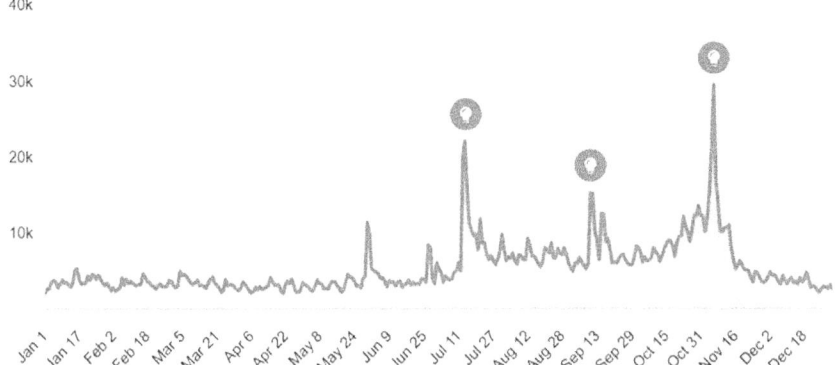

Figure 3.1a. Total of 1.93 million Social media mentions of "Trump" by Kansans in 2024.
Source: Al x Media Institute/Meltwater

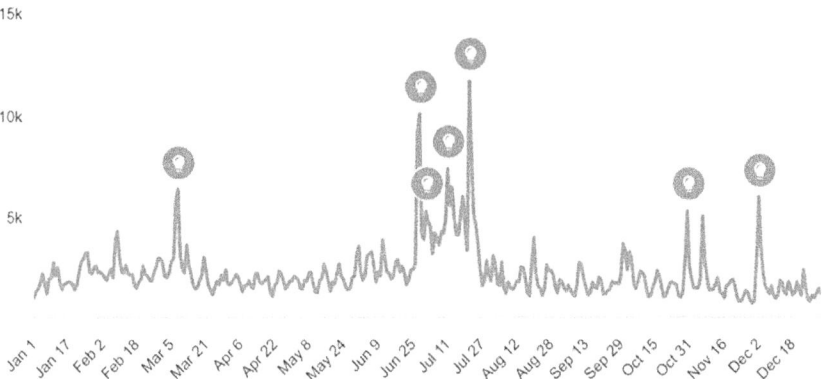

Figure 3.1b. Total of 798,000 social media mentions of "Biden" by Kansans in 2024.
Source: Al x Media Institute/Meltwater

As part of this consumption, certain types of news were frequently mentioned. The two most cited types of news were politics and local. Political news was mentioned by 15 respondents, and local news was mentioned by 13 respondents. A 37-year-old female educator assigned the alias of Sarah explained the appeal of local news this way: "I think local journalism is important to share information about the community, to highlight things, to let people know if something bad

CHAPTER 3

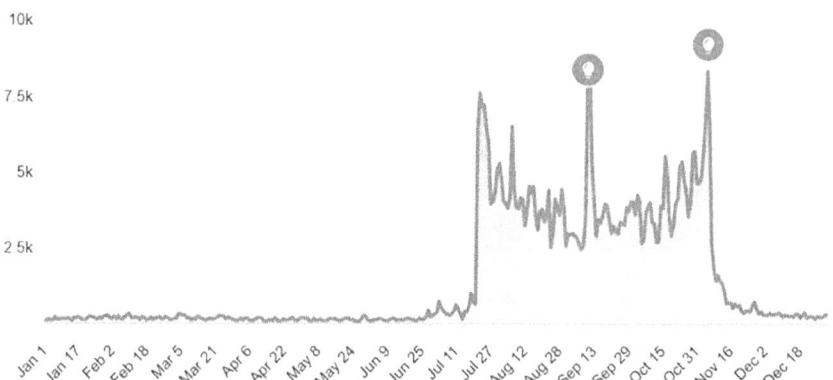

Figure 3.1c. Total of 515,000 social media mentions of "Harris" by Kansans in 2024.
Source: AI x Media Institute/Meltwater

or unfortunate or scary has happened, to bring awareness to that too. So, I think local is really important too just to share information and to highlight things too for your community." Likewise, sports and weather were each driving factors of news consumption for nine people. World and national news were also cited, being mentioned seven and five times respectively.

Similarly, the majority of survey respondents indicated they also seek out two distinct types of news and information: national and local. With 32.9% of the responses, national news was the top category of news individuals desired to consume. Close behind was local with 24.9%. Other popular types included weather (9.3%), professional sports (7.2%), politics (5.1%), agriculture (4.6%), and entertainment (4.6%). There was no statistical significance ($\chi^2(9) = 3.74, p = 0.93$) between rural and urban respondents.

Though Marvin was one of only three respondents who mentioned *The New York Times* specifically, all individuals described diverse pathways to the news they take in. For most, this included four primary avenues—radio, television, print, and online. Such a finding was validated by the survey data, which indicated that social media and the websites of news outlets ranked as the most popular avenues to news for respondents with 32.5% and 22.8% respectively. These were followed by cable/satellite television and local/antenna television, which received 11.4% and 9.7% of the choices respectively. AM radio, FM radio, and podcasts combined to make up 13.5% of the responses. Additionally, streaming television was the top choice for 4.2% of survey participants, daily newspapers accounted for 3.4%, weekly newspapers were chosen by 1.7%, and magazines received 0.8%

of the responses. The data revealed no statistical significance ($\chi^2(11) = 17.20$, $p = 0.10$) between urban and rural Kansans in terms of these pathways to news. However, it is notable that zero urban residents indicated using local antenna television, podcasts, or streaming television as their primary medium. Similarly, 5.4% of rural individuals highlighted newspapers as their preferred pathway to news, compared to only 3.2% of urban respondents.

As for the interviewees, 13 respondents highlighted radio as an important vehicle for news reception. For the majority, their radio listening consisted of either conservative talk radio or NPR. A 40-year-old male educator assigned the alias of Montgomery, and a 37-year-old male farmer assigned the alias of Cletus were outliers in that they reported listening to both conservative talk radio and NPR; however, most individuals listened to one or the other. Jasper, a 76-year-old rancher, said he listens to conservative talk radio because it's the only content he can tune into while driving through his pastures. Abraham, a 52-year-old male working in the agriculture industry, also indicated conservative talk radio's accessibility is part of its appeal. However, both also indicated they agreed with most of the content, which was a consistent reason for listening among respondents. Abraham summed it up by explaining that talk radio "validates your thoughts."

Radio broadcast became a mass medium in the 1920s, ushering in a movement toward news and entertainment reaching people over the airwaves. National networks such as NBC and CBS went on the air in 1926 and 1927 respectively, which made information even more available as local broadcasters signed up to be affiliates of the networks and gained access to the content being produced (Vaughn, 2008). By the 1930s, politicians began leveraging the medium. Most notably was President Franklin D. Roosevelt, who delivered a regular series of radio addresses that were known as "Fireside Chats" (Vaughn, 2008). In speaking directly to the masses via the radio, Roosevelt was able to engage with the public in a new way, and it set the stage for political communication as it is known today (Craig, 2000). Also, advertising and sponsorships debuted as part of programming, providing a revenue stream for broadcasters (Campbell et al., 2019; Craig, 2000). These commercials supported programming, allowing networks to produce more content that included news and entertainment. As far as entertainment goes, programming such as "Amos 'n' Andy," "The Shadow," "The Lone Ranger," and "The Green Hornet" brought families together around the radio to tune into the latest adventure in the serial stories or to hear the Ed Sullivan Show's comedic offerings (Campbell et al., 2019). Also, one cannot forget the infamous "War of the Worlds" dramatization on Halloween in 1938 that "convinced thousands of people that an army of Martians really had invaded" (Vaughn, 2008, p. 435). Of course, the number of people who truly believed aliens were attacking is disputed (Croteau & Hoynes, 2018), but it highlighted the power of radio as a medium, especially with impending war as a backdrop (Schwartz, 2015).

It was war that elevated radio into a news-dissemination medium beyond mere entertainment. As Vaughn (2008) explained:

> [It] was in December 1941 that everything changed, and news took center stage: when the Japanese attacked Pearl Harbor. It was a Sunday and there was not much news scheduled—mostly religion, soap operas, and sports. But when the news broke and was confirmed, radio news reporters rushed in to work and coverage of World War II began in earnest. (p. 435)

Radio's reporting brought the war into the homes of Americans, making it real and shaping the public discourse (Craig, 2000). The cultural views of the war found support through the radio advertisements that aired on all the networks (Horten, 2002). However, without the news coverage of the war, the advertisements wouldn't have been so prominent or profitable. In fact, thanks to coverage of the world-wide conflict, time spend broadcasting news increased from 2,396 hours in 1940 to 5,522 hours by the end of 1944 (Vaughn, 2008). This solidified the place of news within the radio ecosystem. Likewise, politics and conceptions of community and citizenship were forever changed. As Craig (2000) pointed out, radio provided programming directly into the homes of listeners, which "blurred the distinction between public and private culture and entertainment. Listeners could now participate in public events such as sporting contests, concerts, and speeches without leaving home" (p. 279).

Eventually, music became more of a focus for radio, especially with the development of the FM band and the Top 40 and other radio programming formats (Campbell et al., 2019). However, news radio broadcasting continues. As was the case in the early days of radio, formats of news, commentary, and political talk shows continue to remain popular (Horten, 2002). Though the technology was disruptive to a media world where newspapers were the norm, radio gave news consumers an immediacy that print products couldn't match, and it was more accessible. As Vaughn (2008) pointed out, "it made life easier for people in rural areas who lived far from where newspapers could be bought," and it allowed individuals "to sit in the comfort of their own living room and listen to experts discussing what was going on in the world" (p. 434). In short, radio provided something for everyone, and that became even more clear when talk radio took root.

In general, radio news consumption was popular among respondents due to them being able to listen while driving or operating farming machinery. Only one respondent indicated they do not listen to the radio at all, meaning 96% of the interviewees listen to some form of radio content. In most cases, these individuals explained they listened to KSAL News Radio 1150, a commercial AM station out of Salina, Kansas, or KMUW, the NPR station out of Wichita, Kansas. For those not interested in any form of news or talk radio, the dial was typically tuned to country music, though classical music and oldies were also mentioned. Still, radio isn't the only broadcast medium that was popular. Television also provided a dominant pathway to news.

According to the Pew Research Center (2019), 86% of Americans get local news from television. For all news, 68% of Americans use the television (Matsa & Naseer, 2021; Shearer, 2021). Television provides an important pathway for news dissemination and consumption because of how rapidly information can be delivered and how many people can receive it. For example, in the event of an emergency or disaster television news relays important information regarding actions that need to be taken so a person can remain safe. Research suggests that during a public health crisis, such as an infectious disease outbreak, "media messages should include information about the threat (e.g., likely symptoms) as well as information members of the public can use to protect themselves" (Olson et al., 2020, p. 631). Additionally, the visual aspect of television news can help express the situation people are facing by providing different perspectives, and this can be accomplished through video, as well as photography and drawings displayed during a broadcast (Macdonald, 2021). In this way, television "immerses an audience in an event" (Olson et al., 2020, p. 632).

This immersion also occurs when individuals see people that look like them represented on the screen. The standard way television news accomplishes this is through the use of vox pops. These are brief interviews of ordinary people who have been stopped on the street to be asked questions about particular news events, and through the sharing of their opinions, these people are used as proxies for the general public (Beckers, 2019). Including vox pops in a broadcast encourages engagement with the audience because everyone has the opportunity to be arbitrarily chosen as the interviewee if he or she happens to be in the right place at the right time. However, this form of reporting is problematic because random individuals sharing their opinions tend to be viewed as more influential on viewers' beliefs than experts providing statistical information (Beckers, 2022).

Despite the potential pitfalls of relying on opinions over facts, audiences respond to this type of presentation because it makes the news feel more authentic (Debing, 2016). When something feels real to the consumer, it becomes more accessible and believable. The medium itself helps with that because it "shortens audiences' senses of distances to spaces and places of news" (Gutsche, 2019, p. 1037). Rather than having to travel to another country, the television brings that locale to the viewer. Accomplishing this compression of time and spatial separation gives the news legitimacy by making the events unfold on the screen relate more to the individual experiences of the viewers (Kopytowska, 2015). When television news also incorporates content (video, photos, vox pops, et cetera) from the viewers, the legitimacy builds because the audience is engaged and contributing their experiences to the coverage (e.g., Almgren & Olsson, 2015; Bergillos, 2019; Niekamp, 2009; Peterson-Salahuddin, 2021).

Of course, legitimization of news does carry the potential for harm. This is particularly true in relation to coverage of politics. Television journalism exists as a key source of political knowledge creation among viewers (Gutsche, 2019; Ksiazek et al., 2019; Yamamoto et al., 2021). Thanks to cable television, consumers have a plethora of channels they can turn to that provide news. The big three options are CNN, the Fox News Channel, and MSNBC. Despite being news-oriented, each of these channels is on 24 hours per day and actively seeks profit, which influences the types of programming they produce (Jones, 2012). To fill the timeslots, the channels produce a large quantity of commentary and opinion programming, which they were able to do thanks to Reagan-era deregulation that resulted in the repeal of the Fairness Doctrine's requirement of "equal time" being given to competing political voices (Vaughn, 2008; Young, 2021).

Only seven respondents indicated they don't use television to keep up with the news. For example, a 44-year-old female educator assigned the alias of Edna explained she only uses the television to watch DVDs she borrows from her local library. Similarly, a 21-year-old female college student assigned the alias of Helen pointed out she only uses streaming services such as Netflix, Amazon Prime, and Disney+ for television-related content, making this type of news inaccessible. As an avenue to news, television was fairly popular, though. Only six respondents indicated they don't watch any television for informational programming, and Patty, a 64-year-old farmer and rancher, said she doesn't like to watch television. However, she explained that the television is on a lot in her home because her husband likes to watch it, and his preferred channel is Fox News.

Of the national cable news outlets cited by individuals in this study's population, Fox News was mentioned most frequently. For five of the interviewees, Fox News served as a primary news source, and those individuals discussed watching it often and for longer periods of time. For example, Monroe, a 50-year-old male educator, said he watches Fox News when he is at the gym. Yet when Fox News was mentioned by others, it was within the context of believing the content was biased and untrustworthy. CNN, MSNBC, and Newsmax TV were discussed with various interviewees, but those outlets were often mentioned only in passing, if at all. Instead, most respondents suggested they consume more localized television news. Specifically, most individuals said they watch KWCH, the CBS affiliate in Wichita, Kansas. The ABC and NBC affiliates also had viewers.

Relatedly, survey participants were asked about their television consumption habits as well. They were asked to separate cable and local news watching habits. For cable news, CNN led with 25.3% of the responses, and Fox News followed closely behind with 24.5%. With 17.7% of the responses, BBC World News came in third, and the fourth choice was MSNBC with 13.1%. Newsy was reported to be the least watched outlet, garnering only 0.4% of the responses. As far as differences between rural and urban individuals go, there was a statistical significance ($\chi^2(12) = 21.71, p = 0.04$). With this, there was a notable point concerning the watching habits of these two types of respondents. No urban individuals reported watching RFD-TV, which is "the nation's first 24-hour television network featuring programming focused on the agribusiness, equine and the rural lifestyles, along with traditional country music and entertainment. RFD-TV produces six hours of live news each weekday in support of rural America and is a leading independent cable channel available in more than 52 million homes" (RFD-TV, n.d., para. 2), while 6.3% of rural residents selected it as their most-watched channel. Additionally, in terms of local television news, 37.6% of the survey respondents said they do regularly watch, 36.7% said they do not, and 25.7% said they sometimes watch. No statistical significance existed ($\chi^2(2) = 2.20, p = 0.34$) between rural and urban individuals.

When it comes to local news, the interviewees also discussed weekly newspapers as a source of news. These are considered community media outlets. Of course, there are several definitions for these types of operations. Some scholars defined the concept as local-oriented news that helps people feel like they are part of a community by covering matters and people and institutions of importance (Lowrey et al., 2008; Smith & Schiffman, 2018; St. John III, 2013). More technical definitions describe community media in terms of frequency of publication and scope of coverage areas (Bressers et al., 2015; Pauly & Eckert, 2002; Smith, 2018). Howley (2007) defined community media as "locally oriented, participatory media organizations that provide groups and individuals whose voices and perspectives are excluded from mainstream media with access to the tools of media production and distribution" (p. 3).

Regardless of the definition one adopts, community media provides important information to and about residents. Howley (2007) explained this form of journalism as being uniquely focused on covering and promoting local culture while also encouraging civic engagement and social integration in the form of local access radio and television, alternative newspapers, and computer networks, among others. The coverage community journalists provide ranges from weather

CHAPTER 3

and disaster coverage (Perreault, 2021), local schools and athletics (Bressers et al., 2015), and local government (Karlsson & Rowe, 2019). Such coverage by local journalists provides a perspective unique to the community. When outsiders attempt to cover a news event, the coverage is often different than that produced by those who are part of the community (Goldfarb, 2001). Variations in reporting stem from the proximity local journalists have to the news itself. Local journalists must work with community members to report the news, and they must build relationships with those people in order to cultivate an audience that will support the journalistic endeavors of the operation. This type of collaboration is key for "the formation and perpetuation of community, trust, and social capital" (Belair-Gagnon et al., 2019, p. 560). As such, "news organizations can help build stronger communities and further cement their roles in those communities by considering the community's expectations as inextricably bound with their own" (Lewis et al., 2014, p. 11).

Therefore, community news outlets provide a form of camaraderie. Nygren (2019) highlighted "the social role of local media" (p. 53) as it brings people together and builds relationships due to coverage of shared experiences. Leupold et al. (2018) referred to this as social cohesion. This is how society is developed, through communication processes such as journalism. Referring to American philosopher John Dewey, Huntsberger (2020) suggested, "Dewey's theory of knowledge considers communication to be the key to the development of shared intelligence and the formation of cultural and political life. For Dewey, acts of communication are necessary steps required to build the foundations of any community" (p. 193).

Due to this, community media supports democracy. At the most basic level, local news consumers experience greater interest in, expanded knowledge about, and increased participation within their communities' democratic processes (McLeod & Daily, 1996). "Studies show that hyperlocal media play an important democratic role in helping people root themselves in the local community as well as providing the geographic location with meaning," meaning these outlets provide information needed for democracy to thrive and hold local power accountable for its actions (Jangdal, 2019, p. 73). Nygren et al. (2018) pointed out that "hyperlocal media can become new platforms for social action, for defending local communities and giving them voice in the public sphere" (p. 46).

As far as the subjects of this investigation go, ten people indicated they read their local papers in order to stay informed about what was happening locally. That number increases to 14 when including people who read the paper periodically at work, at the doctor's office, or at the grocery store. As a 42-year-old marketing professional assigned the alias of Sherri explained, "Usually it's all local and I keep up with that every week. I read that as soon as it comes out."

To that end, a driving factor of local news consumption was proximity, as many respondents expressed that they found local news more applicable to them and their lives because they were living it. Despite this high interest in national and local news, 78.5% of the survey participants indicated the news being reported had little to no importance to their everyday lives. There was no statistical significance between the responses of rural *(M = 2.80, SD = 1.00)* and urban *(M = 3.00, SD = 0.83)* participants *(t(235) = -0.61, p = 0.54, equal variances assumed)*. Yet, 89.0% reported they generally believe the news outlets cover the important stories. Again, there was no statistical significance between the responses of rural *(M = 3.20, SD = 1.00)* and urban *(M = 3.42, SD = 0.90)* participants *(t(235) = -1.40, p = 0.16, equal variances assumed)*.

Still, online avenues also provide rural residents with access to news. This includes social media and websites. In terms of social media, Facebook was the most popular platform among respondents as 19 of the 25 said they had an account. Facebook was also most popular among survey respondents as 67.5% reported using the platform. YouTube was also popular with 44.3% using it, and Instagram followed closely with 43.1% of participants choosing the photo-sharing application. Twitter was the fourth most popular service with 36.9% of the responses, and 34.1% indicated they were Snapchat users. Additionally, 31.8% of the respondents said they used LinkedIn, and 5.9% indicated they don't use social media at all.

Of the survey participants, 70.1% indicated they look at social media regularly, saying they do so almost hourly or hourly regardless of whether or not they were urban *(M = 3.32, SD = 1.35)* or rural *(M = 3.30, SD = 1.20)* *(t(235) = -0.20, p = 0.84, equal variances assumed)*. For the majority that entailed looking at Facebook, which 39.7% said was the platform they used the most. Instagram was the second-most used, garnering only 12.7% of the responses, but there was no statistical significance $(\chi^2(11) = 13.70, p = 0.25)$ between rural and urban residents in terms of preferred social media platform.

However, the majority reported that they only received the news via these pathways if one of their connections shared something. Of course, a few of the individuals who were interviewed said they do follow local news outlets on Facebook, so they end up getting a fair amount of news that way. Several respondents also highlighted Twitter as an important news pathway, especially for headlines. Overall, though, only five respondents indicated social media was their primary news conduit. Interestingly, Helen said she not only gets most of her news via social media, but the primary platform she uses is Snapchat, which makes her the only interviewee who uses that particular service in this fashion.

These comments algin with the survey data. Those individuals reported using social media primarily for entertainment (35.4%). General communication (18.1%), consuming news and information (14.8%), and building and/or maintaining relationships (13.1%) were also popular reasons for use. Relatedly, 46.0% of survey participants indicated they rarely, if ever, use social media for news and information consumption. Furthermore, only 28.7% said they do so half the time, and only 25.3% reported regularly or often using social media for news and information consumption. In this regard, there was no statistical significance between the responses of rural *(M = 2.80, SD = 1.22)* and urban *(M = 2.90, SD = 1.10)* participants *($t(235) = -0.49, p = 0.62$, equal variances assumed)* in terms of using social media for news and information consumption.

While on various social media platforms, interviewees said the news they encounter usually leads them to click on links and visit the websites of news outlets. For 12 of the respondents, this meant navigating to local news sites. However, 15 interviewees indicated the links in their social media feeds lead them to national or international outlets. The most popular outlets among the respondents were Fox News, *The Wall Street Journal*, the BBC, NPR, CNN, Reuters, and *Yahoo! News*. A 39-year-old male construction worker assigned the alias of Herman said that in addition to Fox News, he also looks at *Breitbart News*, *The Epoch Times*, and *The Gateway Pundit*, which he referred to as "independent media" outlets. Similarly, a 39-year-old male farmer assigned the alias of Kent said he reads CNN, Fox News, *Newsmax*, and *One America News*, and Helen made clear her news consumption consisted of conservative outlets. "I take in a lot of right-wing media," she said.

When looking at these patterns on social media in the last year, Kansans publicly mentioned "Fox News" or "Wall Street Journal" or "Breitbart" 43,700 times on social media (again excluding private Facebook and Instagram posts). Interestingly, they also mentioned "BBC" or "NPR" or "CNN" 147,000 times. In short, this demonstrates that far from the narrative of rural Kansans being self-selectively locked in radical right-wing echo chambers, they were in fact more actively posting on or about liberal news organizations and outlets.

To better explore reasons why Kansans posted more regularly about liberal news outlets than conservative ones, we engaged AI to de-duplicate posts and help highlight trends over a year's worth of posts and found that the increase in volume about liberal news organizations on social media by Kansans is due to the controversy surrounding the exclusion of Jill Stein and Kennedy from the debate stage by CNN, leading to calls for them to be included and criticism of CNN's

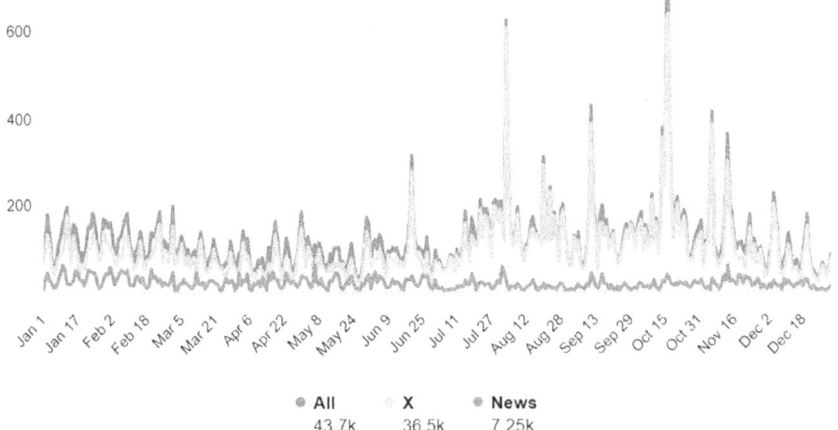

Figure 3.2a. Total social media mentions of "Fox News" or "Wall Street Journal" or "Breitbart" by Kansans in 2024.

Source: AI x Media Institute/Meltwater

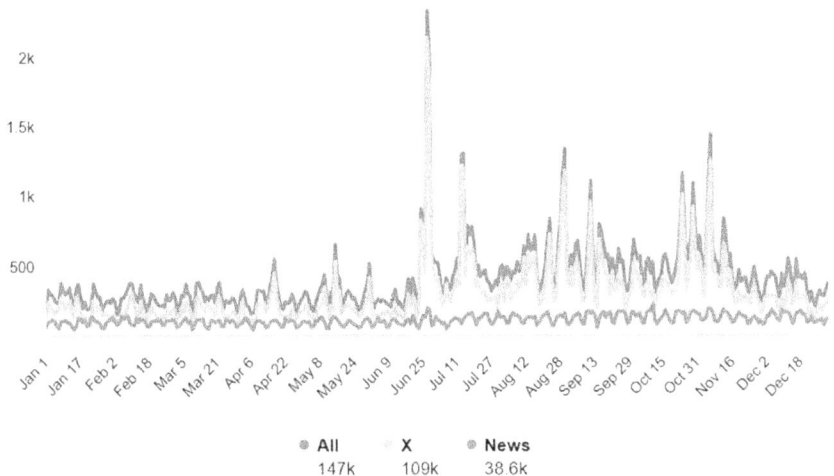

Figure 3.2b. Total social media mentions of "BBC" or "NPR" or "CNN" by Kansans in 2024.

Source: AI x Media Institute/Meltwater

decision. Additionally, there is a debate about the validity of Joe Biden's claim that all of Trump's election challenges were baseless, with evidence presented to the contrary. The Real Debate, a parallel stream produced by Kennedy, gained significant viewership, further fueling the discussion. There are also claims of CNN's failure to fact-check Trump during the debate and calls for Biden to withdraw from the race. The indictment of former Uvalde school police chief and an officer over the failed response to a shooting is also contributing to the spike in volume.

Yet it's possible the solitary nature of rural life created an environment where selective exposure—the tendency for people to prefer information and sources that align with their previously held beliefs and opinions while simultaneously avoiding content that counters those views (Hameleers & van der Meer, 2020; Pearson & Knobloch-Westerwick, 2019; Weaver, 2017)—to partisan media outlets develops powerful echo chambers and filter bubbles. Based on the interviews conducted for this study, that seems to be the case but does not neatly square with the social media data. Nonetheless, podcasts, newsletters, and aggregation applications also serve as important avenues to news and information for many of the individuals interviewed.

Interactions in Isolation: Gravitating Toward Preferences

It's possible the solitary nature of rural life created an environment where selective exposure—the tendency for people to prefer information and sources that align with their previously held beliefs and opinions while simultaneously avoiding content that counters those views (Hameleers & van der Meer, 2020; Pearson & Knobloch-Westerwick, 2019; Weaver, 2017)—to partisan media outlets develops powerful echo chambers and filter bubbles. Based on the interviews conducted for this study, that seems to be the case. To that end, podcasts, newsletters, and aggregation applications also serve as important avenues for news and information for many of the individuals interviewed.

Of the 25 respondents, 11 cited podcasts as key platform for news and information consumption. Nine individuals specifically mentioned programming with distinct political alignments. For instance, Monroe highlighted conservative commentator Ben Shapiro's podcast as one of his favorites, and Herman mentioned *The Health Ranger Show*, which is hosted by Mike Adams as a subsidiary of his *NaturalNews* website that has been accused of trafficking in disinformation (Institute for Strategic Dialogue, 2020) and conspiracy theories "like the *InfoWars* of alternative health" (Banks, 2013, para. 3). Other podcast listeners focused on true crime, religious, personal development, and academic-oriented content. For example, a 59-year-old male educator assigned the alias of Chalmers explained he listens to religious podcasts and sermons, along with sports news via ESPN, and Montgomery indicated he listens to the *TED Talks Daily* podcast. Of course, the number of people consuming audio content that doesn't come through the radio is increased to 13 if audiobooks are included. However, the types of audiobooks being listened to was not explored, meaning the content may or may not be informational in nature.

On the other hand, batch disseminations of email newsletters and aggregation applications do provide information. Two individuals — Marvin and Chalmers — specifically mentioned subscribing to email newsletters and receiving news from those sources. Similarly, Maude and Monroe mentioned using the Apple News aggregation application as a way to receive news. Combining those with *Yahoo! News*, which also aggregates news from across the internet, results in five people using these pathways to consume news. This equates to 28% of the interviewees getting their news via batch disseminations.

As the interviewees pointed out, the podcasts, email newsletters, and aggregation applications the utilize allow them to select the type of content they will receive, which can put them in echo chambers where they encounter content that confirms their biases as it aligns with their previously held beliefs and opinions. The reason these individuals gave for choosing these forms of programming, along with the prevailing uses of radio and social media mentioned previously, was accessibility. These pathways to news can be navigated from anywhere. Several individuals cited using radio and podcasts during their commutes, while driving farming equipment, or while accomplishing other mundane tasks such as household chores or exercising. For example, Kent said, "Well, and that's the other thing about being a farmer and pumping wells is a lot of driving around. I mean, no other way to say it. Checking cows can be a lot of driving around. I've always been a huge radio fan, a huge talk radio fan. I do tons of audio books." Even those who said they do not listen to podcasts indicated they are interested in exploring such an option because such content is becoming more available and specific to certain interests, suggesting they believe podcasts will be become as ubiquitous as radio. After all, as Monroe pointed out, "Podcasts. That's like modern radio, I guess."

Therefore, it is clear that rural residents in Kansas get most of their news via national outlets and social media platforms that focus on opinion-oriented content. Both the survey responses and the interviews highlighted that a majority of the respondents do receive news from national outlets and social media platforms. Likewise, the radio is a primary avenue for content, which aligns with research from Cramer (2016) who found people she interviewed also "reported that a main source of news is radio" (p. 106). Additionally, 13 of the 25 interviewees consumed news from objectively partisan outlets (Ad Fontes Media, 2023; Jurkowitz et al., 2020) that tend to rely on commentary for content. This can be attributed to a pervasive lack of trust in the media.

CHAPTER 4

Unearthing Rural Roots of Media Distrust

Every year in the rural town of Canton, Kansas, the local American Legion Post hosts a fundraiser that consists of a meal and an auction. Cold cans of beer sell for just a couple of bucks, and the crowd of men crammed into the main hall take advantage of the cheap refreshments. The real star of the show is the meal, though. The main course is a delicacy—mountain oysters. The sliced and deep-fried bull or lamb testicles give the event its unofficial name of "The Canton Nut Fry."

While standing in line to get his plate of fries and accompanying sides of baked beans and potato salad, a local journalism teacher struck up a conversation with the man in front of him. The gentleman was in his late 40s or early 50s and said he had just moved back to the area to take over the family farm. He asked the teacher what he did for living, and the teacher told him.

"Journalism, huh?" the man said. "I hope you teach them the right kind of journalism."

The teacher was confused and said, "Well, I try to."

"Good," the man said. "We don't need more CNN or New York Times journalism going on. We need the truth to get reported."

The implication was clear. Any news outlet that didn't fit the man's taste wasn't good or real journalism. It was "fake news" or at least not worth listening to. Though such events—if there are livestock, there's a supply of oysters—and interactions happen in more places throughout rural America than just Canton, Kansas, this anecdote epitomizes the general skepticism and outright distrust many rural citizens have toward the media.

Cultivation of Contempt: Encouraging Disbelief

As farmers shape the terrain of their fields by tilling, or cultivating, the soil, media platforms shape reality through the messages they deliver to audiences.

From this information dissemination sprouts the concept of Cultivation Theory (CT). This theory fits within the realm of media effects. Its chief focus centers on television and how that medium shapes and distorts viewers' perceptions of reality (Rubin & Haridakis, 2001). As primary developers of CT, Gerbner and Gross (1976) argued that the "substance of the consciousness cultivated by TV is not so much specific attitudes and opinions as more basic assumptions about the 'facts' of life and standards of judgment on which conclusions are based" (p. 175).

This social construction of reality is a complex process that requires more than just a consumer or just a content producer who exercises some form of power or overt influence over the other. It is a two-way street. Gerbner et al. (1986) explained "that cultivation is not conceived as a unidirectional process but rather more like a gravitational process […] Cultivation is thus part of a continual, dynamic, ongoing process of interaction among messages and contexts" (p. 24). As such, CT investigates the long-term effects of television viewing as it relates to the shaping of general beliefs regarding society and the moral values of viewers (Mosharafa, 2015).

Perhaps the most notable use of CT, though, concerns how depictions of violence on television shape viewers' beliefs about their safety in society. Gerbner et al. (1986) referred to this as the "mean world" syndrome and suggested that "television may cultivate exaggerated notions of the prevalence of violence and risk out in the world" (p. 29), which means that "one lesson viewers derive from heavy exposure to the violence-saturated world of television is that in such a mean and dangerous world, most people 'cannot be trusted' and that most people are 'just looking out for themselves'" (p. 28).

Fabiansson (2007) argued that concerns about safety at the community level become conflated with national or international events, especially following the September 11, 2001, terrorist attacks on the United States and the media's subsequent focus on violence, crime, and war, which cultivated a looming sense of fear within society. With television being dependent on visual imagery, safety concerns are exacerbated when viewers are inundated with depictions of war and its aftermath (Gadarian, 2014).

However, this distorted view of reality presented by television is problematic. As Alitavoli and Kaveh (2018) highlighted, fear about crime rises even as crime rates actually decrease. This demonstrates how the media has socially constructed a reality in which crime appears to be prevalent and becoming more so over time, and that "socially constructed reality of the existence of crime urges the public to prioritize crime as one of the most important issues concerning their community" (p. 7).

Obviously, crime and violence do occur. For example, one of the earliest examples of modern homegrown extremism and domestic terrorism directed at politicians came in 1995 with the bombing of the Alfred P. Murrah Federal Building in Oklahoma City (Schaller & Waldman, 2024). Timothy McVeigh—the 26-year-old former Army Sergeant who orchestrated the blast—murdered 168 people, including 19 children, using a rented Ryder truck loaded with a 4,800-pound ammonium nitrate-fuel oil bomb. McVeigh, a native of New York, had Kansas ties. He was stationed at Fort Riley in Junction City, and he rented the Ryder truck from a body shop in Junction City. Additionally, much of the fertilizer used for the bomb was purchased from around the State of Kansas (Michel & Herbeck, 2001).

Even so, some news consumers reported that they feel too much attention is placed on crime coverage (Reber & Chang, 2000). Furthermore, one must admit that other issues facing society are just as pressing. Luckily, CT can help explain the media's interactions with other topics as well. Gerbner et al. (1986) explained this broad connection in the following way: "Culture cultivates the social relationships of a society. The mainstream defines its dominant current. We focus on the implications of accumulated exposure" (p. 21). This means that television viewers tend to adopt a worldview constructed by the images, values, and ideologies put forth by television even if such a worldview is not accurate but based on an individual's subjectivity stemming from personal experiences and beliefs (Bilandzic, 2006).

Due to the reliance on personal attributes, choice and preference play a role. White (2022) argued belief in conspiracy theories and other forms for misinformation stem from confirmation bias, which Lee et al. (2021) defined as "the act of purposefully seeking out information that confirms our preexisting beliefs" (p. 166). Serving as a mechanism for cultivation to take place, narratives provide an avenue to shape the beliefs, attitudes, opinions, and values of media consumers. Bilandzic and Busselle (2008) argued that being transported via a narrative can help speed up the cultivation process due to the human affinity for storytelling. Through storytelling, relationships are formed, and that allows social capital to be built.

Social capital concerns social bonds that dictate communal norms and serve as the foundation for community trust and cohesion (Putnam, 2001). From this fertile soil sprouts civility and civic engagement.

Democratic Drought: Mistrusting News and Hindering Society

When individuals fail to engage with each other in this fashion, social capital fails to grow, and democracy is damaged because the development of trust among society members collapses. As societal trust erodes, it pulls media trust down with it, and journalism requires public trust if it is to function properly within a democratic society. As Karlsen and Aalberg (2021) pointed out, "trust in news is essential for the ideal of the informed citizen" because "citizenship only works on the basis of common knowledge" (pp. 2–3). Individuals must believe the news in order to use it in their performances of citizenship (Swart & Broersma, 2022). This is especially true during politically divisive times where "fake news" is used as a cudgel to bash any sort of media coverage that is not favorable to previously held beliefs and opinions.

Out of the 25 individuals interviewed for this study, only five described their trust in the news as more than "half," "average," or "medium," and only two of those people described their trust as "high." Abraham succinctly summed up his views: "I think they're full of shit." A 43-year-old male dairy farmer assigned the alias of Eddie went a step further. He said he had zero trust in the news. "The media is a propaganda arm for their owners, the deep state cabal, George Soros, all of those group of guys, Klaus Schwab, any of those that are connected," he said. Helen agreed: "I don't trust them at all."

When looking at these patterns of trust in media as discussed on social media by Kansans over the course of 2024, it was clear that they expressed less trust when they mentioned the "BBC" or "NPR" or "CNN" in their social media. An AI de-duplicated summary of these 2,290 posts found that there was an increase in volume due to a CNN poll that shows a shift in voter trust on the economy from Kamala Harris to Donald Trump after the debate. The poll indicates that Trump's percentage of voters who trust him more than Harris on the economy increased from 53% to 55%, while Harris's percentage decreased from 37% to 35%. This shift in trust has caused a spike in discussions and reactions online.

Similarly, when doing cluster analysis of co-occurring words in the 898 instances in 2024 that Kansans mention "trust" in addition to "Fox News" or "Wall Street Journal" or "Breitbart" we found that the emphasis was on multiple retweets of a post featuring Ben Shapiro's fiery congressional testimony on the trust crisis in the world of media. The post highlights the loss of trust in legacy media due to their alleged lies and left-leaning narratives, using as an example President Biden's recent mental collapse. It happened during the televised debate with Donald Trump when Biden struggled to express himself or answer questions in a "lucid" manner, causing panic in the Democratic Party and confirming "the country's worst fears about his fitness for office" (Megerian, 2024, para. 29). The post suggests that despite the loss of trust, legacy media continue to gain share in the advertising market.

Even so, trust can be understood as a relationship between social actors that involves an orientation toward the future, includes risk due to unknown futures, and works to reduce the complexity found in social interactions (Prochazka & Schweiger, 2019). Specific to the news media, Strömbäck et al. (2020) suggested a viable conceptualization of trust as a concept, which was adopted for this study and is articulated as follows:

> [A]t the broadest conceptual level, there is significant consensus that news media trust refers to the relationship between citizens (the trustors) and the news media (the trustees) where citizens, however tacit or habitual, in situations of uncertainty expect that interactions with the news media will lead to gains rather than losses. (p. 142)

To that end, Usher (2018) described trust as a constructed object within journalism and communication more broadly because it must be negotiated by all social actors, which includes journalists, audiences, and sources. Without this construct, the informed citizenry necessary for a democracy fails to come to fruition thanks to choosing partisan sources of information that align with their predetermined beliefs. "When people do not trust news, they are more likely to choose nonmainstream, alternative news sources," which leads them "to rely on their political predispositions" more heavily (Kalogeropoulos et al., 2019, pp. 3672–3673). Furthermore, Hopmann et al. (2015) found that when individuals were exposed to political coverage that was framed like a game or competition, such as a horserace, those people ended up trusting the news less.

In alignment with such research, the feelings of distrust pervaded the opinions of all respondents to this investigation, regardless of their political alignment or preferred news outlets. Individuals representing both sides of politics ideologically speaking expressed such sentiments, and some directed their criticism toward outlets they viewed as representing political views that were opposite their own. For example, Murphy, a 46-year-old dairy farmer, explained it this way: "I think of sitting in high school government class and hearing about, this sounds terrible, the German Nazi propaganda machine with the news and everything. And I almost feel like in some minds that's kind of what *Fox News* is in a way." Others described the issue more generally as not being tied to politics. Bart, a 37-year-old male educator, suggested he doesn't feel like he always gets the full story. A 73-year-old male farmer assigned the alias of Quimby agreed, suggesting it is difficult to get clear and reliable information because too much of the information being presented is conflicting. Barney, a 34-year-old male financial professional, viewed the media's focus on being first instead of right as a major factor in cultivating distrust.

For a majority of the respondents, though, the level of trust in the media can be broken down between national and local outlets. Sixteen of the 25 interviewees suggested they trust their local outlets more than national outlets, even if the difference was marginal. In many instances, this stemmed from views that national outlets were more focused on entertainment, political alignments, and ratings as they tried to persuade audiences, while local outlets avoided political partisanship and focus on news that has a more direct impact on the lives of interviewees. This seems to fertilize trust because, as Cletus explained, "If it's not in your backyard, you really don't know. So that's why it's easier to trust your locals because you're in the same community with them." Ned and Sarah expressed similar views.

Likewise, whether survey respondents trust a given news outlet or journalist also depends on whether or not the outlet is national and local in nature. For national outlets and journalists, trust leaned toward "none" as 78.6% ranked their confidence anywhere from average to zero. There was no statistical significance between the responses of rural *(M = 3.22, SD = 1.03)* and urban *(M = 3.50, SD = 0.90)* participants *(t(223) = -1.34, p = 0.09, equal variances assumed)*. Locally, though, trust trended in the opposite direction as 77.8% ranked their confidence anywhere from average to high. Still, there was no statistical significance between the responses of rural *(M = 2.71, SD = 1.00)* and urban *(M = 3.03, SD = 0.90)* participants *(t(223) = -1.76, p = 0.08, equal variances assumed)*. This aligns with research by Newman et al. (2021) that found local television news to be the most trusted news source, ranking at least 10% higher than the likes of CBS News, ABC News, BBC News, CNN, The New York Times, NPR, the Washington Post, and Fox News. Regardless, 81.9% of the participants disagreed with the idea that the "press is the enemy of the people," and there was no statistical significance between the responses of rural *(M = 2.40, SD = 1.24)* and urban *(M = 2.42, SD = 1.15)* participants *(t(223) = -0.14, p = 0.89, equal variances assumed)*. Additionally, 50.2% of the respondents indicated journalism is "extremely" important for society, and there was no statistical significance between rural *(M = 4.30, SD = 0.95)* and urban *(M = 4.10, SD = 1.14)* respondents *(t(223) = 0.83, p = 0.41, equal variances assumed)*.

Even though local news seemed to be more trusted than national news, several interviewees suggested local news could do better. "We all can't be at our local county commission meeting, or the State House in Topeka, or even in D.C. So, there has to be someone there to tell the story," Murphy said. "And it would be nice if they would just be there unbiased, telling the story of what happened today. But anymore, I think that's a pipe dream." From the perspective of a 31-year-old female veterinarian assigned the alias of Maude, including more perspectives from local residents would benefit the local news environment. "I love reading the opinion pieces that get submitted to the paper," she said. "I would like more opinion in a thoughtful manner, and I think when you type something out and submit it to a paper, maybe it's a little bit more thoughtful because of the time and effort that goes into it." Sarah also expressed a desire for a localized focus, specifically on high school athletes. She explained it this way: "When I was growing up, the local newspaper covered everything. All the different school events and community events, and it was in the paper. And now there's not much in there. I would always read about games and stuff like that for sports, and you could find out about opponents and things like that. And now I know it's all on technology. There are grandmas and grandpas who don't have access to that stuff. I think they really do miss the newspapers because otherwise they have no idea what happened."

Highlighting this issue, the survey data also pointed to a need for improvement, particularly in the manner of being present within the local community. The majority of respondents (68.4%) reported rarely or never seeing local journalists or reporters talking to community members, and there was no statistical significance between the responses of rural *(M = 3.23, SD = 1.40)* and urban *(M = 3.52, SD = 1.23)* participants *(t(235) = -1.10, p = 0.28, equal variances assumed)*. Similarly, 83.1% of the individuals indicated they see local journalists or reporters covering community events only sometimes, and here was no statistical significance between the responses of rural *(M = 3.10, SD = 1.12)* and urban *(M = 3.23, SD = 1.02)* participants *(t(235) = -0.79, p = 0.43, equal variances assumed)*. To improve this, 60.3% of participants said they wished local journalists or reporters would work with the communities they serve to develop story ideas or contribute content in order to provide more news of local importance, and 26.2% were open to such an idea. Also, 45.6% reported they would actively participate if such an opportunity arose, and 35.4% would consider it. For this, there was no statistical significance $(\chi^2(3) = 6.91, p = 0.75)$ between rural and urban respondents.

Another way local news could improve would be to document and showcase the history of the community. Abraham shared that he enjoys reading about what happened five or ten or more years ago, which he argued helps the community members see how connected they are. "I think it builds the community," he said. "I think it makes it stronger." Similarly, Chalmers suggested he would like to see more uplifting news about the local community. He explained it this way: "I get a lot of enjoyment out of just the human-interest stories of things that people are doing either for other people or things that they're doing out in the community that helps support the community. So those are things that I really enjoy reading about and am sometimes not even aware of that people are doing certain things, and I think that's really neat. And sometimes reading those types of things encourages other people to get involved with things if they may not even be aware that it's a need. Let's say they do a human-interest story on a family in town that really needs this, that or the other because they're in crisis, I think that's really important and things I'd like to know about." Along those same lines, a 47-year-old female educator assigned the alias of Doris argued for more inclusive and well-rounded reporting. "I think the more homogenous your community is, the more important it is to highlight the diversity of your community, whatever it is that exists," she said.

Jasper expressed sadness for the loss of local news, specifically mentioning how his hometown paper got purchased by a chain, losing its individuality and local focus. Clancy, a 37-year-old male manufacturing worker, agreed: "I hate to see these local newspapers die off. I think a lot of people enjoy them. They want to know what's going on locally; however, social media's really taking that apart. Sometimes the tangible piece of paper is … It's something to hold onto, and it's nostalgic." Quimby seemed to agree, but he reiterated the need for the news to be presented transparently and without bias.

To that end, the interviews show that rural residents in Kansas struggle to discern between credible and unreliable news outlets. Overall, individuals viewed the news as more trustworthy when looked at only through their preferred news outlets. This relates to concepts of reliability. In terms of television viewing, the survey respondents selected BBC World News as the most reliable outlet as it received 29.5% of the responses. CNN followed with 22.4%, and Fox News ranked third in terms of reliability with 19.4% of the responses. Also, MSNBC was viewed as reliable by 9.7%. The least reliable outlet was a four-way-tie among NewsNation, Free Speech TV, Newsy, and One America News Network (OANN) as each received 0.8% of the responses. Based upon this, there was no statistical significance ($\chi^2(13) = 14.67$, $p = 0.33$) between rural and urban respondents. However, it is notable that 7.3% of the rural residents indicated RFD-TV was the most reliable option, while zero urban individuals agreed.

Table 4.1. Survey Respondents' Top Four Most Reliable Cable News Outlets

Rank	Outlet Name	Percentage of Responses
No. 1	BBC World News	29.5%
No. 2	CNN	22.4%
No. 3	Fox News	19.4%
No. 4	MSNBC	9.7%

For Marvin, trustworthy and reliable sources of information can be described as "legitimate media," while several others suggested their levels of trust increased if the outlet was "recognizable" and "reputable." Also, seeing the same story being reported by multiple outlets increased trust for the interviewees. Still, Murphy cautioned that even an individual's preferred or "trusted" source needs to be viewed critically, paying attention to whether the language being used is slanted, biased, or otherwise polarized.

However, even recognizing potential biases in the content does not change the minds of some individuals. For example, Helen explained she leans on outlets that align with her beliefs, which are conservative, but that recognition does not change her level of trust in the information she consumes. "I'm aware of it. I know what I take in is biased," she said. "Everyone has a bias."

Despite the lack of trust described by the interviewees, 15 believe the news is largely accurate. According to Sarah, the accuracy comes from the access reporters have: "I think, well, they're just sharing what they see or what they know. Their eyes and ears of places that we don't have, we can't be, or maybe don't want to be." Overall, though, the view on the news being accurate or not broke on lines of local versus national organizations and outlet preferences. Clancy expressed the opinion that the information within news content is accurate but that the outlets present it in a way that attempts to persuade or convince the audience. Moe, a 35-year-old service worker, agreed: "I think, for the most part, the news media is accurate at giving the information. I think the news should just be told as information. And when you start going away from information, it becomes more inclined to whatever whoever's telling the news wants you to maybe think or hear." Doris echoed such sentiments. She suggested the content of the reporting is accurate, but she has a problem with the presentation of the information, arguing it is often sensationalized, out of context, and lacking verifiable sources. "It's opinion I have a problem with. I love a book with 30 pages of endnotes," she said.

Biased Branding: Seeking Accuracy Over Opinion

This indicates that rural residents in Kansas distrust the news due to a belief that media outlets are not telling the truth about what is really going on in the world. The perceived amount of opinion and bias caused the other respondents to believe the news is inaccurate. Though there may be kernels of truth presented in the reports disseminated by these outlets, Jasper said, "They're clearly quite colored with the particular author's viewpoints. I think so much of it is agenda driven now." Bart agreed: "What we are being told and what's going on isn't the same thing." Likewise, Sherri believes the news "is too skewed," and several respondents discussed how they believed the media exaggerates or sensationalizes the news. For example, Patty explained it this way: "They can make a big deal about nothing. It doesn't amount to piddly dink."

For Kent, the concept of accuracy doesn't factor into his trust in the media because the coverage might be the same, but the way it is presented is different. "It's not really a matter of being accurate or inaccurate," he said. "Everybody's cheering for their side to be right. Everything's right versus left instead of right versus wrong." To that end, several interviewees mentioned they do their own research, which often entailed looking at multiple news sources and using internet searches in an attempt to suss out the truth. Quimby alluded to this as well: "You have to get both sides of the story."

The quest for truth was another commonality among the respondents. "I'm after truth," Herman explained. Kent agreed. "I'm looking for the truth. It isn't readily available. No one's really after the truth. They try to persuade you to see it through a lens," he said. For some, such as Edna, truth is information that is "fact-based and you can verify it." However, for others, true news is determined by the source. Ned explained his perspective in this fashion: "If you see it on TV, you have to trust it's real."

In short, the truth seems to be in the eye of the beholder. This cultivates fertile ground for misinformation to take root.

CHAPTER 5

Misinformation Taints Media Diets

Farming in rural America can be lonely. Hours tick by while plowing fields, cutting wheat, or checking cattle, and seeing another human being might be rare. Finding ways to socialize becomes crucial for mental health and the development of connections. Cramer (2016) found rural citizens often gather around a pot of coffee. Sometimes this happens at the local diner, the town's gas station, or in the community lumber yard. For Kent, it happens at the co-op. Co-ops are an essential part of any farming community. They "are producer- and user-owned businesses that are controlled by—and operate for the benefit of—their members, rather than outside investors. Farmer-owned co-ops help producer-members market and process their crops and livestock, and secure needed production supplies and services" (USDA, n.d., para. 1). Without a co-op, farmers wouldn't have a place to sell their crops, and in small towns, those same farmers wouldn't have a place to interact with their neighbors. Of course, these same exchanges take place at high school sporting events, which serve as another cornerstone of rural community life. At one high school volleyball match that took place in September 2024, two men in attendance to watch their daughters managed to miss the entire competition as they chatted. Church functions also provide a place to come together and talk with neighbors.

Back at the co-op, Kent said they discuss everything, such as the weather and the news. Undoubtedly, the topic of eating pets surely came up following the Sept. 12, 2024, presidential debate between Republican nominee former President Donald Trump and Democratic nominee Vice President Kamala Harris. That is when Trump repeated a thoroughly debunked rumor about Haitian immigrants in Springfield, Ohio: "They're eating the dogs. They're eat the cats. They're eating the pets of the people that live there" (Catalini et al., 2024, para. 3). This anti-immigrant rhetoric, of which Haitians have been the subject before (Dize,

2024), caused far-right extremist group The Proud Boys to descend on the town (Wendling, 2024). According to a post-debate poll by YouGov, more than half of Trump's supporters believe that Haitians in Ohia are eating pets (Crisp, 2024).

In the case of lies about Haitians, the rumor started online via platforms such as YouTube and X, the platform formerly known as Twitter. It entered popular discourse thanks to the nationally televised debate. News outlets heavily covered the remarks, so even if a person hadn't watched the debate, they were sure to have heard about it. Cable television channels discussed it, and so did talk radio stations, which can be one of the only forms of media rural residents like Kent can access depending on where their work takes them.

Radio Rumors: Hearing Misinformation

Talk radio consists of opinion-based programming, and it is often cited as the most popular format on the radio (Campbell et al., 2019). Since American adults spend almost 12 hours per week listening to traditional radio (Nielsen, 2019), the likelihood that individuals are spending at least some of that time listening to news or talk radio seems high. Of course, talk radio in its current form would not exist if it weren't for Reagan-era deregulation that resulted in the repeal of the Fairness Doctrine's requirement of "equal time" being given to competing political voices (Vaughn, 2008; Young, 2021). "Radio was now free to air programs that only presented one side, without the obligation to let the other side be heard. By the end of the 1980s, partisan talk shows, mostly from the right-wing conservative viewpoint, were proliferating" (Vaughn, 2008, p. 436). One notable name in the talk radio game was Rush Limbaugh.

In February 2021, a year after receiving the Presidential Medal of Freedom during President Donald Trump's 2022 State of the Union Address, Limbaugh died of lung cancer at the age of 70 (Folkenflik, 2021), but he left behind an indelible mark on the radio and media worlds. His style of promoting conservative and Republican ideals while simultaneously attacking anyone and anything remotely viewed as liberal turned talk radio into a powerful political force (Jones, 1998). He rarely had guests on the show and only allowed a handful of callers to speak on the air, opting instead to opine about politics and the news of the day through a largely solo performance (Dori-Hacohen, 2013). Through this, he became one of the most prominent voices in politics (Jones, 1998). According to Boyd (1994), Limbaugh's influence over individuals and conservative political talking points stemmed from information distortions he used to convince others to adopt his point of view, and those distortions included the following: Ad Hominem, or attacking a source of an argument instead of the argument itself through name calling and ridicule; Mind Reading, or second guessing motives of an individual; Numbers Distortion, or using numbers vaguely or misusing statistics as a way to impress the audience without providing the proper context; Thinking for Others, or telling people what they should think and believe; and Not Quoting Sources, or not citing any references or sources to support the positions and opinions being expressed.

Limbaugh's approach and influence clearly worked. His show cultivated a massive fan base that even led to his devotees meeting together in real life at locations referred to as "Rush Rooms," which were spaces in restaurants where individuals gathered together to listen to Limbaugh's show and interact with each other (Dori-Hacohen, 2013). For what it's worth, Limbaugh attributed his popularity to the idea that he symbolized Middle America and its rejection of elitism because the "enemy of the plain people, of good ol' red-state America, is intellectuals. They are the haughty liberal elite under whose tyranny 'Middle America' suffers" (Frank, 2004, p. 192). Regardless, his pioneering programming inspired the likes of conservative talk radio stalwarts Sean Hannity, Michael Savage, Glenn Beck, and Mark Levin (Campbell et al., 2019). Such individuals, as Weaver (2013) argued, have throttled public dialogue and debate because their brand of content "strangles free thinking and obstructs self-agency and participation on both the local and national level. It goes against the basic dialogic principles of communication and thwarts the outcomes for basic education and literacy policies" (p. 298).

It's worth noting that liberal talk radio did exist, but it failed to find a sustainable audience (Campbell et al., 2019; Vaughn, 2008), which is why the medium became the sole domain of conservatives. The reason for conservative talk radio working remains unclear, though, but within conservative circles, the partisan messages clearly struck a nerve. By tuning in to conservative talk radio, listeners "could quickly and easily get detailed, informed assessments from someone they generally agreed with, a fellow conservative—a charming, articulate, well-informed one" (Jones, 1998, p. 370).

This again feeds into the idea of filter bubbles and echo chambers that serve as vehicles to reinforce previously held beliefs and opinions (Flaxman et al., 2016; Geiß et al., 2021; Torres-Lugo et al., 2020). Also, the messages are delivered with emotion and energy, which pulls listeners in and excites them. For example, Michael Savage is known for his high intensity (Stiegler, 2014). The passion exhibited by personalities like Savage or Limbaugh typically leverages outrage aimed at opposing political beliefs or institutions (Shrader, 2013; Young, 2021).

Often, this outrage results in the use of hateful and derogatory language that can be viewed as a form of hate speech (Noriega & Iribarren, 2014; Stiegler, 2014).

Through looking at the language used between conservative (the right) and liberal (the left) media outlets, Sobieraj and Berry (2011) found "that the right uses decidedly more outrage speech than the left. Taken as a whole, liberal content is quite nasty in character, following the outrage model with emotional, dramatic, and judgment-laden speech. Conservatives, however, are even nastier" (p. 30).

The partisan and polarizing discourse of conservative media damages democratic society. It fosters incivility in audiences, resulting in increased use of uncivil language when discussing political issues (Gervais, 2014), and shapes knowledge, attitudes, and perceptions about political issues and political actors (Lee & Cappella, 2001). Such impacts are not always positive, which is why Hemmer (2016) highlighted that conservative media permanently altered American politics.

Additionally, Gastil and Keith (2005) argued that "the viciousness of talk radio reveals the popularity of a decidedly nondeliberative form of citizen participation" (p. 12–13). It also distorts the shape of the public sphere, which is the communicative space where members of the public can discursively interact with each other (Habermas, 1991), by altering the ability of citizens to acquire the information necessary to effectively participate in dialogue and debate over matters of public concern (Mwesige, 2009).

Furthermore, selectively exposing oneself to partisan media shapes a person's political behavior and overall media use, which has implications for civic engagement (Weaver, 2017) and how dialogue is constructed within society (Lee, 2012). If citizens cannot communicate civilly, democracy fails to function. This results in a communication landscape fertile for the cultivation of misinformation.

Lynchets of Lies: Endangering Democracy

As Vincent and Gismondi (2021) argued, "Misinformation is a grave concern for democracy, and it is the responsibility of us all to be proactive in discerning fake news and misinformation and reducing their virality online" (p. 94). Failure to do so degrades society's information environment (de Ridder, 2021), which "impedes civic dialogue" (Damasceno, 2021, p. 2). This causes individuals to make poor political, policy, and health decisions (de Ridder, 2021; Ecker et al., 2022; Jain, 2021). Misinformation reaches beyond the radio dial, though. It weaves its way through television, online, and social media as well. Such an insidious societal force destroys trust in the media and among neighbors.

Our research found that 84% of the survey respondents indicated they believe misinformation are a problem in society, and there was no statistical significance between rural *(M = 4.34, SD = 0.90)* and urban *(M = 4.32, SD = 0.90)* respondents $(t(223) = 0.73, p = 0.94,$ *equal variances assumed*$)$. Additionally, all interviewees also indicated they believe misinformation exists. However, not all of them agreed that it was a problem for society. Five of the 25 interviews suggested it either isn't a problem or isn't a full-blown problem yet. Both Ned and Kent explained it isn't a problem because inaccurate information and politically motivated news have always existed. Kent cited examples of World War II propaganda and the newspaper wars of yellow journalism between William Randolph Hearst and Joseph Pulitzer. From her perspective, Sarah believes it is sometimes a problem because of social media, which allows anyone to share anything just because they want to regardless of its accuracy. Helen agreed for identical reasons. Quimby, on the other hand, struck a more optimistic tone. He suggested misinformation is just starting to become a problem: "I think you're hearing too much one-sided stuff."

In contrast, the 20 other respondents all agreed that misinformation is a problem for society. Maude argued that its existence damages communities and social ties, especially when a person pushes back against inaccurate information. She explained it this way: "I think it breaks down trust and it makes trust harder to build from the beginning. If you're always saying like, no, I don't think that's right or I don't agree with that, I think it's harder to build those bonds with individuals. I think some people when you say, yeah, I don't agree, that maybe is a trust-building thing, but I think for the majority of individuals disagreeing prevents trust or impeaches trust." According to the respondents, a lack of trust can lead to division and polarization. "I think it's largely responsible for our division in this country, which seems to keep getting deeper all the time," Marvin said. In terms of politics, this was a common refrain from the interviewees. For example, Sherri suggested each political "side" has its own media. "It makes us more heated against each other," she said. "I think it pits us against each other instead of seeing each other as allies when one side has to be wrong if you're right." Doris agreed and argued that social media is a powerful force driving a wedge between members of society and injecting confusion into public conversation.

When looking at these patterns on social media in the last year, Kansans publicly mentioned "misinformation" or "disinformation" or "fake news" 70,500 times on social media (again excluding private Facebook and Instagram posts). When looking at what drove spikes in the increase in volume, clustered network analyses found it was due to expressed concern over the spread of misinformation and conspiracy theories about fake news and disinformation. These posts and tweets are accusing media outlets like 60 Minutes of being fake news, propaganda, and spreading disinformation. These posts also criticize politicians and government officials for using the term "disinformation" to suppress criticism and label it as unpatriotic. This has sparked a debate about the role of the media and the manipulation of information for political purposes. Based even on this

CHAPTER 5

high-level view, we begin to see evidence of the Misinformation Finds Them (MFT) perception taking shape.

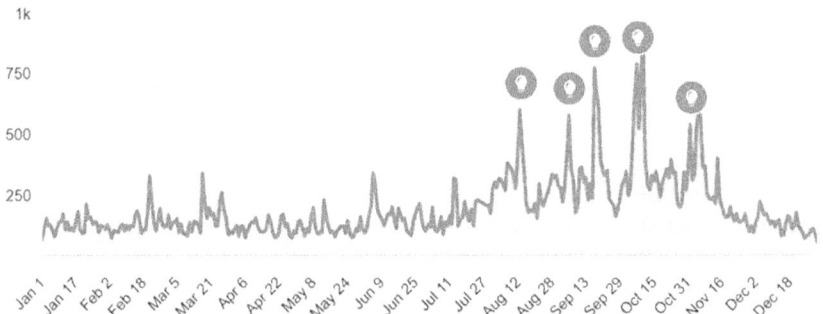

Figure 5.1. Total social media mentions of "misinformation" or "disinformation" or "fake news" by Kansans in 2024.

Source: AI x Media Institute/Meltwater

Producing this type of content serves the business interests of the channels carrying such programming. Those who manage a station's purse strings seem to ignore the social responsibility of radio (Shrader, 2013), and advertisers don't seem to care about the messages being broadcast either. "They're buying them because their audience buys tractors, their audience drinks soda, and their audience needs data backup. And that's the place to get those types of customers" (Weinger, 2013, para. 5). Additionally, this type of content breeds incivility—understood to be disrespectful and hyperbolic claims toward a target that are delivered in a purposeful and confrontational manner—within society's political discourse by using emotional appeals that activate negative political beliefs and opinions (Gervais, 2014). Research from Conway and Stryker (2021) found people from all political beliefs recognized the incivility, especially when it came from talk radio show hosts or other broadcast political pundits, but Republicans seemed to be unfazed by the hostility and outrage while Democrats demonstrated more concern about the language being used.

Using Cultivation Theory (CT), Shrum (2017) highlighted how media consumption, especially television viewing, can cultivate interpersonal mistrust. Earlier research also found a correlation between television viewing and a lack of trust (Gerbner & Gross, 1976; Jin & Kim, 2014). Of course, television isn't the only type of media that relates to ideas of cultivation. This is because, at its core, CT is used "to determine what, if anything, viewers absorb from living in the world of television" (Gerbner & Gross, 1976, p. 182), but society is saturated with media, such as social media.

In terms of social media, some research shows that the online worlds created by these platforms cultivate opinions based upon the user-generated content to which a user is exposed (Nevzat, 2018). This is important because social media platforms "provide individuals interpersonal connect with others, relational satisfaction, and a way to learn about the surrounding cultural milieu" (Croucher, 2011, p. 261). If these connections radicalize an individual toward destructive behavior, the cultivation of attitudes and beliefs becomes problematic. Furthermore, as Eddington (2018) found, social media networks create an avenue for hate groups and other like-minded individuals to find each other online, further spreading harmful discourses that can then inculcate others.

Therefore, CT is applicable to all forms of communication because people can absorb messaging via all media platforms because it provides a way to make sense of the effects of various media types and a lens through which to look at the news usage and opinion. As such, the cultivation ability of mass media messaging is wide-reaching, and if one isn't aware of the impacts their media consumption has on them, they can become confused about where to place their trust.

This is why many respondents suggested it is difficult to know what is true or what can be trusted. Barney pointed out that this causes a snowball effect, leading to multiple issues. One such issue is apathy, and that leads members of society to simply stop paying attention to the news, according to Jasper. Chalmers also expressed the idea of apathy by explaining that he doesn't do much digging into whether something is accurate when it gets reported, instead relying on his trust level of the outlet doing the reporting. Additionally, Edna pointed out that democratic decision-making suffers if misinformation flourishes: "If decisions are made on either the local, state, national, or international level based on misinformation, then those policies affect the safety and well-being of people. Yeah, it's a problem." Such a sentiment was of key concern to Nelson, a 55-year-old male who works in the manufacturing industry. He expressed the view that misinformation inhibits an individual's ability to make their own decisions, which stems from the power of media to manipulate and shape people's opinions. Doris also shared such worries and feared it could be catastrophic for society: "Worst case scenario, it's the end of our democracy."

Knowing this, an increased call for media literacy education efforts seems warranted. Increasing media literacy by "providing audiences with information and critical thinking skills to assess, evaluate, analyze, and process media messages" (Stamps, 2021, p. 234) could help counter the effects of television viewing as they relate to reality construction. One step people could take is turning off the television. Gerbner and Gross (1976) found college education and regularly reading newspapers diminished mistrust because those "who do not read newspapers regularly have a high level of mistrust regardless of TV viewing" (p. 193).

Part of being media literate is understanding where reliable news comes from and where the misinformation is germinated. According to the people we interviewed, politics spreads numerous seeds of misinformation.

Murphy explained it this way: "Politics clouded the judgment of otherwise good people." From Abraham's perspective, misinformation spreads because "it's too easy to confuse people." Such a statement aligned with the general consensus of the interviewees that social media and national news outlets are leading spreaders of this faulty information. Maude pointed at talk radio as a vocal part of the problem. According to Marvin, outlets like Fox News, *Newsmax*, and *One America News* are prime examples of the issue as well. "That's where I believe disinformation bloomed," he said. Cletus agreed, adding CNN to the list of perpetrators. Kent also laid the blame at the feet of cable news, but he had a different perspective. He explained his views this way: "I think the left has a lot bigger voice through a whole lot more stations, TV personalities or whatever, to put it out there. I mean, talk radio is completely, I mean, conservatives dominate talk radio, English, Spanish, whatever. But, TV, I mean, MSNBC, NBC, ABC, CBS, all that legacy media, they all lean left and lean left hard, which is why they all hate Fox News so much. It's the one that's not."

Relatedly, interviewees discussed where they believe they are most likely to encounter misinformation, which is to say how they believe it spreads. They pointed to television as a primary purveyor of this content, and the survey data aligned with that finding. In fact, television was deemed to have a lot of misinformation as 85.8% of the survey participants indicated the medium has an "average" to "an extreme amount" of this type of content, and there was no statistical significance between the responses of rural *(M = 2.44, SD = 1.00)* and urban *(M = 2.16, SD = 0.90)* participants *($t(223) = 1.50, p = 0.13$, equal variances assumed)*.

Of the major cable networks, Fox News was viewed to be the outlet that spreads the most misinformation as 38.7% of the survey respondents chose it. CNN came in second with 22.2%, and MSNBC checked in with 9.8%. There was no statistical significance ($\chi^2(12) = 14.14, p = 0.29$) between rural and urban respondents. On the flip side, BBC World News was reported to spread the least amount of misinformation with 38.7% of the responses. Despite the results of what outlets spread misinformation, CNN and Fox News were the second and third choices for also spreading the least amount of misinformation with 16.4% and 12.0% respectively. Again, there was no statistical significance ($\chi^2(14) = 15.92, p = 0.32$) between rural and urban respondents.

Outside of television, respondents cited social media often when discussing how misinformation spreads. Several of them pointed out that because anyone can post, the content is often more inflammatory and one-sided. "The negativity can really suck you in," Doris said. This leaves a void of honest and reputable sources of information, according to Moe. "Opinions seem to be overpowering what the real news is," he said. The survey data aligns with 46.2% of respondents indicated they believe "an extreme amount" of misinformation is present on social media. An additional 47.1% reported they believe the amount is "average" or higher. There was no statistical significance between the responses of rural *(M = 4.11, SD = 1.00)* and urban *(M = 4.50, SD = 0.90)* participants *(t(235) = -1.85, p = 0.07, equal variances assumed)*.

When examining differences in the concern over misinformation in social media data posted by Kansans in 2024, we found that residents of both urban and rural areas contributing approximately 70,500 posts that mention "misinformation" or "disinformation" or "fake news" on publicly available platforms. Here we see that while nearly half of all posts were from Kansas City, there is otherwise a near even split between rural counties with 13,822 posts and all other urban counties with 19,348 social media posts on the topic. When taking into account the relative population distribution in urban versus rural counties, it is fair to observe that rural Kansans' concern over misinformation seems to be in line with that of their urban counterparts.

Table 5.1. Total Social Media Mentions of "misinformation" or "disinformation" or "fake news" by Kansans in 2024 (Source: AI x Media Institute/Meltwater)

City	Posts	County
Kansas City	31326	Urban
Wichita	6931	Urban
Topeka	3314	Urban
Overland Park	2759	Urban
Olathe	1685	Urban
Lawrence	1354	Urban
Lenexa	1088	Urban
Derby	576	Urban
Prairie Village	427	Urban
Shawnee	389	Urban
Leawood	326	Urban

(Continued)

Table 5.1. *(Continued)*

City	Posts	County
Gardner	291	Urban
Lake Quivira	208	Urban
Anthony	2479	Rural
Andover	2281	Rural
Liberal	2119	Rural
Sterling	1135	Rural
Manhattan	1032	Rural
Pittsburg	647	Rural
Protection	614	Rural
Hutchinson	479	Rural
Salina	310	Rural
Atchison	279	Rural
Ottawa	273	Rural
Moundridge	266	Rural
Hays	240	Rural
Junction City	240	Rural
Leavenworth	235	Rural
Pretty Prairie	229	Rural
El Dorado	206	Rural
Coffeyville	193	Rural
Bird City	154	Rural
Ellsworth	142	Rural
Humboldt	136	Rural
Garden City	133	Rural

While we do advance more on the Misinformation Finds Them (MFT) perception in Chapter 8 as a mechanism where the threat of misinformation can exacerbate polarization due to its presumed differential effects, the notion that misinformation alone radicalized rural populations because they were either overly concerned or caught unaware simply is not supported by the social media data in this corpus.

Divisive Discourse: Feeding Polarization With Misinformation

Trust in the media can be heavily influenced by the discourse found on social media networks, especially in terms of politics. This is due to the fact that social media networks exist as user communities (Walker et al., 2019). As such, these channels provide an avenue for political discussion, so political ideology and perceived political affiliation of information disseminators via the platforms influence the trust of news found in those spaces (Karlsen & Aalberg, 2021). Furthermore, political actors weaponize social media to increase partisanship by spreading polarized messages, which contributes to the erosion of trust in democratic institutions (Walker et al., 2019). Additionally, opinion leaders, whether politicians or not, permeate social media and spread whatever thoughts and opinions they are promoting. This makes it difficult to know who to trust in the online spaces (Swart & Broersma, 2022). As Dubois et al. (2020) highlighted:

> Opinion leaders can serve as a trusted source for information and thus have the potential to insulate their followers from threats of problematic information flows on social media but they could also amplify the effects of disinformation and echo chambers if their political information verification practices are poor. (pp. 8–9)

Such findings could be explained by a general sense of skepticism social media users have toward information found via those platforms (Park et al., 2020), especially considering people tend to bump into news without intentionally seeking it out online (Swart & Broersma, 2022). Therefore, as research by Kalogeropoulos et al. (2019) found, "choosing social media as the main source of news is correlated with lower levels of trust in news" compared to the trust in mainstream sources of news such as television, print, and other legacy media outlets (p. 3682), and Karlsen and Aalberg (2021) echoed this idea.

Banning or blocking conspiratorial content or other forms of misinformation could help, but research by Innes and Innes (2021) found doing so does not eliminate such content completely. Of course, this makes sense. Social media algorithms amplify misinformation (Ingram, 2021), and when a user encounters that content, his or her brain engages psychological mechanisms to process the information, which both affects and is affected by emotions and attitudes (Lee et al., 2021). Based upon this information consumption, value judgments are made concerning the reliability and credibility of the news being disseminated. Research clearly shows that belief in the news stems from political ideology (Bauer et al., 2022; Gaultney et al., 2022; Vincent & Gismondi, 2021). After all, according to survey research highlighted by Lee et al. (2021), "people were much more likely to believe fake news stories that cast their preferred candidate in a good light" (p. 169). The result is political polarization and division.

For example, Recuero et al. (2019) found that social media creates polarization due to the proliferation of opinion statements, which are sometimes unsubstantiated, spreading on the platforms. Most recently, the 2016 United States Presidential election highlights how polarization, understood to be entrenched beliefs and opinions related to politics or other subjects of public discussion that divide individuals (Gaultney et al., 2022), can be fostered. "Social media, by acting as portals of shared information determined to be sought (algorithmically or otherwise) by users, may have helped Trump win by cultivating ideological filter bubbles that lacked cross-cutting information" (Groshek & Koc-Michalska, 2017, p. 2). Furthermore, social media can shape perceptions of news because users see comments and opinions of others before being able to consume the news themselves (Gearhart et al., 2021).

Polarization occurs when there is a void of reliable information or when individuals do not feel like their voices are being heard. Darr et al. (2018) found loss of local newspapers increased community division as evident by down-ballot voting patterns. People become less knowledgeable about politics if no journalists are covering the local politics. Community news outlets can help diminish polarization and increase the democratic practice of voting by focusing editorial writing on local issues (Darr et al., 2021), and the research of Chapp and Aehl (2021) found "local papers have a tremendous impact on what happens after voters have registered their presidential preference" (p. 247). One reason for this is that "weekly newspapers are the only steady source of local news for rural communities […], thereby making their role even more critical" (Finneman & Thomas, 2021, p. 335).

Correcting inaccurate information helps, but if a person is repeatedly exposed to false information, he or she is likely to believe it due to the illusory truth effect (Maresh-Fuehrer & Gurney, 2021). Journalists can help in the effort of countering polarization-inducing mis- and disinformation by reporting on the falsehoods and directly debunking them, but it is the polarization itself that prevents such actions because some individuals will see this type of reporting as evidence of media bias (Saldaña & Vu, 2022).

From Montgomery's perspective, this results in a domino effect that perpetuates misinformation and causes more of it to spread. "I think that's sad because I think people just see that information right away and they believe it. And it's sad. Maybe it shows the uneducatedness of the United States of America. Or the dumbification." What's more, this was not a unique view. The sentiment of education levels being related to believing and spreading misinformation came up with a few different respondents.

Maude suggested less educated, lower socioeconomic individuals, who are typically white males, are some of the worst offenders. Marvin and Murphy agreed and suggested religious beliefs can play a role, which Montgomery agreed with. Doris shared parallel views: "I think it's White Christian nationalists. The White conservative men. But I do think both sides are guilty. I absolutely do. Extremists on both sides want to get their headlines and all that too. So it's certainly not just White Christian nationalists that are fanning the flames, but I feel like it's more prominent coming from them." Similarly, several interviewees argued rural, small-town citizens spread misinformation more than their urban or suburban counterparts due to the previously highlighted education and socioeconomic concerns, as well as a narrower worldview stemming from less exposure to a diversity of thoughts and opinions.

Additionally, perceptions of money and power influenced respondents' views of how misinformation spreads. For example, Nelson explained that those with the most wealth and influence get to dictate what is reported, whether it is accurate or not. Herman, as well as several others, related this idea of money and power to ratings, which they acknowledged news outlets needed to make money and stay in business. Bart took this a step further. He suggested news outlets twist facts to make stories "juicier" and more interesting, which increases audience attention and results in more profitability. As Sherri argued, "They know who their viewers are, and they know what sells and they know what gets them to come back. And I feel like some of it is reported in that way for that purpose." This relates to the views of radio and printed media that were shared by the survey participants.

In terms of radio, most survey takers (47.6%) reported believing only an "average" amount of misinformation was going out on the airwaves, but 34.3% indicated radio carried little to no misinformation. In this case, the difference between the responses of rural and urban Kansas residents is statistically significant, though, because the results of a t-test found that $(t(223) = -2.60, p = 0.01$, *equal variances assumed*) rural respondents believe there is more misinformation on the radio $(M = 2.81, SD = 0.87)$ than their urban counterparts $(M = 3.30, SD = 1.03)$.

Additionally, survey respondents reported printed news products such as newspapers and magazines as having the least amount of misinformation as 82.6% indicated they believed those products contain an average amount of misinformation or less. Again, the difference between the responses of rural and urban Kansas residents is statistically significant because the results of a t-test found that $(t(223) = -2.00, p = 0.05$, *equal variances assumed*) rural respondents believe there is more misinformation in these printed products *(M = 2.73, SD = 1.00)* than their urban counterparts *(M = 3.10, SD = 1.00)*.

Media Monoculture: National Outlets Sowing Dissent

To that end, it appears rural citizens do not use community media as a primary source of news in their daily lives. In discussing misinformation, local news outlets rarely came up. The focus remained entirely on national media organizations. This indicates the primary news sources of the respondents were not community-based. Though the interviews highlighted a desire for local news, national sources are the dominant players in the media ecosystems of these individuals.

Thanks to the selective exposure that constructs filter bubbles and echo chambers, conservative media outlets fuel polarization and division. It accomplishes this by exaggerating fringe opinions to motivate those who have low trust in the government to engage with politics (Hollander, 1997; Johnson & Kaye, 2013). Again, relying on outrage (Shrader, 2013; Sobieraj & Berry, 2011; Young, 2021), partisan pundits pontificating over the airwaves and via digital avenues broadcast messaging designed to rally the like-minded consumer and shore up the conservative ideals being put forth. For the diehard, these political messages confirm previously held beliefs. They can spur action that can be dangerous, such as the insurrection at the Capitol that happened on January 6, 2021.

In this way, the national news outlets are planting seeds of dissent that will lead to a crop of audience members who can be harvested for profit. All that is needed, then, is to cultivate the existing fertile soil that consists of religion and social capital found in politically favorable fields.

CHAPTER 6

Religious Beliefs Plant Political Views

Nearly 25 people packed into the small city council room on June 10, 2024. It was the regular monthly meeting for a small, rural Kansas town, but the turnout was anything but regular. Though ten were there as part of their official capacities with the city or the council and a few citizens attended to voice concerns they had about their water bill, a majority of the audience filling the seats or standing at the back of the room were there for one reason—the public library.

On the night's agenda was to approve a new library board member. A seemingly innocuous and pro forma matter, the individual nominated for the position had drawn ire for his stance on a recent push by some in the community to have certain books removed from their places on the shelves. The book in question was *Queer: The Ultimate LGBT Guide for Teens* by Kathy Belge and Marke Bieschke. It wasn't required reading for anyone, and, according to the head librarian, the book had only been checked out a couple of times, which made the nominee question why people were taking umbrage with the book since it didn't seem it was impacting the community that much. Furthermore, the book had mysteriously disappeared from the library without being checked out, making it completely unavailable. According to the nominee, the attempted ban of this particular title seemed to have political motivations.

The man leading the charge against the book and the board nominee stood during the public comments section of the meeting and reiterated his concerns. "Most of you have heard me speak in the past and know that I'm concerned about the sexualization of our children. By the strength of Jesus Christ, I've been able to speak out on this issue," he said. "There are three current library board members who will resign if I'm granted the opportunity to become a library board member, but if I am given the opportunity to serve on the board I'm willing to work with them concerning the other functions that the board performs to keep

CHAPTER 6

the library going. However, by God's strength, I am not willing to compromise on this issue. My goal is to protect the innocence of our youth and stand against their sexualization."

Another individual also stood to share his opposition to the board nominee: "I'm concerned that this nominee is too agenda-driven to be thoughtful."

The nominee then expressed his views on libraries and books. He explained a deep reverence for the First Amendment and free expression, which he said were under attack when books were banned or other forms of censorship were enacted:

> A library is a very special place in a given community. It's the democratization of knowledge. Anybody can go in. They're not forced to read anything. It's all available. They can pick, and they can educate themselves. I think that's an important thing to maintain and preserve and protect in a community. It's not my place to tell the rest of the community what they can't have access to. There should be this free exchange of ideas and knowledge. That's how we can develop a greater knowledge about the world around us and understanding of each other. Currently, we're in such a divided time that that doesn't always work, but a library can be one of those centers where that is allowable. And if we lean on that type of idea, we need to ensure that people have access. That's something that is key to our democracy and something that we should uphold and protect. To pick a side and only allow certain things from either political perspective would be antithetical to what the First Amendment exists for, and why public libraries exist, which is to help people gain knowledge.

More back and forth between the nominee and the opposition ensued. Council members asked questions, and another board member stood and spoke in favor of the nominee. Eventually, nominee's admission to the library board was brought to a vote. The nominee was approved 4–1.

Despite the arguing that the nominee had a political agenda, the opposition articulated their agenda in detail. It was all about religion.

Religious Radicalism: Leveraging Beliefs to Instigate Action

For example, in July 2023 the Sterling Free Public Library—located in Sterling, Kansas— made national headlines and faced widespread condemnation when its board fired the library director for her decisions on what books to display and how to decorate the library, especially during June's Pride Month. Such a decision stemmed from religious beliefs held by library board members, according to news reports (e.g., Alatidd, 2023), and lawsuits resulting from these actions have been filed against the city, mayor, and library board members. Similarly, the library in Dayton, Washington, came under attack by book-banning groups in 2023. As Abramsky (2023) explained:

movements that seek to ban books with LGBTQ+ or racial justice themes have picked up steam in GOP-controlled states around the country. Pro-censorship groups have sprung up at both the local and national levels, pioneered by a Florida outfit with the Orwellian appellation Moms for Liberty. The organization is endorsed by Steve Bannon, the Heritage Foundation, and other avatars of the hard right and has more than 200 local chapters. (para. 2)

In this case, the effort to ban or reshelve books focused on titles with LGBTQ+ themes, and the controversy became so heated that residents gathered signatures to force a ballot measure calling for the dissolution of the county's library system (Flatt, 2023). The courts blocked the proposition, deeming it unconstitutional according to the state's constitution (Hanlon, 2023). Ultimately, the library won a lawsuit and avoided being shut down (Gutman, 2023).

The battle over books in Dayton occurred because would-be censors were motivated "by religious and political objections to the content of certain books" (Abramsky, 2023, para. 6). Unfortunately, this type of script has been used in many other states, such as Montana, Missouri, North Carolina, and Iowa, among others (Cineas, 2023; Kim, 2023; Melotte, 2023; Schermele, 2022). No matter where it happens, though, an undercurrent of religiosity flows beneath the outrage.

Only one person interviewed for this investigation indicated they had no religious affiliation. The remaining 24 claimed Christianity as their chosen religious belief structure, making this particular belief system the choice of 96% of the participating people. This aligns with survey data. For the majority, religion was reported to be highly impactful as 54.4% indicated it was more than "average" in terms of importance. Importantly, the difference between the responses of rural and urban Kansas residents is statistically significant because the results of a t-test found that $(t(215) = 2.02, p = 0.05$, *equal variances assumed*) rural respondents see religion as important more *(M = 3.52, SD = 1.50)* than their urban counterparts *(M = 2.94, SD = 1.61)*.

As such, religion appears to be an important aspect of life for rural Kansans. This speaks to what Wuthnow (2012) highlighted as "the social role of churches" in rural life (p. 195). However, 84.4% of the survey respondents indicated their religious beliefs only have some impact on their political views, and there was no statistical significance between rural *(M = 2.81, SD = 1.41)* and urban *(M = 3.10, SD = 1.50)* respondents $(t(215) = -1.04, p = 0.30$, *equal variances assumed*) in this case. In contrast, those interviewed for this study often cited their religious affiliations as key to numerous aspects of their lives. For example, Chalmers said, "I believe my religious views shape everything I think about."

The social media data collected over the past year in 2024 supported that Kansans are enthusiastic about sharing their faith online, and there were over

CHAPTER 6

181,000 posts that mentioned "faith" or "religion" or "Christian" during this time. Moreover, hybrid AI analyses based on natural language processing models informed by human coding found that the increase in volume was due to an ongoing discussion and debate surrounding the intersection of religion, politics, and freedom of speech. The articles and posts touch on topics such as Trump's statements on Christianity and law-abiding Americans, the use of religious imagery in performances, the role of religion in politics, and the renaming of terms related to domestic violence. These discussions have sparked controversy and differing opinions, leading to a spike in online conversations.

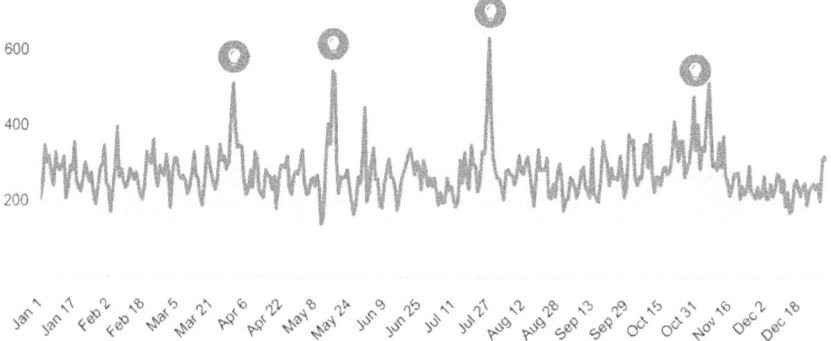

Figure 6.1. Total social media mentions of "faith" or "religion" or "Christian" by Kansans in 2024.

Source: AI x Media Institute/Meltwater

Also, nearly every individual who defined themselves as either conservative or Republican suggested their political alignments stemmed from their religious beliefs. This was especially true when it came to social issues such as abortion, immigration, gun control, parental rights, and marriage equality, among others. Using abortion as an example, Herman argued that a person cannot call themselves a Christian and be OK with abortion. "There's always a way for God to help, whether adoption or whatever the case may be. There's plenty of ways to help," he said.

How any of these individuals came to align with a religious belief such as Christianity appeared to be consistent across the board. Everyone said they were raised in Christian households, and many shared they had been baptized in their churches, especially if they specifically aligned with Catholic or Lutheran denominations. For some of them, even if they grew up with religion being part of their lives, their affiliation with Christianity was solidified by personal examination.

For example, Helen said, "The more that I explored it myself in high school and college, the more that I agree with the values of caring about people and loving people." Similarly, Montgomery discussed how he has studied several different religions, and though he considers himself a Christian, he tries to learn from all belief systems because each has value to society. He explained it this way: "I think that I try to take the strengths from each one of those religions. I think that it's something that we've lost in America, and I don't mean that we have to have religion. I think we have to have some type of identity where people understand that service, some type of giving back are so important."

However, not all the individuals professed to be devoted Christians for their entire lives. For example, Abraham said, "Am I a believer? Yes. I'm a believer in Christ and God, but I do not attend any formal church. I've never been sewn to any one religion." Nelson shared a similar sentiment. After growing up Catholic, he explained he fell away from the church a bit, but he maintained his faith. For him, it is a focus on morality. "It comes down to the moral things of right or wrong," he said. Bart also expressed the idea that being a good person was his focus rather than a particular religion. "I think all religions have that," he said.

He's right. Religious discourse and iconography represent certain morals and values, and followers of a given belief system hold those attributes closely and personally (Chimuanya & Igwebuike, 2021; Putnam, 2010; Wuthnow, 2012). Such values include, but are not limited to, giving back to the community and helping others. This is the essence of community engagement.

Regardless of their devotion to a given belief structure or simply a desire to be a good human, all but three of the individuals represented in this study are involved in their community in ways not related to their professions, equating to 88% of the people being active in their communities. Seven people related their involvement to their religion associations and participation within their chosen churches. Such activities ranged included, but were not limited to, participating in charitable drives, helping with afterschool programs, volunteering at vacation bible school, and supporting local chapters of the Fellowship of Christian Athletes. Also, ten individuals discussed being involved through agriculture-related organizations such as 4-H, county fair boards, cattleman associations, the Farm Bureau Federation trade association, state and national crop and dairy boards, farm credit unions, local water boards, and county extension offices, to name a few. Being involved with local schools and military organizations also came up often, along with helping the needy with a given community.

CHAPTER 6

Collective Communities: Developing Relationships With Neighbors

This is how rural residents in Kansas create relationships with their neighbors and communities. A majority of people suggested being involved locally was important to foster such relationships. Patty explained it this way: "I think that it pulls your community together, makes it a tighter-knit community, and I think it's important." For Eddie, being active locally means being heard. "I've always found grassroots involvement and involvement in the community, that's always been important, and even then, in organizations as far as having a voice, you can't argue or complain if you're not willing to take part and let your voice be heard," he said. Maude echoed such sentiments by suggesting that a larger impact can be made at the local level, and Barney argued helping one's community is important to help the area grow and thrive, which builds trust within the community as individuals become acquainted by working together on community issues.

This positions trust as a fruitful and connective aspect of community life. Yet the survey data suggests concerns for the rot of distrust harming such relationships. According to the responses, 20.3% of the participants indicated they trust their neighbors an average amount. However, 58.5% said they trust their neighbors more than average and "a lot." In this instance, though, the difference between the responses of rural and urban Kansas residents is statistically significant because the results of a t-test found that $(t(215) = -2.33, p = 0.02,$ *equal variances assumed*$)$ rural respondents trust their neighbors more $(M = 2.32, SD = 1.16)$ than their urban counterparts $(M = 2.84, SD = 1.10)$.

Such data argues that rural residents have more social capital than their urban counterparts. Social capital is a key component of community and democratic society since it focuses on how members of society interact with each other. Putnam (2001), who made the concept famous even if Loury (2020) argued he created the term, referring to social capital as a web of mutual trust and cooperation derived from the participation in community groups and organizations. Gastil and Keith (2005) built upon this to define the term as "the social networks and mutual trust that sustain democratic institutions" (p. 6). This requires investment within the community. This does not need to be in terms of financial contributions, though. Capital can be any resource used to make progress toward goals (Lin, 2002), such as through engagement.

Putnam's research led him to see how social capital as he defined it as a crucial component for social and civic engagement (Maras, 2006). As Loury (2020) explained, "all human development is socially situated and mediated," which means the "development of human beings occurs inside social institutions. It takes place as between people, in the context of human interactions" (p. 178). Mutz (2006) pointed out that there are two types of social capital that Putnam discussed—bridging social capital between social groups and bonding social capital within a social group—and "the conditions likely to promote bonding social capital may be precisely the opposite of those that facilitate bridging social capital" (p. 34).

Due to these two types, social capital isn't necessarily positive in all instances. For example, bonding social capital can cause individuals to become more insular and less open to outside thoughts and opinions, retreating into the comfort of their in-group relationships (Chakraborty, 2016; Mou & Lin, 2017; Yang & Hanasono, 2021). This can result in more polarization and division, which further erodes society and democracy. On the other hand, though, bridging social capital "is likely to be fostered in environments where information flows freely across the groups," and that communicative transaction "leads to higher social trust" that "makes connections between social networks and promotes widespread relationships" (Lee, 2017, p. 5).

If members of society recognize the value of being connected through bridging social capital, positive change can be realized. How those connections are built and maintained, though, may not always look the same over time. "Social, demographic, and technological changes have all put stress on older forms of socializing, but they may also drive the evolution of new ones that are better suited to modern times" (Hudson, 2020, para 57).

Technological Trappings: Seeing the Positive and Negative Implications

Giddens (2013) pointed out that "technological innovation stimulated by capitalistic development alters basic aspects of social life" (p. 116). Putnam (2001) saw a decline in social capital by noticing fewer people were joining bowling leagues and other community organizations, which he attributed to increased television consumption. Despite the fact television news can be a source of political information (Bucy & Grabe, 2010), the issue with television consumption, as some research suggests, is that it can cause viewers to be desensitized, especially to societal ills such as poverty or violence (Edgar & Edgar, 1971).

Outside of television, other technologies can have a negative impact on the creation of social capital. This is especially true in the realm of newer technologies, such as the internet and social media. A cause of this could be that users focus more on their digital lives than the social and civic opportunities around them (Maras, 2006). The research on this, however, is varied. Some scholars believe "online communities will make possible new social arrangements, more democratic and more inclusive," while others believe "social groups facilitated by the computer revolution will, in fact, destroy traditional social bonds, leading to weak social ties" (Matei, 2003, p. 3). This can lead to a society with less civility, which can negatively impact democracy functioning properly due to the lack of connectivity between citizens (Putnam, 2001).

Even so, communication supported by the internet can be beneficial, especially when it comes to organizing, activism, and socializing. "In fact, there are examples of digital communication building social capital and promoting democratic ideals in unprecedented ways" (Hudson, 2020, para. 49). Furthermore, it can happen anywhere or any time. "No longer is social capital constrained by time or space; cyber networks open up the possibility of global reaches in social capital" (Lin, 2002, p. 227). Abdullah et al. (2016) highlighted a case where online forums have allowed people to come together and discuss issues their communities are facing. Interacting online can help reduce limitations of participation that are inherent in face-to-face interactions (Beauvais, 2018). Using technology can also help individuals "connect with their neighbors online. It helps them break down social isolation" (Abdullah et al., 2016, p. 4).

No matter what, how a given media impacts individuals and society can be attributed to the amount of knowledge being available, which is tied to how individuals engage with the information ecosystem and each other (Edgar & Edgar, 1971). In this case, knowledge is crucial. Without this knowledge, which is important for being active in a democracy, reasons to become civically engaged dwindle because the idealism, instilled responsibility, and enjoyment of political participation becomes nonexistent (Putnam, 2001).

However, social capital has not died. In the aftermath of the September 11, 2001, terrorist attacks, the public's interest in civic life seemed to be renewed. This is because "critics have found other wellsprings of public spirit beyond the more traditional civic activities that Putnam traced over time. Charitable giving, volunteerism, and more diffuse civic networking may be supplanting lodges, PTA meetings, and bowling leagues" (Gastil & Keith, 2005, p. 15).

Local media plays an important role in connecting and informing the communities it serves. Despite the world being digitally connected, "most journalism continues to serve audiences closer to home" (Hess, 2015, p. 482). In fact, the reading of local print products is pointed to as being an indicator of having higher levels of social capital (Hess, 2015; Maras, 2006). Print journalism helps counter the feelings of social and geographical isolation that rural residents can experience (Gilbert et al., 2010). Such isolation could contribute to the fact television and other media privatized leisure (Putnam, 2001). The effects of which could be more impactful in rural areas because there is less to do, and television viewing in one's own home is more convenient (Maras, 2006).

Furthermore, rural individuals seem to adopt new technologies quite readily, which could be due to a desire to minimize isolation (Gilbert et al., 2010). This is especially true due to social media allowing various individuals to connect over any distance. Even so, rural social media users tend to connect with those closer to themselves geographically (Gilbert et al., 2010). This is because social media platforms allow individuals to surround themselves only with opinions and views they already agree with (Turkle, 2012). This allows for confirmation bias and misinformation to exist. As such, using technology to increase social capital could create possible drawbacks for individuals in rural communities that focus more on a print product for news. A resulting clash of social norms could hinder the development of social capital (Sass, 2016). This relates to the correlation between increased technology use and decreased social capital Putnam (2001) suggested. It should be noted, though, that correlation cannot empirically mean causation.

Therefore, social capital is important for a functioning democratic society. Unfortunately, aspects of society get in the way of social capital formation, even something like religion that is intended to bring people together. This is due to the passions associated with religion. The topic can be a hot-button issue that can cause disagreements, full-blown arguments, exclusion, or even violence, and media consumption can cultivate this type of animosity (Alkazemi, 2019).

The biggest issue in this regard, as Hofstetter and Gianos (1997) suggested, is when media personalities leverage passions, such as religion, to convince vulnerable people to view the world from their perspectives. This deepens division and cultivates mistrust of the other side. Even though something like talk radio or prime-time cable television is more about entertainment than news (Bennett, 2002), audiences often internalize the messaging differently. "When considering elite talk show hosts, they engage in one-sided, monolithic conversation. Their commentary is often passed on as fact. Hardcore listeners embrace their opinion leaders as a primary source for making sense of what is happening in America" (Weaver, 2013, p. 298). As such, despite the ability of broadcast and digital media to disseminate news and information quickly and efficiently, they distort reality, which endangers democracy.

So then why do people pay attention? It must be because the audience gets something out of it.

Bushels of Benefits: Exploring Media's Appeal

To that end, Uses and Gratifications Theory (U&G), which fits under the umbrella of media effects theories, attempts to understand the "how" and "why" people actively choose certain media to satisfy their needs (Valkenburg et al., 2016).

Communication and media scholars Elihu Katz, Jay G. Blumler, and Michael Gurevitch developed U&G to its current form (Severin & Tankard, 2000). In their review of the state of gratification research, Katz et al. (1973) laid the groundwork for the full development of U&G by arguing the following:

> Our position is that media researchers ought to be studying human needs to discover how much the media to or do not contribute to their creation and satisfaction. Moreover, we believe it is our job to clarify the extent to which certain kinds of media and content favor certain kinds of use—to thereby set boundaries to over-generalization that any kind of content can be bent to any kind of need […] Though audience oriented, the uses and gratifications approach is not necessarily conservative. While taking account of what people look for from the media, it breaks away from a slavish dependence of content on audience propensities by bringing to light the great variety of needs and interests that are encompassed by the latter. (p. 521)

However, prior to this work, McQuail et al. (1972) outlined four categories of media use, which included the following: Diversion, which includes an escape from routine or problems and serves as an emotional release; Personal Relationships, which considers the media as a substitute for companionship as well as a social utility; Personal Identity, which looks at self-reference, reality exploration and a reinforcement of values; and Surveillance, which entails information seeking.

These categories allowed Katz et al. (1973) to propose five assumptions regarding the relationship between media and audience, and these include the idea that the audience is conceived as active, linking gratification and media choice lies with the audience, the media and other sources of satisfaction compete with one another, the goals of mass media use can be determined through research that utilizes data coming from individual audience members, and judgments regarding the cultural significance of media should be separated from audience orientations toward the media. This led to the suggestion that media goals can be grouped into uses such as informing or educating, identifying with characters, entertainment, enhancing social interactions, and escapism to avoid daily life stress (McQuail, 2010).

To that end, U&G applies to a variety of news and information content (e.g., Sherry, 2006; Towers, 1985; Wei, 2009). "Specifically, attitudes such as news affinity, perceived news realism, and informational viewing motivations" have been the focus of this type of research (Haridakis & Whitmore, 2006, p. 770), which positions U&G as a valuable lens for investigating the spread of misinformation and how partisan media plays a role. Key to this is the important role of Computer-Mediated Communication (CMC) (Ruggiero, 2000), which considers the process of communication creation and exchange using networked computers and digital media such as email, social media, video conferencing, and other internet-facilitated forms of discourse (Kiesler et al., 1984; Luppicini, 2007; Romiszowski & Mason, 2013).

This stems from the theory's focus on individual differences that drive media use behaviors (Haridakis & Whitmore, 2006). Within media studies, a scholar might be looking at cultural contexts, the people that make up the audience, the individual behavior of those audience members, or the society in which the media exists (McQuail, 1984). U&G provides an avenue to connect all four of these lines of inquiry. As McQuail (1984) suggested, the goal of U&G "has been towards the construction of a major highway which serves to link all four purposes in one investigative enterprise" (p. 191).

Religious Routes: Motivating via Beliefs

Though for rural residents it would be more of a country road rather than a major highway, religion also serves as a link for people. This is especially true considering what participants of this study said. By considering the importance of religion in their lives as they described it, clearly their faith plays a significant social role, which aligns with previous research. Dingemans and Van Ingen (2015) found "that religiosity is an important determinant of social trust" (p. 752), but whether one's faith increases or decreases that social trust is debatable.

Even so, our interviews showed that rural residents maintain strong religious beliefs and connect to their communities by being involved in community organizations and causes. The high number of individuals who both express religious beliefs and place a high value on being involved in their local communities paints the picture that these two concepts go hand-in-hand. Cletus suggested it comes down to "Midwest values" that bind people together. This indicates bonding social capital, which can foster hostility toward out-groups due to the insular nature of the tight-knit bonds in this form of social capital (e.g., Frank et al., 2004; Jin & Kim, 2014; Putnam, 2001; Yang & Hanasono, 2021). Prior research supports this (Wuthnow, 2019) and focuses on shared "work ethic or values" (Cramer, 2016, p. 165). Furthermore, as many individuals explained, these religious beliefs and value of community involvement led them to their political beliefs. Combined with media consumption, this sets the stage for political activity.

CHAPTER 7

Partisanship Cultivates Radical Political Engagement

Driving along the dirt roads of rural America, there are certain sites one is almost guaranteed to see. Livestock and fields of row crops are omni-present. Telephone wires line the roads, and birds and insects lazily float through the sunshine-filled air. It's also common to see American flags waving in the breeze and religious iconography on display. In some cases, those flags and crosses are accompanied by signs sharing political preferences. For example, a flag flying in central Kansas read, "Trump 2024 No More Bullshit."

When it comes to religion, Republicans appear to have the market cornered. According to Korhonen (2024), "56 percent of surveyed Republicans identifying as Protestants compared to 38 percent of Democrats" (para. 1). Along with Protestants, the majority of Catholics and Mormons are also Republicans, and they attend religious services more frequently than their Democratic counterparts (Doherty et al., 2024). As Newport (2023) argued, "Everything else being equal, the more religious the individual in the U.S. today, the higher the probability that the individual identifies with or leans toward the Republican party. I called this the 'R and R rule'" (para. 1).

It makes sense then that most of the rural residents who participated in this study aligned with the Republican Party and considered themselves religious. After all, religious beliefs often contribute to a large part of a person's core identity. It would be understandable, then, if those religious beliefs shaped how people viewed politics, even influencing the political stances of individuals and the Republican Party (Wuthnow, 2012). However, that isn't necessarily the case. Rather, most citizens seem to be in agreement that religion shouldn't have much influence on political policy (Smith et al., 2019; The Associated Press-NORC Center for Public Affairs Research, 2018). This speaks to the idea that political party affiliation is more powerful than religious beliefs in the minds of people. Some refer to this as tribal partisanship (Etelson, 2020). Westwood et al. (2018) called it "partyism," and it is derived from their findings that political party identification creates stronger bonds than other forms of social or cultural identity, which can be attributed to the idea that people can choose their politics but not their cultures.

Undoubtedly, though, religion feeds into politics. Even though a majority think religion isn't influencing public life as much as it used to (Rotolo et al., 2024), nearly half of U.S. adults believe the country should be a Christian nation (Smith et al., 2022). This is at the core of Christian Nationalism. This concept can be understood as a "concern for symbolic boundaries and the belief that Christianity should play a prominent role in the public sphere" (Whitehead et al., 2018, p. 3). Put more simply, it is the melding of religious and national identities to the point where the church and state are not separated despite the Establishment Clause of the U.S. Constitution's First Amendment (Rotolo et al., 2024; Walker & Haider-Markel, 2024). Acolytes of this belief system rely on the United States motto of "In God We Trust" to prove their views (Lee, 2022), and the use of religious rhetoric by politicians only solidifies Christian nationalists' ideals (Lee, 2020).

Of course, this belief structure didn't develop overnight. It has gained traction among MAGA Republicans. For example, Rep. Marjorie Taylor Greene (R-Ga.) adopted the idea and promoted it: "We need to be the party of nationalism and I'm a Christian, and I say it proudly, we should be Christian nationalists" (as cited in Golgowski, 2022, para. 2). Here comments were met with so much support that she started selling T-shirts that had a cross and "Proud Christian Nationalist" emblazoned on the front (Olmstead, 2022).

This zealousness can be dangerous, especially when it morphs into white Christian Nationalism. As Gorski and Perry (2022) pointed out, White Christian Nationalism spawned the insurrection at the Capitol. It's also a driving force behind book bans, states' rights arguments, freedom of speech and expression battles, and other elements of the so-called "culture wars" (Burke et al., 2023; Davis et al., 2023). Such beliefs damage democracy. They approve of political violence, promote racism, and are inherently anti-democratic (Whitehead, 2022). That's because white Christian nationalists "degrade democratic institutions and norms, including transparency, accountability, the rule of law, and civil liberties and rights" (Schaller & Waldman, 2024, p. 140).

Without those elements, democracy as we know it can cease to exist.

Information Inputs: Creating an Informed Citizenry

Democracy occurs in the public sphere. This concept is most closely associated with German philosopher and sociologist Jürgen Habermas, and according to Finlayson (2005), "The public sphere is a space where subjects participate as equals in rational discussion in pursuit of truth and the common good" (p. 12). A key component of such interactions concerns the intersection of democracy and journalism. Since journalists write the first draft of history, which includes the activities of the democracy, the news media supports the public sphere.

As technology has progressed and media outlets have adopted new methods of information dissemination, the journalism-supported public sphere has evolved. Dahlgren (2005) highlighted how the internet has expanded the public sphere and created more space for public interactions. Turkle (2012) argued that despite the connective promise of such technologies, users end up more isolated. This leads to fewer meaningful interactions and exchanges of information. As Dahlgren (2018) explained, the internet and social media platforms carve out numerous spaces in which democratic participation can occur, but it can also limit participation due to structural and other limitations. Despite the promise of information access and equal participation, these platforms have not lived up to their ideals due to a variety of institutional influences (Kruse et al., 2018).

Carson (2021) suggested "that a functioning democracy consists of a tripartite classification of government, market, and civil society" (p. 86). If democracy is done right, individual voices can be heard in authentic ways. Goodin (2018) pointed out that accepting different forms of communication creates a more inclusive atmosphere, which is more democratic and allows for information to be conveyed to and from diverse members of society. Furthermore, as Gutmann and Thompson (2018) explained, "there should be many different ways of expressing political views including protests, demonstrations, and strikes" (p. 905). Through this, decisions that impact society can be made. These decisions emerge from the sharing of information that would otherwise be obscured if not for the open communication deliberation creates space for (Goodin, 2018).

Media help facilitate this. As Carson (2021) highlighted, the media's role in democracy "includes providing quality information so that citizens are informed and able to meaningfully participate in the democratic process" because "a well-functioning democracy depends on the public being able to monitor its representatives and on the state accepting criticism of its own exercise of power" (p. 12). Chapp and Aehl (2021) suggested that "local journalism is uniquely equipped to meet basic democratic needs" (p. 249) because "declines in local news corresponded to declines in both political knowledge and engagement" (p. 237). This is because, as Darr et al. (2021) explained, "Communities have critical information needs that help members live safely, access opportunities, and participate in civic life, and local media are the best sources for that information" (p. 8), which provides the necessary knowledge to deliberate and make decisions.

Unfortunately, the political climate in the United States makes this difficult. Too much of the country experiences polarization, voter apathy, institutional distrust, and misinformation (Farrell et al., 2019). Still, journalism can help facilitate the exchange of ideas with the added benefit of increasing unification, especially at the community level. According to research, more local news coverage exposure causes individuals to become less polarized (Darr et al., 2021).

In line with the fact that so many of the individuals interviewed for this project expressed alignment with a particular political party, only four of the 25 people indicated they don't vote at all or don't vote regularly. Abraham indicated he doesn't vote because he believes politicians don't vote for their constituents, making voting pointless. "It just doesn't matter," he said. "I just have never felt like my vote really makes a difference where I live." Sarah and Moe both shared that they don't vote on a regular basis, primarily because they feel uninformed despite high levels of news consumption.

Though Monroe also reported that he doesn't vote regularly, he suggested his reason for not voting was due to having recently moved. However, when he does vote, he said he takes a unique approach. "I like to look up all the judges that you are voting to retain or not to retain. Because I feel like a lot happens locally based on whether or not judges are prosecuting certain things or the positions that they take on certain things," he said.

As for the remaining 21 interviewees, they stated they vote regularly and in nearly every election. Three specifically expressed a focus on local and state politics. The prevailing sentiment was that local politics was where people felt they could have a larger impact. Murphy explained it this way: "It's your local politics. It affects you every day, all day. And the national, I mean, what are you going to do? I mean, I vote, but at the end of the day what are you going to do about a decision that's going on in D.C.?" In *The Left Behind*, Wuthnow (2019) hit on this idea as well: "The basis of small-town life is not only that it is 'rural' but that it is small, which means what happens is close enough to witness firsthand and to experience intimately enough to understand and have some hope of influencing" (pg. 98).

Also, people expressed the feeling that voting is necessary as part of democracy. For example, Ned said, "I think it's important just because of duty as a citizen of the United States, regardless of whether your county has 2,000 or 200." To complete their duty, nine individuals reported they vote the party line or straight ticket each time they enter the polls.

This aligns with the survey data as 72.4% of the respondents reported voting in every election, both national and local ($\chi^2(6) = 7.94$, $p = 0.24$). For example, in the 2012 presidential election, 30.9% voted for the Democratic Party ticket, and 27.6% said they voted for the Republican Party ($\chi^2(4) = 2.81$, $p = 0.59$). In 2016, though, 38.2% voted Republican, while 28.1% voted Democratic ($\chi^2(6) = 9.45$, $p = 0.15$). Then, in 2020, more individuals voted for the Democratic Party (41.5%) than the Republican Party (38.7%) ($\chi^2(4) = 6.49, p = 0.17$). On average, only 23.8% indicated they did not vote in any of the elections. As far as these forms of engagement go, there was no statistical significance between the political actions of rural and urban respondents.

Relatedly, during the summer of 2022 Kansans were faced with a state constitutional amendment vote that sought to overturn the Kansas Supreme Court's ruling that abortion was legal (Gowen, 2022; Smith, 2022; Smith, 2021). The amendment was defeated (Kusisto & Barrett, 2022; Ollstein, 2022; Smith & Glueck, 2022; Smith & Becker, 2022), and 49.3% of the survey respondents reported they voted against it, which contributed to the amendment not passing. Of course, 18.4% said they did not vote. To that point, how rural and urban participants voted was statistically significant according to a Chi-Square Test ($\chi^2(2) = 11.68, p = 0.003$). This is because 21.5% of the rural respondents did not vote in this instance, while all urban respondents did. Also, 74.2% of the urban individuals voted "no," and 45.2% of the rural individuals voted "no." When it came to voting "yes," the percentages were closer as rural residents in this sample outweighed urban 33.3% to 25.8%. The perspective of Kansas voters seems to be favored nationally.

Despite frequently voting, a majority of the individuals expressed distrust of politicians. In fact, 98.2% of the survey respondents indicated they have little to no trust in politicians, and there was no statistical significance between rural *(M = 2.10, SD = 0.80)* and urban *(M = 2.13, SD = 0.81)* respondents ($t(215) = -0.40$, $p = 0.70$, *equal variances assumed*). Additionally, only a few interviews suggested they trust politicians in general, though some did stipulate that they trust local politicians more. "I actually know those people," Sherri said. However, the majority of interviewees discussed how they believed politicians only looked out for their own interests instead of the people they are representing. "I have much more respect for the populace than I think that many politicians have," Jasper explained. Moe agreed and suggested politicians were too focused on transactive relationships: "They're only in it for people as long as the people give them something in return."

Barney took a more critical approach. "I feel like most of the time they talk out of both sides of their mouths. They want to appease their audience, and that's it," he said. Monroe summed up his views succinctly: "They all lie." Ned agreed, saying, "I don't think they're going to follow through. I think they're just telling us what we want to hear so they get elected." Helen also viewed politicians in a similar way. "I just hate politicians. I just think there's too much secrecy," she said. "Politics in general has just become about putting on a face and just putting on your best face. Well, that's not real. And social media and online, everything anymore has made that possible because you can put whatever you want online without people knowing what actually is going on."

Doris suggested the way the system is set up creates an environment where trust can't be built because "with no term limits, it's self-preservation for them." Political agendas also seemed to erode trust. Chalmers explained it this way: "I don't know that it's smart to put complete trust in any politician just because I think everybody has their own agenda so to speak. And I believe that in the political world there's a lot of pressures and things that people are trying to do for their own purposes. And no human is pure enough to say that everything that they do has to do with in the best interest of other people."

Eddie and Herman argued for a reset of the political system to solve the trust problem. "They're freaking crooks. The best thing we could do as a country is wipe out the whole damn system. Get rid of the IRS, get rid of it all and start from scratch," Herman said. "So, I don't trust them as a far as I can throw them. I think we need to gut the whole system and start from scratch. And I mean both sides of the spectrum, not just one, and not the other. Tank them all, start from scratch. We don't need government governing us. They work for us." Eddie echoed such views. "I think we need a blank slate, a clean slate. I think we need term limits and anybody who's been there for very long has been corrupted by the system and they're no good," he said.

However, 73.8% of the survey respondents described their trust in the government as average to "extreme." Again, there was no statistical significance ($t(215) = -0.16$, $p = 0.88$, *equal variances assumed*) between rural ($M = 2.94$, $SD = 1.10$) and urban ($M = 2.30$, $SD = 1.14$) respondents. Similarly, 83% indicated they largely were satisfied with democracy as a method of self-governance, and having roots in a rural ($M = 3.61$, $SD = 1.10$) or an urban ($M = 3.42$, $SD = 1.03$) area of Kansas presented no statistical significance difference in how the participants responded ($t(215) = 0.90$, $p = 0.40$, *equal variances assumed*).

The extant individuals trust either their neighbors or the elected officials is often influenced by their media diets. Misinformation and conspiracy theories spread by partisan sources create political division and polarization, and that erodes trust. These forms of unreliable and untruthful content spread via numerous pathways. Wuthnow (2019) suggested that for residents of rural American it "is driven by the conservative media they find appealing because it speak to their frustrations" (pg. 110).

However, according to the interviewees, the ways such content trickles down through the populace came down to social media and conversation. Of the 25, only four individuals indicated they share news and information via social media on a regular basis. Eddie, who reported he shares content via social media all the time, argued he has to do so because "I feel some sort of obligation to share a balance of what is out there." On the other hand, nearly everyone interviewed reported they share information in conversation, whether with family and friends or other people they encounter throughout their days.

Aversion to Awkwardness: Refusing to Correct Misinformation

Regardless of whether they share via social media or personal conversation, most people explained they are cautious about doing so because of existing political divisions and polarization within society. It seems people tend to heed Minnesota governor and Democratic vice-presidential nominee Tim Walz's advice: "Mind your own damn business" (Grabenstein, 2024, para. 4). Several individuals shared concerns about being attacked for their views on various issues. Such comments speak to the spiral of silence theory, which suggests that people don't speak up if they believe their views go against the dominant opinions on a given subject, especially if it is a controversial or value-laden subject, and the ensuing silence stems from a fear of being ostracized, isolated, or other negative consequences (Alkazemi, 2019; Kolotouchkina et al., 2021; Noelle-Neumann, 1974). For example, Doris said, "I recognize that among our social group, the small social group that it is. I am an outlier politically, and it's just easier to not talk about it."

Similarly, the majority of the individuals reported they will not correct people when they share incorrect information, even when such content could be classified as misinformation. Monroe explained his hesitancy this way: "I mean, nobody has ever felt better after getting into a heated Facebook debate. Nobody ever shut their laptop and were like, 'Yes. That was really helpful.' Usually, you're still fuming, or, usually, you haven't changed any minds."

Societal Slurry: Molding Individual Beliefs and Opinions

Even so, nearly all respondents believed the news and information they consume shapes their opinions and beliefs. Marvin suggested such an impact was most evident in other people. However, Jasper admitted his content consumption has a more personal effect. He explained it this way: "I do see I make changes in where I'm at politically or philosophically because of outside sources of information." Quimby agreed. "Well, if you consume that stuff, if you listen, it could affect the way you'd vote for, well, anything."

For some, the impacts news and information consumption have on individuals were viewed as problematic. Abraham argued the amount of news and information available "desensitizes people and makes for everything being just a little more acceptable." Alternatively, others believed the impact was positive. For example, Edna suggested that consuming news and information gives people a wider perspective and allows them to see the bigger picture. Chalmers agreed. "It keeps me cognizant of the things that are going on around the world. And I think that can affect how you think about your own faith and maybe what's going on with certain things in the world," he said.

Such impacts can be amplified when conspiracy theories are added to the mix. Seven individuals claimed to believe, or at least be open to, what others might deem to be conspiracy theories. From Edna's perspective, individuals believe conspiracies due to fear of the unknown. She explained it this way: "Anxiety was a big one on the list. People want a sense of certainty and having some knowledge that everything's explainable, and that there's a single source for all this powerlessness that we feel that makes us anxious."

This seemed to be the reason Patty didn't believe it. "I don't want to deal with it," she said. "It gives me anxiety." However, Patty did indicate she believed that schools were allowing students to identify as cats and were providing litterboxes for them. Outside of that, a few individuals said they find conspiracy theories entertaining, and others indicated they could be convinced of their veracity if they were presented with credible evidence. Still, skepticism remained the primary stance on the subject. "If it doesn't sound right, it's probably not right," Sherri said. For some, their disbelief in such theories stemmed from simply not caring. As Helen explained, "I don't know. I'm never going to know. I don't care."

In line with these responses, a series of six survey questions presented various conspiracy theories respondents as a way to gauge levels of belief in these types of statements. The majority of the survey participants reported not believing them. Only one conspiracy theory presented received more "neutral" responses, and that one read as follows: "Lee Harvey Oswald did not act alone in President John F. Kennedy's assassination." Of the respondents, 33.8% reported they are unsure about what occurred, yet there was no statistical significance between rural *(M = 3.00, SD = 1.24)* and urban *(M = 3.00, SD = 1.20)* respondents *($t(223) = -0.07, p = 0.95$, equal variances assumed)*.

For his part, Jasper explained that he believes in some of conspiracy theories because of their accuracy. "Some of those conspiracy theories have proven to be true, which I find pretty scary." Eddie agreed and discussed theories concerning child sex trafficking and the terrorist attacks of September 11, 2001. For his part, Kent also suggested he believed in some conspiracy theories and echoed the idea that some of them are true. He specifically discussed the stories of Ghislaine Maxwell, the assassination of President John F. Kennedy, the World Economic Forum and Klaus Schwab, George Soros, and the COVID-19 pandemic, among others.

COVID-19 came up frequently among interviewees. Kent explained his suspicions about the pandemic like this: "Are we really supposed to believe that COVID come out of a guy eating a bat soup that wasn't cooked right? Or out of a big virology institute that does this sort of thing, that had employees that worked there, that said it came out of this lab, and then a week later these employees are gone and nobody knows what happened to them? I mean, those are all facts. That's not a theory or anything conspiracy." Similarly, Eddie described the pandemic as a key component of his views. "This COVID and everything else, that truly sent me down a path of questioning everything. I question everything, everything that we have thought was, whether it be history or whatever. I don't know what's coming exactly. That's why I like to listen to some of these things, is because it's like, well, if I see some indicators of some things happening, I'm not going to be completely caught off guard. Maybe that means that I'll have some silver stored up or whatever. I've got to be able to protect my family, provide for them," he said. "I'm not worried about food because we have freezers full of beef and a tank full of milk. I'm not a doomsday prepper, but, at the same time, you can still look at what's going on in the world and take small steps to be prepared. We saw what happened with the toilet paper shortage. Well, I mean, it'd only take one week of nobody having food in grocery stores before people start coming out of the big cities to the country looking for food. It's like, I hope I never have to witness that, but it's not far from reality. It doesn't take much for something to happen."

For Doris, COVID-19 lead to her "break up" with Facebook. She said she permanently logged off the platform when the discourse surrounding the pandemic reached a point where she couldn't stand to subject herself to it any longer. Likewise, Sherri explained she stopped watching the nightly news because of the depressing nature of the coverage, which at the time focused heavily on COVID-19. Maude also shared a similar experience. She said she got into more heated discussion on social media because of the pandemic, causing her to scale back how much she used the platforms.

In the case of Murphy, though, COVID-19 and people's reactions to it resulted in a crisis of faith. "I'm Catholic, a very devout Catholic, and again, really had my, I guess, faith shaken by how our local diocese handled or did not handle the pandemic," he said. "Our response was totally different than others, and I think a lot of the way ours was is because of the bishop that's in charge of our diocese. Even prior to the pandemic, he was anti-vax and anti-science. I also feel that because when we shut down the state, and rightfully so, and inside church attendance wasn't allowed, I think it was the lack of tithing that the church started getting nervous. That's why they wanted to open everything back up just because, well, they want the money, which is sad. And, we had one local priest who is actually from my home church, and he'd been on this big 'Democrats are ruining our country and they're turning us into the communists' kick, and when the pandemic hit and Governor Kelly took the steps that she did to keep us all safe, that just gave him a louder platform to speak from. It just was like a snowball rolling down the hill at that point." As his wife worked in the medical field and saw the pandemic as a serious concern, Murphy found it disheartening that his faith community, as well as that of his friends and neighbors, refused to take COVID-19 seriously and listen to science. He explained it this way: "I guess that was the biggest disappointment for me being in the agriculture profession was we as an ag community have been trying to tell our urban neighbors, 'Your food is safe. We eat the same food you guys do. We're not harming the earth. We're not doing anything to poison you or the food supply or damage the environment.' And then here comes the pandemic, and what's the first thing some in the ag community start doing? Popping horse pills to prevent COVID."

COVID-19 also came up in terms of being an indicator of political beliefs. A few interviewees mentioned that masks were used to determine where a person stood on the political spectrum. For example, Kent said, "This issue turned into left versus right. If I see somebody walking in a mask, I'll just almost bet that that person's going to pretty much vote Democrat." From Nelson's perspective, this kind of division causes communities to fracture, and such fissures are widening, he said, because now people are discouraged from congregating together, whether at work in the breakroom or elsewhere.

Pastoral Politics: Engaging Civically from Ideological Stances

Therefore, it became clear that rural residents in Kansas engage in political actions and discussions on a regular basis, generally adhering to conservative political ideology. The interviewees described sharing and discussing news and politics on a regular basis. These discussions are often framed within conservative political ideologies. Also, political action in the form of voting is high, and those individuals hold their political views tightly. The majority of the individuals indicated their political activity is confined to voting or serving on the boards of community and industry-related boards. However, a minority of respondents did

Figure 7.1. "Trump 2024" roadside sign.

Source: Todd R. Vogts, Ph.D.

This photo provides an example of political messaging that can often be seen along the highways and byways in rural Kansas. This sign was photographed on April 2, 2023, at the Ellsworth, Kansas exit on Interstate 70.

say they put political signs in their yards or have run for public office, and one individual even held public office—Quimby reported he was a former county commissioner. Likewise, survey respondents indicated they have not run for an elected office (91.2%) ($\chi^2(12) = 14.14, p = 0.29$) or ever held an elected office (89.4%) ($\chi^2(1) = 0.20, p = 0.65$).

Such findings demonstrate the concept of civic engagement. Being civically engaged is crucial for a democracy. It means being aware of the happenings within and being involved in the community. Berger (2011) suggested this umbrella term—which can be broken apart into political, social, and moral components—entails "political participation, social connectedness, associational membership, voluntarism, community spirit, [and] cooperative and tolerant moral norms" (p. 2–3). This could mean being on the local school board or city council because it is at the local level where a difference can be made. Awareness can be attained through information consumption, such as via local media. This is important for community health because the decisions made locally have far more bearing on everyday life than national politics.

To that end, Matei (2003) suggested that "social capital is the nutritive tissue from which civic organizations and collective action grow" (p. 6). Put another way, a functioning democratic society requires socially connected individuals. This is evident when looking at today's politically divided landscape. As Talisse (2020 December 22) argued, "Bitter partisanship has rendered Americans unable to treat their opponents as democratic partners" (para. 5).

This type of polarization "leads to the erosion of moral capacities we need in order to enact democracy well" (Talisse, 2021, p. 17). Of course, this isn't new. Giddens (2013) mentioned how social ties are coming undone due to political differences, but a possible solution for this is the rebuilding of communal life. This suggests the remedy could be increasing social capital. This could be developed in youth through educational initiatives and programming, such as journalism curricula (Bobkowski et al., 2012; Killenberg & Dardenne, 1997; Lamberth & Aucoin, 1993; Robinson, 2017; Vogts, 2023).

Such considerations are germane to the discussion because a society's culture is formed and informed by the mass media consumed as it shapes public knowledge and beliefs (Potter, 2014). Digital technologies create a portion of the mass media as it exists in society today. As Groshek (2011) pointed out, "it is possible that new media might alter information flows and reshape democratization process precisely because of greater forms of media participation and creation" (p. 1,176).

Engagement with the news provides an indicator of civic engagement, and the user-generated content found on social media sheds light on how individuals engage civically offline, providing an understanding of their feelings of political empowerment by considering how the consumption and creation of online content provides gratifications (Leung, 2009). Furthermore, This concept can be used to examine how the use social media impacts the frequency of political discussion among people within the same political party (in-group members) and people from different political parties (out-group members) related to motives for using traditional and social media for political information (Ponder & Haridakis, 2015), which is important for understanding "political socialization" (Haridakis & Whitmore, 2006, p. 770).

Pathway Pivots: Using News Uniquely

Research by Song et al. (2020) that looked social media users' perceptions of how informed they are about politics even as they come across news that "finds" them, making social media use more gratifying even if their feelings of being informed are false. Some people might avoid the news entirely. The reason for such behavior can be attributed to a variety of factors, such as time, money, or a perception that all the news is negative (Toff et al., 2023). Still, information about current events and society finds its way to them. Along the way, seeds of misinformation get planted. They take root and sprout in the information fields. Rather than growing into nutritious grains of knowledge, they bloom into noxious weeds that mimic edible morsels. At that point it is too late. Individuals consume these news sprouts, but it poisons the system. This influences decisions people make at the ballot box and in other aspects of daily life. Society suffers and democracy falters.

It's because, despite best efforts, misinformation finds them. Sargent (2018) argued this is because "conservative voters are far more reliant on a single partisan media source—yup, you guessed it, Fox News—than are liberal voters, who tend to rely on more media sources, including major news organizations" (pgs. 69–70). As a result, rural Americans become more radical in their political beliefs. Their religious preferences confirm those beliefs (Alkazemi, 2019), and the conservative media echo chambers reinforce the message by serving a steady diet of misinformation.

It would be surprising if misinformation didn't find them.

CHAPTER 8

Pathways Forward When "Misinformation Finds Them"

Just as agriculture reshapes the land, the hybrid media system is shaping the opinions and beliefs of rural Kansans. That means their realities are being constructed through the social interactions they have with each other and the media messages they consume. This is the essence of social constructionism (e.g., Ackermann, 2001; Berger & Luckmann, 1966; Burr, 2015; Pass, 2004), which was the primary lens through which this research investigated how pathways of news provide fertile ground for misinformation to spread in rural America. As the results indicated, most of the media being consumed by rural Kansans is biased and partisan. This is a problem as it allows misinformation and outrage to seep into the public discourse with little resistance. That damages social capital, or the web of mutual trust and cooperation needed for a democratic society to succeed (Gastil & Keith, 2005; Putnam, 2001) and has been shown to lead to greater polarization and division among individuals.

Such societal splits occur due to bonding social capital, which cultivates homogenous social groups that are resistant to outside beliefs and opinions of others, particularly out-group others that have competing views or values (Arachchi & Managi, 2021; Heath & Waymer, 2014; Heath & Lowrey, 2021). Through such groups, mis- or disinformation can spread more easily if it aligns with the beliefs of the members (Bringula et al., 2022; Pearson & Knobloch-Westerwick, 2019; White, 2022). This is problematic. The further spread of misinformation can occur because "media foster cynicism or distrust on the part of media consumers and thus alienate them from political or civic activities" (Zhang & Seltzer, 2010, p. 157), whereby the information put forth through the contemporary hybrid media content infiltrate society, in part, via the web of connections created by social capital (Putnam, 2001). As respondent Marvin said, "Misinformation is going to further split our country." Without taking steps to stem the flow, such a prediction undoubtedly will come true—and since the 2024 election all indications point to a widening divide between citizens along ideological lines.

Effectively combating dis- or misinformation is not easy. Considering the microcosm of rural Kansans and their news consumption habits, several hurdles to combating faulty and inaccurate information become evident. Respondents in this study indicated they consume news at high rates. Most of the interviewees said they read, watch, or listen to the news nearly constantly, and more than half of the survey respondents indicated they do so at least daily. However, the pathways they use seem problematic. A large portion relies on partisan and biased news outlets to become informed about what is going on in the country and the world. As such, dis- and misinformation taints their media diets, which causes distrust to grow.

Misinformation Finds Them: Extending the "News-Finds-Me" Perception

The findings of this study suggest that rural Kansans are particularly vulnerable to misinformation, not because they actively seek it out, but because of the ways in which they consume news and interact with their social networks. This aligns with and expands upon the News-Finds-Me (NFM) perception (Gil de Zúñiga et al., 2017), a phenomenon where individuals believe they do not need to actively seek news because they assume that important information will reach them through their social circles or digital feeds. This passive approach to news consumption fosters an environment in which misinformation can flourish unchecked. When individuals rely on news to "find me" rather than critically engaging with a diverse set of sources, they become more susceptible to receiving and spreading misleading or false narratives, particularly as algorithms and AI become more and more embedded in news distribution systems that seek only to cater maximizing user engagement with personalized content.

This study suggests a parallel phenomenon, which we term the Misinformation Finds Them (MFT) perception. Just as the NFM perception shapes passive news habits, the MFT perception suggests that rural Kansans are not only exposed to misinformation simply by participating in their usual media and social ecosystems but—more importantly—that they consider the threat of misinformation serious precisely because they see that misinformation finds them, and, when it does, it has great impact on *others*, but not necessarily themselves. Here, because their primary news sources tend to be partisan, and because their social circles often reinforce rather than challenge these sources, misinformation is absorbed and internalized with little scrutiny, and thus the impact on *others* in a hybrid media system that ranks low in trust but is high. The problem is compounded by the very nature of social capital and media use—particularly bonding social capital and the third-person effect—which strengthens trust within homogenous groups while fostering skepticism toward outside perspectives, and overestimating the impact of media on others unlike the homogenous group (Arachchi & Managi, 2021; Heath & Lowrey, 2021; Putnam, 2001).

In practice, this means that misinformation is not just something rural Kansans may encounter—it is something that actively reaches them, embedding itself within their media consumption habits and social interactions despite their belief that *others* are more susceptible to falsehoods. Algorithms on social media amplify this effect, reinforcing confirmation bias by prioritizing content that aligns with users' existing beliefs (Guess et al., 2020; Pariser, 2011). Meanwhile, partisan media sources often blur the line between opinion and fact, making it difficult for consumers to distinguish between legitimate reporting and misleading narratives (Pearson & Knobloch-Westerwick, 2019), a view exacerbated in the MFT cycle This creates an environment where misinformation does not need to be actively sought out—it is simply there, woven into the very fabric of daily information consumption and a vector in polarizing individuals and social groups.

This dynamic poses a significant challenge to democratic discourse. If individuals believe they are informed and others are not, when in reality all media users are consuming a distorted version of reality, efforts to combat misinformation become even more difficult. Traditional fact-checking and media literacy campaigns may have limited effectiveness in these communities because they operate under the assumption that people are actively engaging with a range of news sources. However, when misinformation "finds them" passively through trusted social connections and familiar media outlets, attempts to correct it may be met with resistance or outright dismissal (Lewandowsky et al., 2012).

To address this challenge, interventions must go beyond merely increasing access to factual information but also by challenging the knowledge base of media effects and the third-person effect in particular. Here, citizens can learn to better account for the ways in which misinformation is integrated into social and media networks. Solutions may involve fostering training through accessible on-demand mobile apps that can encourage connections between different ideological or social groups to promote exposure to a wider range of perspectives (Putnam, 2001). Additionally, promoting critical media literacy in these communities may help individuals recognize misinformation and better gauge its relatively limited individual effect, rather than passively absorbing it as part of their daily news consumption and overestimating the reach and impact of misinformation on others (Vraga & Tully, 2021).

As a new pathway forward, the Misinformation Finds Them perception helps explain why the risk of misinformation is not just its presentation or content—it is the belief that misinformation is pernicious and has greater effects on others. As long as misinformation is embedded in the pathways through which rural Kansans receive their news, and it is buoyed by the MFT perception, it will continue to spread, deepening polarization and eroding trust in democratic institutions. Addressing this issue requires not only correcting falsehoods and reshaping the ways in which information flows through these communities, which is unlikely, but providing better public campaigns on NFT and MFT such that the similar, rather than differential impact media consumption has on *all* media users becomes conventional wisdom.

Self-Selective Exposure: Cultivating Misinformation Media Effects

The tendency to consume partisan and biased news as the default can be attributed to selective exposure. This concept explains that people tend to prefer information and sources that align with their previously held beliefs and opinions, and, consequently, people avoid content that runs counter to those views (Hameleers & van der Meer, 2020; Pearson & Knobloch-Westerwick, 2019; Weaver, 2017). Those beliefs and opinions are further developed and embedded into the minds of people thanks to a process of cultivation, which suggests perceptions of reality are shaped and attitudes altered because of media exposure (Gerbner & Gross, 1976; Gerbner et al., 1986; Good, 2009; Harmon et al., 2019; Mosharafa, 2015). Such impacts are amplified by heavy and long-term exposure (Callanan & Rosenberger, 2016; Morgan et al., 2015; Weiss, 2020).

Some might believe this doesn't affect them. In fact, respondent Abraham claimed as much. However, nearly all interviewees admitted the news they consume impacts their views on society in some fashion. For example, Jasper, who explained that he believes abortion is morally and biblically wrong, said his perspective has changed slightly to the point where now he is more comfortable with allowing abortions up to 15 weeks of pregnancy if such an option has to be pursued. Previously, he thought four weeks was the maximum window during which the procedure should be allowed. He attributed this change in views to some of the news he consumed. Also, Sherri described the impact news consumption has on her by explaining that she had to stop watching the news each night because it was impacting her mental health. One reason for this could be the type of content she and others are focusing on.

Across the board, political news ranked high on the list of what people indicated they consume, and most of that comes from national sources via social media and news websites, television, and radio. However, those mediums are rife with misinformation. Because of the easy access and ability for anyone to create content, study participants placed a lot of blame on social media for the spread of misinformation. Since nearly everyone uses such platforms at least some of the time, it should come as no surprise that this contributes to political polarization (Kubin & von Sikorski, 2021; Vincent & Gismondi, 2021).

Notably, though, nearly half of this study's survey respondents reported not using social media for news and information consumption, which countered the consensus of the interviewees who often used social media for news and information consumption. Regardless, as Collins et al. (2021) pointed out, the nature of social media allows messages to "rapidly spread" (p. 247), and if those messages are inaccurate or false, they can cause "enormous damage to our society and […] democracy as well" (p. 248). The worst part is that verifying social media messages can be tough to do. As Xiao (2021) suggested, "Because of this challenge to interpret and evaluate a social media message, social media users are found to be persuaded by views that have no factual basis" (p. 213).

Even though Ned said that seeing something on television made it true, that is not necessarily the case. Television can be manipulative and also leverage persuasion to push an agenda. Benkler et al. (2018) referred to this as the "propaganda feedback loop," which positions the media, political actors, and the public "in a self-reinforcing feedback loop that disciplines those who try to step off of it with lower attention or votes, and gradually over time increases the costs to everyone of introducing news that is not identity confirming, or challenges the partisan narratives and frames" (p. 79). Additionally, technology has made it easier for visual content to be manufactured (Thomson et al., 2022). Now, people cannot simply trust what they see.

Mediating Uses: The Gratification of Misinformation

Even in the so-called post-truth era, "television is identified as the most trusted source of accurate political information for adults in the United States" (Yanich, 2020, p. 23). Arguably, this can be attributed, in part, to the fact that views feel gratified by the content, which again relates to Uses and Gratifications Theory (U&G). According to McQuail et al. (1972), people use media for one of four reasons: Diversion, which includes an escape from routine or problems and serves as an emotional release; Personal Relationships, which considers the media as a substitute for companionship as well as a social utility; Personal Identity, which looks at self-reference, reality exploration and a reinforcement of values; and Surveillance, which entails information seeking. Considering that, U&G focuses on individual differences that drive media use behaviors by exploring how and why people choose the content and platforms they do (Haridakis & Whitmore, 2006; McQuail, 1984; Weiyan, 2015).

Similarly, U&G helps explain the popularity of radio (Laor, 2022; Lazarsfeld, 1940; Ullah, 2018) and podcasts (Berry, 2015; Perks & Turner, 2019; Perks et al., 2019). Podcasts were mentioned with some frequency in the interviews for this study. One reason was because everyone can find a podcast about something they are interested in or passionate about, and they can listen from anywhere at any time. The same goes for terrestrial radio. There's a station out there for everyone. All it takes is a twist of the dial, point to the gratification of convenience.

In rural Kansas, radio provides a key pathway to news and information because individuals can listen while they work, whether that involves driving or operating farming machinery or accomplishing other tasks. Like its audio descendant podcasts, radio is a passive activity. In many ways, though, radio's impact on public discourse is more sinister than social media or television. Misinformation spread without consequence because it is fleeting. As Phil Boyce, a conservative talk radio veteran and a program director for Salem Communications, said during a special podcast series called "The Divided Dial" that was produced by *On the Media*, "It's almost better to say it on the air than to post it in a Tweet because you post it in a Tweet, it's out there for the end of time. You say it on the air, maybe they didn't hear it" (as cited in Thornton, 2022b).

Additionally, radio lives and dies on opinion-based programming. As Hemmer (2016) highlighted, talk radio has been leveraged as a political platform since the 1930s. These early political pundits laid the groundwork for the modern-day commentators. Then, in the 1980s, highly divisive and emotionally charged content started to take hold by hosts who came to be known as "shock jocks" (Thornton, 2022a). These gurus of gab leveraged passion, regardless of whether or not it was in support or opposition of the points they were making, and it worked. The result was an enduring focus on outrage, which fires up and exploits the emotions of individuals with certain political beliefs to maintain viewership and increase profitability (Shrader, 2013; Young, 2021).

With a captive audience of farmers stuck in combines slowly rolling through the harvest fields and ranchers sitting in pickup trucks bouncing through pastures in order to check their cattle, the impacts of this content can be significant. Political beliefs become ingrained, and the indignant shouting coming from the speakers starts to feel normal and right. Intolerance for opposing views becomes deep-seated, which alters how people interact with each other. Polarization and division take root and grow.

Therefore, it comes as no surprise that some of this study's respondents expressed a feeling of helplessness in terms of the news. Both Sarah and Patty didn't see how worrying about the news could matter because they couldn't do anything to change what was occurring. Sarah did say she prays about those issues, though, which speaks to the deeply held religious beliefs found in rural Kansas. Similarly, Bart suggested what he consumes stays in his mind, and that would undoubtedly affect his thought processes. Ned agreed, and he also brought up that where he lives plays a role in how the news impacts him. "You're not engaged down here in the middle of the country," he said. "Yeah. It affects us, or just our overall thought process. But it doesn't change how I carry on."

No matter the rationalization, these impacts stem from the type of news these individuals consume. As the survey results and interviewees revealed, this consists of a fair amount of biased and partisan media outlets. A few individuals even pointed this out. They discussed how the news they trust and distrust are guided by their political beliefs. As Herman said, "People want to hear what makes them feel warm and fuzzy." This speaks directly to the root of this study. It highlights how and why misinformation is believed and spread in rural Kansas. It is about selective exposure and confirmation bias (Hameleers & van der Meer, 2020; Knobloch-Westerwick et al., 2015; Lee et al., 2021; Pearson & Knobloch-Westerwick, 2019).

Distrusting the Messenger: More Media, More Misinformation

Every person interviewed shared certain news outlets they trusted more than others, and the survey specifically asked respondents to choose their preferences. "Rather than not trusting any media, […] the public indicates that it trusts only some media and not others" (Yanich, 2020, p. 23). For many, it was the difference between local and national. However, a majority of the individuals also said they trusted, at least to some degree, specific national news organizations. In nearly every instance, these outlets are known to have a political bias (Ad Fontes Media, 2023; Jurkowitz et al., 2020). Therefore, if those are considered to be trusted news outlets by the rural residents, they will continue to consume the content those organizations produce. The result is the construction of an echo chamber where individuals are only being exposed to messages that agree with their pre-existing beliefs and opinions. To borrow from Barney, this creates a snowball effect. Political beliefs influence the media being consumed, and then the media being

CHAPTER 8

consumed reaffirms political beliefs. It becomes a perpetual motion machine that results in distrust of news and information that doesn't come from the selected outlets, and that breeds misinformation.

Figure 8.1. "Ask For A Paper Ballot" roadside sign.
Source: Todd R. Vogts, Ph.D.
This photo provides an example of political beliefs fueled by conspiracy theories and misinformation. This sign was photographed on April 2, 2023, at Wilkens Manufacturing Inc., which is located south of Stockton, Kansas.

Of course, interviewees seemed to understand how this works, but they also considered themselves immune to the effects, as outlined in our newly advanced Misinformation Finds Them perception. Several respondents made it a point to suggest they see others being influenced in this way, but they believed they weren't impacted. For example, Patty said she was exposed to Fox News regularly because her husband watches it, but she said she didn't pay any attention. Then she expressed her disgust at schools putting litter boxes in bathrooms for students who identified as cats, which is a debunked hoax pushed by Republican political candidates (Kaczynski, 2022; Stanford, 2022).

Similarly, though he said he only trusts certain people he follows on Facebook, Eddie's entire perspective on the world was changed during the COVID-19 pandemic when he watched the "26-minute video called 'Plandemic,' a slickly produced narration that wrongly claimed a shadowy cabal of elites was using the virus and a potential vaccine to profit and gain power" (Frenkel et al., 2020, para. 3). Eddie repeatedly expressed the belief that he didn't blame others for not being better informed because he had been misled before too, but he said people needed to open "their eyes and start to connect dots, which isn't very difficult to do."

Such discussions highlight the problem of conspiracy theories. Muirhead and Rosenblum (2019) defined these ideas in the following way:

> Classic conspiracy theory, whether it is true or not, tries to make sense of the political world. There are no accidents, no unintended consequences […] classic conspiracism insists on proportionality and undertakes painstaking detective work: it is a kind of investigation that at least pretends to follow journalistic or even scientific standards. (p. 20)

Though the majority of the respondents to this study claimed no belief in such ideas, those who do believe these "answers" seemed to do so out of an apparent need for order. They don't want to live in a world of the unknown. As respondent Edna suggested, anxiety might drive people to believe conspiracy theories because they want a sense of certainty that tells them everything is explainable. Thus, the trajectory toward radical becomes more probable.

God, It's Brutal Out Here: Religion, Conspiracy, and News Deserts

Regardless of the reasons, though, these ways of looking at the world can be damaging. Extreme belief structures rooted in misinformation and conspiracy impact public discourse, which can further divide society (Mahl et al., 2021; Ross et al., 2006). Muirhead and Rosenblum (2019) argued conspiracy theories often have political and partisan links, and "the corrosive effects […] are distinctive: to delegitimate foundational democratic institutions and, in a more personal mode, to disorient us" (p. 169). Innes and Innes (2021) highlighted this by investigating how COVID-19 was discussed on Facebook.

Even more disturbing is the idea that religious leaders have been shown to support conspiracy theories. As Chimuanya and Igwebuike (2021) argued, "Religion can be a functional force, helping to promote civil society, community values, and education. Still, it can also become a dysfunctional influence, stifling rational discourse and promoting the belief that only faith and devotional life will solve our myriad of national problems" (p. 402). Since religion plays such an important role in the lives of rural Kansas as the results of this study indicated, it seems plausible that individuals can be exposed to and influenced by conspiracy theories without even realizing it because they trust their pastors or priests. In fact, Murphy shared this type of experience. It caused him to start questioning his faith, which made him question his identity.

With misinformation and conspiracy theories existing as a part of the media ecosystem, it makes it hard for individuals to trust the news and information they consume. The results of this study highlighted this as nearly everyone expressed lower levels of trust in the media. One reason for this was attributed to the perceived amount of opinion and bias rural Kansans see in the news, and they aren't alone. Research literature often highlights these attributes as drivers of mistrust (e.g., Fisher et al., 2021; Strömbäck et al., 2020; Swart & Broersma, 2022; Usher, 2018; Zimmermann & Kohring, 2020). Accuracy in reporting is also important. Individuals want to be able to verify what they are being told is correct, and, if they can, mistrust can be decreased (Kalogeropoulos et al., 2019; Park et al., 2020; Saldaña & Vu, 2022; Wenzel, 2019).

Unfortunately, too often that means these individuals turn to their preferred sources of information for fact-checking and debunking claims they feel are inaccurate. Doing so further embeds them into their echo chambers and filter bubbles. This activity of "doing their own research" isn't research at all. It is relying on lay opinion instead of expert knowledge, which can result in people making uninformed and harmful decisions about their health or on other issues (Carrion, 2018). Even so, individuals don't see this as a problem, believing they know the truth and can't be swayed by unreliable content.

Statements made by interviewees who claimed to be immune to misinformation's detrimental impacts speaks to a couple of ideas. First, it alludes to the Misinformation Finds Them perception and the third-person effect hypothesis, which "deals with an individual's tendency to believe that the effect of a message on others will be greater than on himself or herself" (Guo & Johnson, 2020, p. 2). Whenever an interviewee suggested they see others being influenced by media messages more than they are influenced, the MFT perception was invoked. This highlights a lack in understanding how content impacts them. This brings up the second idea, which is media literacy.

Media literacy is the ability to understand and analyze media messages (Gaultney et al., 2022; Matthews, 2022; Potter, 2016). Several interviewees also mentioned this idea. Generally, it came up in the context of looking at multiple sources and doing the "research" necessary to verify the information. Cletus and Montgomery even explained that they intentionally listen to outlets from both sides of the political spectrum in order to develop a more complete picture of what is happening in the world. However, that wasn't the norm for most interviewees. Instead, they tended to rely on partisan news outlets or local.

A lot of local television news is aired each day (Yanich, 2020). With its wide availability, it comes as no surprise that the medium is popular. Furthermore, the fact that local was viewed as being more reliable and trustworthy can be attributed to the perception that those outlets and their journalists understand rural residents more. Sherri explained it this way: "I don't know, sometimes in rural areas I feel like we're kind of throwaway in terms of media, in terms of big cities reporting on us." A component of this is that local news organizations represent the values of their audience. This representation also applies to national outlets, though. If Fox News or MSNBC aligns with an individual's beliefs and values, that person feels seen, which cultivates a sense of belonging and affiliation. As Cramer (2016) argued, people who feel misunderstood or misrepresent tend to retreat back into their comfort zones because they believe they are being ignored or not taken seriously. That sows the seeds of distrust that are fertilized by the misinformation spread by partisan media outlets as they plow through the fields of the media ecosystem available to rural Kansans.

To that end, it makes sense to instigate a local news revival in the spirit of religious tent revivals. Such an analogy fits because those tent revivals focused on the spatial relationships of individuals (Burchardt, 2020), and local news is inherently tied to concepts of proximity, community, common interest, and place (e.g., Harte et al., 2017; Jenkins & Nielsen, 2020; Usher, 2019; Wenzel et al., 2020). Also, it's at the local level where impactful change can be made (e.g., Darr et al., 2021; Katz & Nowak, 2018; Sullivan, 2020). Through both the interviews and survey underpinning this study, respondents indicated they wanted their local media outlets to do more, especially since they trusted community news more than the national products. There are several ways this improvement could take place, and revitalizing local news would be an important and productive venture.

Of course, doing so will require media organizations and communities to confront the increasing spread of news deserts, which are areas where there is a lack of local news coverage (Abernathy, 2018a) brought about by newspaper closures stemming from disruptions to the media business models induced by the internet and other technologies, and these news deserts are spreading as corporate owners continue to seek profitability over quality journalism (Bartelme, 2022; Stites, 2018). Kansas fits into the category of having areas where residents do not have journalists dedicated to reporting on their communities (Abernathy, 2018b), and, since Kansas is largely rural, such a finding aligns with other reports. For example, Brounstein (2017) highlighted that news deserts are often found "in rural and economically distressed areas of the country, where for so long local newspapers were the main source of news for small communities, and which now are disappearing at an alarming rate" (para. 1).

News deserts aren't the only issue, though. A drought of journalism can also come in different forms. For instance, some areas have news outlets that have been reduced so greatly in terms of coverage, staffing, and resources that they can barely fulfill their journalistic duties. These are referred to as "ghost newspapers" (Sullivan, 2020). However, whether a news outlet disappears completely or just becomes a shell of its former self, the reasons underlying the change are what matter. Demographic changes in communities and other economic considerations could be at play (Claussen, 2020b), or a change in the news consumption habits of audiences could be blamed (Claussen, 2020a). Regardless, the lack of dedicated and reliable local news damages communities and democracy. Research shows that communities without local news are more polarized (Darr et al., 2018), while the presence of a local newspaper can counteract polarization (Darr et al., 2021). Furthermore, as Chapp and Aehl (2021) suggested, community media consumption impacts levels of social and civic engagement, such as voting.

Since the results of this study pointed to a strong desire for local news that is reliable and not just what random community members post on social media, change must be pursued. Such a need is evident from the research of Smethers et al. (2021) who found that community members see "a centralized source of professionally sourced news" (p. 384) as vital. Therefore, due to the current media environment, the business models must be re-imagined. Rather than relying on advertising or subscriptions, new ways of funding news must be explored. After all, younger news consumers, such as 21-year-old Helen, indicated they don't want to pay for it because they can get information and news content from other sources. Luckily, innovations are taking place. Some news outlets are pursuing nonprofit business models (Birnbauer, 2019; Bodrozic & Paulussen, 2018; Konieczna & Robinson, 2014), and politicians have floated ideas of tax-based funding mechanisms for local media (Klein, 2025). In other cases, college and university classes are creating news outlets to cover community news and bring a little informational rain to the drought-stricken news deserts (Finneman et al., 2022). Also, some community members are banding together to keep news alive through volunteerism (Bressers et al., 2015; Smethers et al., 2017).

Putting Humpty-Dumpty Back Together Again: Social Civic Media

For any of these or other efforts to work, though, trust must be rebuilt. Though nonprofit news organizations might aim to do that (Konieczna & Robinson,

2014), more needs to be done. This could be accomplished through visibility and interaction via social media (Fisher et al., 2021), but research has shown that use of social media as a primary pathway to news is an indicator lower levels of trust (Kalogeropoulos et al., 2019), which is a finding this study supports. Instead, news organizations need to engage with the local audiences more and actually listen to the needs of those individuals (S. Lewis, 2020). Engaged journalism (Batsell, 2015) or participatory journalism (Borger et al., 2013) provide avenues for this type of audience-focused work to occur. In these models, the proverbial doors are thrown open, and the community members are invited in to help cultivate the news harvest. It is done with an eye toward serving the public in a transparent and responsive fashion, and this type of effort has roots in Kansas media. In fact, it grew out of the Wichita Eagle, located in Wichita, Kansas.

It is called public or civic journalism, and former Wichita Eagle editor Davis "Buzz" Merritt and media scholar Jay Rosen developed the idea. Lowrey (2012) explained that public or civic journalism typically "(a) seeks 'citizen voices' through feedback, articles, forums; (b) represents diverse views; (c) enables citizen involvement; and (d) helps solve community problems by offering solutions" (p. 95). Merritt (1997) positioned the concept as a desire for journalism to do more and present the news in a manner that benefits society and supports public life. Meyer and Daniels (2012) described it as "the late 20th-century movement in which some news media actively involved community members in the news process and the media in turn participated in efforts to address community issues," which aimed "to enhance the role of professional news outlets as conduits for communication about important issues" (p. 205–206).

To that end, public or civic journalism centers on listening to and working for the community. Dzur (2002) described this listening as "public listening," which "involves finding out what is of concern in a community and then reporting on how those concerns are or are not being met" (p. 316). Too often, "decisions about online news features and content may be shaped more by routines and resources of the news outlet than by needs specific to the community" or community news outlets "are making less effort to aid communication in fragmented communities" (Lowrey, 2012, p. 99). Public or civic journalism can counter this by further inserting the media as a key component of the community and the citizens, and this would counter the negative effects of Cultivation Theory (CT), which can include the breeding of distrust (Moyer-Gusé et al., 2008).

Doing so could allow journalists to reconnect with communities and refocus on what is important to the people living in those areas, allowing the unique aspects of the individuals in the particular place to drive news decisions (Usher, 2018, 2019; Wenzel et al., 2020). According to the results of this study, such initiatives not only would be welcomed, but they would be supported. What's more, though, this could counteract the mistrust that currently pervades rural communities in America, which is undoubtedly present due to more partisan and opinion-based content being injected into the local public discourse that allows dis- and misinformation to spread and drive wedges between community members.

The result is that the local storytelling networks (STN) become overwhelmed with destructive messages (Wenzel, 2020). STNs are at the core of Communication Infrastructure Theory (CIT), which is "a theoretical framework that differentiates local communities in terms of whether they have communication resources that can be activated to construct community, thereby enabling collective action for common purpose" (Kim & Ball-Rokeach, 2006a, p. 174). As such, local media plays a social role and connects individuals (Nygren, 2019; Smethers et al., 2021). This leads to social capital development, especially through reciprocity (Bressers et al., 2015; Lewis et al., 2014; Richards, 2013; Smethers et al., 2017).

Social capital is a web of mutual trust and cooperation among members of a community or society that are necessary for democracy to function (Gastil & Keith, 2005; Putnam, 2001). With strong social capital comes strong social and civic engagement, and those forms of involvement are also needed for democratic functions. Of course, social and civic engagement can take on many forms. An easy way to look at them is through memberships in community organizations and voting. Based upon the results of this study, rural Kansans are fairly engaged. Nearly all of them reported voting on a regular basis, and even if they weren't actively involved in their communities, they expressed the importance of such engagement.

Such findings showcase, at least at a subconscious level, an understanding of the important role social capital plays in a community. In most cases, that engagement came through participation in their church communities, but a few were involved in local politics even beyond voting or interested in greater involvement. Either way, the underlying current was that they could have more of an impact by giving back to their local communities instead of worrying about what was going on at the national level. This also contributed to the pervasive view that politicians could not be trusted, except for some of the local individuals. Again, such perceptions indicate strong bonding social capital and weak bridging social capital. This combination provides fertile ground for polarization and division to grow as individuals seek refuge in their social spheres that provide them the most comfort and affirmation in relation to their beliefs and opinions (e.g., Docherty, 2020; Lin, 2002; Mou & Lin, 2017; Yang & Hanasono, 2021).

Even so, nearly everyone who participated in this study recognized the existence of mis- or disinformation, and a few showed great concern for what its continued spread could mean for society. That alone should serve as a clarion call for dis- and misinformation to be doused with informational herbicide. More than handwringing is needed. Action is necessary. This is especially true considering that that rural and urban Kansans rarely differed greatly in their thoughts and opinions that were explored in this study.

Therefore, the power of partisan and biased media outlets must be inspected closely, and news consumers need to put a check on the information dissemination practices of these organizations. As ranchers raise and care for their cattle through the process of animal husbandry (Kron, 2014), these agenda-driven media outlets and actors are breeding and feeding news consumers a diet rich in empty content calories in the form of misinformation. With the goal of raising a herd of polarized media consumers. This equates to "societal husbandry," which aims "to cultivate the types of behavior patterns among the populace that the elite behavior-control experts would judge as being for the common good" (Jones & Butman, 2012, p. 166).

Combating misinformation and its effects—both real and perceived—will require the hard work rural Kansans are known for. Then, the notion that something's the matter with Kansas won't be so radical, at all.

Bibliography

Abdullah, C., Karpowitz, C. F., & Raphael, C. (2016). Equity and inclusion in online community forums: An interview with Steven Clift. *Journal of Deliberative Democracy, 12*(2), 1–14. <https://doi.org/10.16997/jdd.263>

Abernathy, P. M. (2018a). The expanding news desert. The Center for Innovation and Sustainability in Local Media. *School of Media and Journalism.*

Abernathy, P. M. (2018b). Kansas. In *The Expanding News Desert*. Center for Innovation and Sustainability in Local Media. <https://www.usnewsdeserts.com/states/kansas/>

Abernathy, P. M. (2023). *The State of Local News: The 2023 Report.* The Medill Local News Initiative. <https://localnewsinitiative.northwestern.edu/projects/state-of-local-news/2023/report/>

Abramowitz, A. I., & Webster, S. W. (2016). The rise of negative partisanship and the nationalization of U.S. elections in the 21st century. *Electoral Studies, 41*, 12–22.

Abramsky, S. (2023, August 7). The small-town library that became a culture war battleground. *The Nation.* <https://www.thenation.com/article/society/libraries-book-banning/>

Ackermann, E. (2001). Piaget's constructivism, Papert's constructionism: What's the difference. *Future of learning group publication, 5*(3), 438.

Ad Fontes Media. (2023). *Interactive Media Bias Chart* <https://adfontesmedia.com/interactive-media-bias-chart/>

Alatidd, J. (2023, September 15). Librarians sue over firing: Lawsuit alleges Sterling leaders confused autism symbol with gay pride. *The Topeka Capital-Journal*, 1 and 3.

Alitavoli, R., & Kaveh, E. (2018). The U.S. Media's Effect on Public's Crime Expectations: A Cycle of Cultivation and Agenda-Setting Theory. *Societies, 8*(3), 58. <https://www.mdpi.com/2075-4698/8/3/58>

Alkazemi, M. (2019). Inner Peace or Piece of Mind? Religiosity, Media Exposure and Tolerance for Disagreement about Religion. *Journal of Media & Religion, 18*(2), 39–49. <https://doi.org/10.1080/15348423.2019.1651574>

Allam, R. (2019). Constructive Journalism in Arab Transitional Democracies: Perceptions, Attitudes and Performance. *Journalism Practice, 13*(10), 1273–1293. <https://doi.org/10.1080/17512786.2019.1588145>

Almgren, S. M., & Olsson, T. (2015). 'Let's Get Them Involved' … to Some Extent: Analyzing Online News Participation. *Social Media + Society*, *1*(2), 2056305115621934. <https://doi.org/10.1177/2056305115621934>

Annenberg Public Policy Center. (2019). *American's civics knowledge increases but still has a long way to go*. University of Pennsylvania. <https://www.annenbergpublicpolicycenter.org/americans-civics-knowledge-increases-2019-survey/>

Annenberg Public Policy Center. (2020). *Amid pandemic and protests, civics survey finds Americans know more of their rights*. University of Pennsylvania. <https://www.annenbergpublicpolicycenter.org/pandemic-protests-2020-civics-survey-americans-know-much-more-about-their-rights/>

Annenberg Public Policy Center. (2021). *Americans' civics knowledge increases during a stress-filled year*. University of Pennsylvania. <https://www.annenbergpublicpolicycenter.org/2021-annenberg-constitution-day-civics-survey/>

Annenberg Public Policy Center. (2023). *Many Don't Know Key Facts About U.S. Constitution, Annenberg Civics Study Finds*. University of Pennsylvania. <https://www.annenbergpublicpolicycenter.org/many-dont-know-key-facts-about-u-s-constitution-annenberg-civics-study-finds/>

Annenberg Public Policy Center. (2024). *A Majority of Americans Can't Recall Most First Amendment Rights*. University of Pennsylvania. <https://www.annenbergpublicpolicycenter.org/most-americans-cant-recall-most-first-amendment-rights/>

Arachchi, J. I., & Managi, S. (2021). The role of social capital in COVID-19 deaths. *BMC public health*, *21*(1), 1–9.

Ballotpedia. (n.d.). *Presidential voting trends in Kansas*. Lucy Burns Institute. <https://ballotpedia.org/Presidential_voting_trends_in_Kansas>

Banks, J. (2013, September 26). Meet the "Health Ranger" who's using pseudoscience to sell his lies. *Mic*. <https://www.mic.com/articles/65075/meet-the-health-ranger-who-s-using-pseudoscience-to-sell-his-lies>

Baran, S. J., & Davis, D. K. (2021). *Mass communication theory: Foundations, ferment, and future* (8th ed.). Oxford University Press.

Bartelme, T. (2022). News deserts are growing. SC's Oasis Project will try to stop this pattern. *The Post and Courier*. <https://www.postandcourier.com/news/news-deserts-are-growing-scs-oasis-project-will-try-to-stop-this-pattern/article_c5facf60-aae4-11ec-87d2-3b010885963b.html>

Bartels, L. M. (2006). What's the Matter with What's the Matter with Kansas? *Quarterly Journal of Political Science*, *1*(2), 201–226.

Batsell, J. (2015). *Engaged journalism: connecting with digitally empowered news audiences*. Columbia University Press.

Bauer, A. J., Nadler, A., & Nelson, J. L. (2022). What is Fox News? Partisan Journalism, Misinformation, and the Problem of Classification. *Electronic News*, 16(1), 18–29. <https://doi.org/10.1177/19312431211060426>

Beauvais, E. (2018). Deliberation and Equality. In A. Bachtiger, J. S. Dryzek, J. Mansbridge, & M. Warren (Eds.), *The Oxford Handbook of Deliberative Democracy* (1 ed., pp. 144–155). Oxford University Press.

Beck, C. D. (2014). Antecedents of Servant Leadership: A Mixed Methods Study. *Journal of Leadership & Organizational Studies*, 21(3), 299–314. <https://doi.org/10.1177/1548051814529993>

Beckers, K. (2019). What Vox Pops Say and How That Matters: Effects of Vox Pops in Television News on Perceived Public Opinion and Personal Opinion. *Journalism & Mass Communication Quarterly*, 96(4), 980–1003. <https://doi.org/10.1177/1077699019843852>

Beckers, K. (2022). Power of the people or the expert? The influence of vox pop and expert statements on news-item evaluation, perceived public opinion, and personal opinion. *Communications: The European Journal of Communication Research*, 47(1), 114–135. <https://doi.org/10.1515/commun-2019-0186>

Belair-Gagnon, V., Agur, C., & Frisch, N. (2017). The Changing Physical and Social Environment of Newsgathering: A Case Study of Foreign Correspondents Using Chat Apps During Unrest. *Social Media + Society*, 3(1), 2056305117701163. <https://doi.org/10.1177/2056305117701163>

Belair-Gagnon, V., Nelson, J. L., & Lewis, S. C. (2019). Audience Engagement, Reciprocity, and the Pursuit of Community Connectedness in Public Media Journalism. *Journalism Practice*, 13(5), 558–575. <https://doi.org/10.1080/17512786.2018.1542975>

Benkler, Y., Faris, R., & Roberts, H. (2018). *Network Propaganda: Manipulation, Disinformation, and Radicalization in American Politics*. Oxford University Press.

Bennett, W. L. (1990). Toward a theory of press-state relations. *Journal of Communication*, 40(2), 103–125.

Bennett, S. E. (2002). Americans' Exposure to Political Talk Radio and Their Knowledge of Public Affairs. *Journal Of Broadcasting & Electronic Media*, 46(1), 72. <https://doi.org/10.1207/s15506878jobem4601_5>

Berger, A. A. (2020). *Media and communication research methods: an introduction to qualitative and quantitative approaches* (5th ed.).

Berger, B. (2011). *Attention Deficit Democracy: The Paradox of Civic Engagement* (1st ed.). Princeton University Press.

Berger, P. L., & Luckmann, T. (1966). *The social construction of reality: A treatise in the sociology of knowledge*. Penguin.

Bergillos, I. (2019). Rethinking Vox-Pops in Television News Evolution of Person-on-the-Street Interviews in Spanish News Programs. *Journalism Practice*, *13*(9), 1057–1074. <https://doi.org/10.1080/17512786.2019.1635042>

Berry, R. (2015). A Golden Age of Podcasting? Evaluating Serial in the Context of Podcast Histories. *Journal of Radio & Audio Media*, *22*(2), 170–178. <https://doi.org/10.1080/19376529.2015.1083363>

Bilandzic, H. (2006). The Perception of Distance in the Cultivation Process: A Theoretical Consideration of the Relationship Between Television Content, Processing Experience, and Perceived Distance. *Communication Theory (1050-3293)*, *16*(3), 333–355. <https://doi.org/10.1111/j.1468-2885.2006.00273.x>

Bilandzic, H., & Busselle, R. W. (2008). Transportation and Transportability in the Cultivation of Genre-Consistent Attitudes and Estimates. *Journal Of Communication*, *58*(3), 508–529. <https://doi.org/10.1111/j.1460-2466.2008.00397.x>

Birnbauer, B. (2019, January 17). The biggest nonprofit media outlets are thriving but smaller ones may not survive. *The Conversation*. <https://theconversation.com/the-biggest-nonprofit-media-outlets-are-thriving-but-smaller-ones-may-not-survive-109369>

Block, M. (2021, January 16). Can the forces unleashed by Trump's big election lie be undone? *NPR*. <https://www.npr.org/2021/01/16/957291939/can-the-forces-unleashed-by-trumps-big-election-lie-be-undone>

Bobkowski, P. S., Goodman, M., & Bowen, C. P. (2012). Student Media in U.S. Secondary Schools: Associations with School Demographic Characteristics. *Journalism & Mass Communication Educator*, *67*(3), 252–266. <https://doi.org/10.1177/1077695812444699>

Bobkowski, P. S., & Miller, P. R. (2016). Civic Implications of Secondary School Journalism. *Journalism & Mass Communication Quarterly*, *93*(3), 530–550. <https://doi.org/10.1177/1077699016628821>

Bodrozic, S., & Paulussen, S. (2018). Citizen Media Practices at the Digital Startup Mvslim. *Journalism Practice*, *12*(8), 1061–1069. <https://doi.org/10.1080/17512786.2018.1493945>

Borger, M., van Hoof, A., Costera Meijer, I., & Sanders, J. (2013). Constructing participatory journalism as a scholarly object. *Digital Journalism*, *1*(1), 117–134. <https://doi.org/10.1080/21670811.2012.740267>

Borter, G., Layne, N., & Clifford, T. (2024, July 14). Suspect came within inches of killing Trump, but left few clues as to why. *Reuters*. <https://www.reuters.com/world/us/heres-what-we-know-about-thomas-matthew-crooks-suspected-trump-rally-shooter-2024-07-14/>

Bötticher, A. (2017). Towards Academic Consensus Definitions of Radicalism and Extremism. *Perspectives on Terrorism*, *11*(4), 73–77.

Boyd, C. (1994). SPEAKING RUSHIAN. *ETC: A Review of General Semantics*, *51*(3), 251–260.

Braun, V., & Clarke, V. (2006). Using thematic analysis in psychology. *Qualitative Research in Psychology*, *3*(2), 77–101. <https://doi.org/10.1191/1478088706qp063oa>

Braun, V., & Clarke, V. (2021). *Thematic Analysis: A Practical Guide*. SAGE.

Brennen, B. S. (2016). *Qualitative research methods for media studies*. Routledge.

Bressers, B., Smethers, J. S., & Mwangi, S. C. (2015). Community journalism and civic engagement in mediated sports: A case study of the open-source media project in Greensburg, KS. *Journalism Practice*, *9*(3), 433–451. <https://doi.org/10.1080/17512786.2014.950470>

Briggs, M. (2007). *Journalism 2.0: How to survive and thrive* (J. Schaffer & Ed), Eds.). The Institute for interactive journalism.

Briggs, M. (2020). *Journalism Next: A Practical Guide to Digital Reporting and Publishing* (4th ed.). SAGE Publications, Inc.

Bringula, R. P., Catacutan-Bangit, A. E., Garcia, M. B., Gonzales, J. P. S., & Valderama, A. M. C. (2022). "Who is gullible to political disinformation?": predicting susceptibility of university students to fake news. *Journal of Information Technology & Politics*, *19*(2), 165–179. <https://doi.org/10.1080/19331681.2021.1945988>

Brooks, D., et al. (2020). *The silenced minority: Conservative students on liberal campuses*. Oxford University Press.

Brounstein, K. (2017, February 14). News Deserts Threaten Rural Areas. *News Media Alliance*. <https://www.newsmediaalliance.org/news-deserts/>

Brouwer, D. C., & Hess, A. (2007). Making Sense of 'God Hates Fags' and 'Thank God for 9/11': A Thematic Analysis of Milbloggers' Responses to Reverend Fred Phelps and the Westboro Baptist Church. *Western Journal of Communication*, *71*(1), 69–90. <https://doi.org/10.1080/10570310701215388>

Brown, T., Mettler, S., & Puzzi, S. (2021). When Rural and Urban Become "Us" versus "Them": How a Growing Divide is Reshaping American Politics. *The Forum*, *19*(3), 365–393. <https://doi.org/doi:10.1515/for-2021-2029>

Brown v. Board of Education of Topeka, 347 U.S. 483 (1954). <https://supreme.justia.com/cases/federal/us/347/483/#tab-opinion-1940808>

Brummette, J., DiStaso, M., Vafeiadis, M., & Messner, M. (2018). Read All About It: The Politicization of "Fake News" on Twitter. *Journalism & Mass Communication Quarterly*, 95(2), 497–517. <https://doi.org/10.1177/1077699018769906>

Bruner, M. L., & Balter-Reitz, S. (2013). Snyder v. Phelps: The U.S. Supreme Court's spectacular erasure of the tragic spectacle. *Rhetoric & Public Affairs*, 16(4), 651–683. <https://doi.org/10.1353/rap.2013.0042>

Bucy, E., & Grabe, M. (2010). Image Bite Politics: News and the Visual Framing of Elections. *Image Bite Politics: News and the Visual Framing of Elections*, 1–332. <https://doi.org/10.1093/acprof:oso/9780195372076.001.0001>

Burchardt, M. (2020). From Mission Station to Tent Revival: Material Forms and Spatial Formats in Africa's Missionary Encounter. In C. Philip & J. Adam (Eds.), *Transnational Religious Spaces* (pp. 35–50). De Gruyter Oldenbourg. <https://doi.org/doi:10.1515/9783110690101-003>

Burke, K. J., Juzwik, M., & Prins, E. (2023). White Christian Nationalism: What Is It, and Why Does It Matter for Educational Research? *Educational Researcher*, 52(5), 286–295. <https://doi.org/10.3102/0013189x231163147>

Burr, V. (2015). *Social Constructionism* (3rd ed.). Routledge. <https://doi.org/10.4324/9781315715421>

Business Insider. (2023). Donald Trump rape case and E. Jean Carroll allegations. Retrieved from https://www.businessinsider.com.

Callanan, V. J., & Rosenberger, J. S. (2016). Cultivation Theory: Gerbner, Fear, Crime, and Cops. In *The Routledge Companion to Media and Race*. Taylor & Francis.

Campbell, R., Martin, C. R., & Fabos, B. (2019). *Media & Culture: Mass Communication in a Digital Age* (12th ed.). Bedford/St. Martin's.

Capelos, T., Chrona, S., Salmela, M., & Bee, C. (2021). Reactionary Politics and Resentful Affect in Populist Times [affect; emotions; populism; radicalism; reactionism; resentment]. *2021*, 9(3), 5. <https://doi.org/10.17645/pag.v9i3.4727>

Carey, M. C. (2020). *Local News and Community Resiliency in Appalachia: How Media Institutions Can Strengthen. Communities by Empowering Individuals, Promoting Inclusive Dialog, and Seeking New Solutions to Problems*. <https://www.journalismliberty.org/publications/local-news-and-community-resiliency-in-appalachia>

Carney, T. P. (2019). *Alienated America: Why some places thrive while others collapse*. HarperCollins.

Carrion, M. L. (2018). "You need to do your research": Vaccines, contestable science, and maternal epistemology. *Public Understanding of Science*, 27(3), 310–324. <https://doi.org/10.1177/0963662517728024>

Carson, A. (2021). *Investigative Journalism, Democracy and the Digital Age* (1 ed.). Routledge.

Catalini, M., Smyth, J. C., & Shipkowski, B. (2024, September 11). Trump falsely accuses immigrants in Ohio of abducting and eating pets. *AP*. <https://apnews.com/article/haitian-immigrants-vance-trump-ohio-6e4a47c52b23ae2c802d216369512ca5>

Chakraborty, D. (2016). Social Networking Sites and Social Capital: A Chandigarh-Based Study of Undergraduate and Postgraduate Students. *Amity Journal of Media & Communications Studies (AJMCS)*, 6(2), 29–39.

Chapp, C., & Aehl, P. (2021). Newspapers and political participation: The relationship between ballot rolloff and local newspaper circulation. *Newspaper Research Journal*, 42(2), 235–252. <https://doi.org/10.1177/07395329211014968>

Chimuanya, L., & Igwebuike, E. E. (2021). From COVID-19 to COVID-666: Quasi-religious mentality and ideologies in Nigerian coronavirus pandemic discourse. *Journal of African Media Studies*, 13(3), 399–416. <https://doi.org/10.1386/jams_00056_1>

Cineas, F. (2023, May 8). The rising Republican movement to defund public libraries. *Vox*. <https://www.vox.com/politics/2023/5/5/23711417/republicans-want-to-defund-public-libraries-book-bans>

Claussen, D. S. (2020a). Continuing to digest the report, News Deserts and Ghost Newspapers: Will Local News Survive? *Newspaper Research Journal*, 41(4), 395–398. <https://doi.org/10.1177/0739532920970807>

Claussen, D. S. (2020b). Digesting the report, News Deserts and Ghost Newspapers: Will local news survive? *Newspaper Research Journal*, 41(3), 255–259. <https://doi.org/10.1177/0739532920952195>

Collier, J. R., Dunaway, J., & Stroud, N. J. (2021). Pathways to Deeper News Engagement: Factors Influencing Click Behaviors on News Sites. *Journal Of Computer-Mediated Communication*, 26(5), 265–283. <https://doi.org/10.1093/jcmc/zmab009>

Collins, B., Hoang, D. T., Nguyen, N. T., & Hwang, D. (2021). Trends in combating fake news on social media—a survey. *Journal of Information and Telecommunication*, 5(2), 247–266. <https://doi.org/10.1080/24751839.2020.1847379>

Connaughton, S. L., Linabary, J. R., Krishna, A., Kuang, K., Anaele, A., Vibber, K. S., Yakova, L., & Jones, C. (2017). Explicating the relationally attentive approach to conducting engaged communication scholarship. *Journal of Applied Communication Research*, 45(5), 517–536. <https://doi.org/10.1080/00909882.2017.1382707>

Conway, B. A., & Stryker, R. (2021). Does a Speaker's (In)formal Role in News Media Shape Perceptions of Political Incivility? *Journal Of Broadcasting & Electronic Media*, 65(1), 24–45. <https://doi.org/10.1080/08838151.2021.1897819>

Craig, D. B. (2000). *Fireside Politics: Radio and Political Culture in the United States, 1920–1940*. The John Hopkins University Press.

Cramer, K. J. (2016). *The Politics of Resentment: Rural Consciousness in Wisconsin and the Rise of Scott Walker*. University of Chicago Press.

Crary, J. (2001). *Suspensions of Perception: Attention, Spectacle, and Modern Culture*. MIT Press.

Creswell, J. W. (2014). *Research design: Qualitative, quantitative, and mixed methods approaches.Thousand* (4th ed.). Sage.

Creswell, J. W., & Poth, C. N. (2018). *Qualitative inquiry and research design: Choosing among five approaches* (4 ed.). SAGE Publications, Inc.

Crisp, E. (2024, September 17). Most Trump supporters believe false claims about Haitian migrants: Poll. *The Hill*. <https://thehill.com/homenews/4883582-donald-trump-jd-vance-ohio-pet-false-claims-survey/>

Crockett, Z. (2016, May 3). If cows staged a revolt against humans, these 9 states would be udderly screwed. *Vox*. <https://www.vox.com/2016/5/3/11504568/states-most-cows>

Croteau, D., & Hoynes, W. (2018). *Media/Society: Industries, images, and audiences* (6th ed.). SAGE.

Croucher, S. (2011). Social Networking and Cultural Adaptation: A Theoretical Model. *Journal of International & Intercultural Communication*, 4(4), 259–264. <https://doi.org/10.1080/17513057.2011.598046>

Currid-Halkett, E. (2023). *The Overlooked Americans: The Resilience of Our Rural Towns and What It Means for Our Country*. Basic Books.

Dahlgren, P. (2005). The Internet, Public Spheres, and Political Communication: Dispersion and Deliberation. *Political Communication*, 22(2), 147–162. <https://doi.org/10.1080/10584600590933160>

Dahlgren, P. (2018). Public Sphere Participation Online: The Ambiguities of Affect. *International Journal of Communication (19328036)*, 12, 2052–2070.

Damasceno, C. S. (2021). Multiliteracies for Combating Information Disorder and Fostering Civic Dialogue. *Social Media + Society*, 7(1), 2056305120984444. <https://doi.org/10.1177/2056305120984444>

Darr, J. P., Hitt, M. P., & Dunaway, J. L. (2018). Newspaper Closures Polarize Voting Behavior. *Journal Of Communication*, 68(6), 1007–1028. <https://doi.org/10.1093/joc/jqy051>

Darr, J. P., Hitt, M. P., & Dunaway, J. L. (2021). *Home Style Opinion: How Local Newspapers Can Slow Polarization*. Cambridge University Press. <https://doi.org/10.1017/9781108950930>

Davis, J. T., Perry, S. L., & Grubbs, J. B. (2023). Liberty for Us, Limits for Them: Christian Nationalism and Americans' Views on Citizens' Rights. *Sociology of Religion*, 85(1), 60–82. <https://doi.org/10.1093/socrel/srac044>

de Ridder, J. (2021). What's so bad about misinformation? *Inquiry*, 1–23. <https://doi.org/10.1080/0020174X.2021.2002187>

Debing, F. (2016). Doing "Authentic" News: Voices, Forms, and Strategies in Presenting Television News. *International Journal of Communication (19328036)*, 10, 4239–4257.

Department of Agriculture. (2022). *Beef—Kansas Ag Growth*. State of Kansas. <https://agriculture.ks.gov/docs/default-source/ag-growth-summit/2022-growth-documents/2022-beef.pdf>

DeRose, J. (2024, July 18). Trump assassination attempt lays bare deep religious division in the U.S. *NPR*. <https://www.npr.org/2024/07/15/nx-s1-5040606/trumps-assassination-shooting-god-religion>

Dickey, C. (2024, July 18). Why the Trump attack has spawned myriad conspiracies (sic) theories—from left and right alike. *The Guardian*. <https://www.theguardian.com/commentisfree/article/2024/jul/18/donald-trump-attack-conspiracy-theories-news-media>

Dingemans, E., & Van Ingen, E. (2015). Does Religion Breed Trust? A Cross-National Study of the Effects of Religious Involvement, Religious Faith, and Religious Context on Social Trust. *Journal for the Scientific Study of Religion*, 54(4), 739–755. <https://doi.org/https://doi.org/10.1111/jssr.12217>

Dize, N. H. (2024, September 17). 'They're eating pets' — another example of US politicians smearing Haiti and Haitian immigrants. *The Conversation*. <https://theconversation.com/theyre-eating-pets-another-example-of-us-politicians-smearing-haiti-and-haitian-immigrants-239032>

Dobbs v. Jackson Women's Health Organization, 597 U.S. _ (2022). <https://www.supremecourt.gov/opinions/21pdf/19-1392_6j37.pdf>

Docherty, N. (2020). Facebook's Ideal User: Healthy Habits, Social Capital, and the Politics of Well-Being Online. *Social Media + Society*, 6(2), 2056305120915606. <https://doi.org/10.1177/2056305120915606>

Doherty, C., Kiley, J., & Asheer, N. (2024). *Changing partisan coalitions in a politically divided nation: Party identification among registered voters 1994–2023*. Pew Research Center. <https://www.pewresearch.org/wp-content/uploads/sites/20/2024/04/PP_2024.4.9_partisan-coalitions_REPORT.pdf>

Dori-Hacohen, G. (2013). "Rush, I Love You": Interactional Fandom on U.S. Political Talk Radio. *International Journal of Communication (19328036)*, 7, 2697–2718. <https://search.ebscohost.com/login.aspx?direct=true&db=ufh&AN=99140391&site=ehost-live>

Dreisbach, T., & Mak, T. (2021, March 19). Yes, Capitol rioters were armed. Here are the weapons prosecutors say they used. *NPR*. <https://www.npr.org/2021/03/19/977879589/yes-capitol-rioters-were-armed-here-are-the-weapons-prosecutors-say-they-used>

Druckman, J. N., Gubitz, S. R., Lloyd, A. M., & Levendusky, M. S. (2019). How Incivility on Partisan Media (De)Polarizes the Electorate. *Journal of Politics*, *81*(1), 291–295. <https://doi.org/10.1086/699912>

Dubois, E., Minaeian, S., Paquet-Labelle, A., & Beaudry, S. (2020). Who to Trust on Social Media: How Opinion Leaders and Seekers Avoid Disinformation and Echo Chambers. *Social Media + Society*, *6*(2), 2056305120913993. <https://doi.org/10.1177/2056305120913993>

Dzur, A. W. (2002). Public journalism and deliberative democracy. *Polity*, *34*(3), 313–336. <https://www.jstor.org/stable/3235394>

Ecker, U. K. H., Lewandowsky, S., Cook, J., Schmid, P., Fazio, L. K., Brashier, N., Kendeou, P., Vraga, E. K., & Amazeen, M. A. (2022). The psychological drivers of misinformation belief and its resistance to correction. *Nature Reviews Psychology*, *1*(1), 13–29. <https://doi.org/10.1038/s44159-021-00006-y>

Economic Research Service. (2007). *Kansas—Rural Definitions: State-Level Maps*. U.S. Department of Agriculture. Retrieved from <https://www.ers.usda.gov/webdocs/DataFiles/53180/25571_KS.pdf>

Economic Research Service. (2022). *State Fact Sheets: Kansas*. U.S. Department of Agriculture. Retrieved from <https://data.ers.usda.gov/reports.aspx?StateFIPS=20&StateName=Kansas&ID=17854>

Eddington, S. M. (2018). The Communicative Constitution of Hate Organizations Online: A Semantic Network Analysis of "Make America Great Again." *Social Media + Society*, *4*(3), 2056305118790763. <https://doi.org/10.1177/2056305118790763>

Edgar, P. M., & Edgar, D. E. (1971). Television Violence and Socialization Theory. *Public Opinion Quarterly*, *35*(4), 608–612.

Etelson, E. (2020). *Beyond Contempt: How Liberals Can Communicate Across the Great Divide*. New Society Publishers.

European Commission. (2018). *General Data Protection Regulation (GDPR) Article 17: Right to erasure ('right to be forgotten')*. European Union. Retrieved from <https://gdpr.eu/article-17-right-to-be-forgotten/>

Fabiansson, C. (2007). Young People's Perception Of Being Safe—Globally & Locally. *Social Indicators Research*, *80*(1), 31–49. <https://doi.org/https://doi.org/10.1007/s11205-006-9020-3>

Fairclough, N. (2010). *Analysing discourse: textual analysis for social research*. Routledge.

Farrell, D. M., Curato, N., Dryzek, J. S., Geifzel, B., Gronlund, K., Marien, S., Niemeyer, S., Pilet, J.-B., Renwick, A., Rose, J., Setala, M., & Suiter, J. (2019). Deliberative Mini-Publics: Core Design Features. *Centre for Deliberative Democracy and Global Governance Working Paper 2019/5*. Canberra, Australia: Centre for Deliberative Democracy and Global Governance.

Ferguson, R. (2021). *Losing Ground: Farm Consolidation and Threats to New and Black Farmers and the Future of Farming*. Union of Concerned Scientists. <https://www.ucsusa.org/sites/default/files/2021-04/losing-ground-white-paper-4-14-21.pdf>

Fertig, N., & Rivard, R. (2024, July 14). Sunday services paint Trump as God's chosen one. *Politico*. <https://www.politico.com/news/2024/07/14/trump-shooting-megachurch-sermons-00168146>

Finlayson, J. G. (2005). *Habermas: A Very Short Introduction*. Oxford University Press.

Finneman, T., Heckman, M., & E. Walck, P. (2022). Reimagining Journalistic Roles: How Student Journalists Are Taking On the U.S. News Desert Crisis. *Journalism Studies*, *23*(3), 338–355. <https://doi.org/10.1080/1461670X.2021.2023323>

Finneman, T., Mathews, N., & Ferrucci, P. (2024). *Reviving rural news: Transforming the business model of community journalism in the US and beyond*. Routledge.

Finneman, T., & Thomas, R. J. (2018). A family of falsehoods: Deception, media hoaxes and fake news. *Newspaper Research Journal*, *39*(3), 350–361. <https://doi.org/10.1177/0739532918796228>

Finneman, T., & Thomas, R. J. (2021). "Our Company is in Survival Mode": Metajournalistic Discourse on COVID-19's Impact on U.S. Community Newspapers. *Journalism Practice*, 1–19. <https://doi.org/10.1080/17512786.2021.1888149>

Fish, S. (1994). *There's no such thing as free speech: And it's a good thing, too*. Oxford University Press.

Fisher, C., Flew, T., Park, S., Lee, J. Y., & Dulleck, U. (2021). Improving Trust in News: Audience Solutions. *Journalism Practice*, *15*(10), 1497–1515. <https://doi.org/10.1080/17512786.2020.1787859>

Flatt, C. (2023, August 26). Rural Washington library could be nation's first to dissolve after book challenges, reshelving requests. *Oregon Public Broadcasting*. <https://www.opb.org/article/2023/08/26/rural-washington-state-library-could-be-nations-first-to-dissolve-after-book-challenges/>

Flaxman, S., Goel, S., & Rao, J. M. (2016). Filter Bubbles, Echo Chambers, and Online News Consumption. *Public Opinion Quarterly*, *80*(S1), 298–320. <https://doi.org/10.1093/poq/nfw006>

Folkenflik, D. (2021, February 17). Talk show host Rush Limbaugh, a conservative lodestar, dies at 70. *NPR*. <https://www.npr.org/2021/02/17/926491419/talk-show-host-rush-limbaugh-a-conservative-lodestar-dies-at-70>

Frank, K. A., Zhao, Y., & Borman, K. (2004). Social Capital and the Diffusion of Innovations Within Organizations: The Case of Computer Technology in Schools. *Sociology of Education*, *77*(2), 148–171. <https://doi.org/10.1177/003804070407700203>

Frank, T. (2004). *What's the Matter with Kansas?: How Conservatives Won the Heart of America*. Metropolitan Books.

Fraser, N. (1990). Rethinking the Public Sphere: A Contribution to the Critique of Actually Existing Democracy. *Social Text* (25/26), 56–80. <https://doi.org/10.2307/466240>

Frenkel, S., Decker, B., & Alba, D. (2020, May 20). How the 'Plandemic' movie and its falsehoods spread widely online. *The New York Times*. <https://www.nytimes.com/2020/05/20/technology/plandemic-movie-youtube-facebook-coronavirus.html>

Frounfelker, R. L., Frissen, T., Miconi, D., Lawson, J., Brennan, R. T., d'Haenens, L., & Rousseau, C. (2021). Transnational evaluation of the Sympathy for Violent Radicalization Scale: Measuring population attitudes toward violent radicalization in two countries. *Transcult Psychiatry*, *58*(5), 669–682. <https://doi.org/10.1177/13634615211000550>

Furedi, F. (2004). *Where have all the intellectuals gone*. Bloomsbury.

Gadarian, S. K. (2014). Scary Pictures: How Terrorism Imagery Affects Voter Evaluations. *Political Communication*, *31*(2), 282–302. <https://doi.org/10.1080/10584609.2013.828136>

Gastil, J., & Keith, W. M. (2005). A Nation That (Sometimes) Likes to Talk. In J. Gastil & P. Levin (Eds.), *The Deliberative Democracy Handbook: Strategies for Effective Civic Engagement in the Twenty-First Century*. Jossey-Bass.

Gaultney, I. B., Sherron, T., & Boden, C. (2022). Political polarization, misinformation, and media literacy. *Journal of Media Literacy Education*, *14*(1), 59–81. <https://doi.org/10.23860/JMLE-2022-14-1-5>

Gearhart, S., Moe, A., & Holland, D. (2021). Social media users (under)appreciate the news: An application of hostile media bias to news disseminated on Facebook. *Newspaper Research Journal*, *42*(4), 433–448. <https://doi.org/10.1177/07395329211047009>

Geiß, S., Magin, M., Jürgens, P., & Stark, B. (2021). Loopholes in the Echo Chambers: How the Echo Chamber Metaphor Oversimplifies the Effects of Information Gateways on Opinion Expression. *Digital Journalism*, 9(5), 660–686. <https://doi.org/10.1080/21670811.2021.1873811>

Gelman, A., Shor, B., Bafumi, J., & Park, D. (2005). Rich state, poor state, red state, blue state: What's the matter with Connecticut? *Quarterly Journal of Political Science*, 2, 345–367.

Geological Survey. (1964). *Geographic Centers of the United States*. U.S. Department of the Interior, Retrieved from <https://pubs.usgs.gov/unnumbered/70039437/report.pdf>

Gerbner, G., & Gross, L. (1976). Living with Television: The Violence Profile. *Journal Of Communication*, 26(2), 172–199. <https://doi.org/10.1111/j.1460-2466.1976.tb01397.x>

Gerbner, G., Gross, L., Morgan, M., & Signorielli, N. (1986). Living with Television: The Dynamics of the Cultivation Process. In J. Bryant & D. Zillmann (Eds.), *Perspectives on Media Effects* (pp. 17–40). Lawrence Erlbaum Associates.

Gervais, B. T. (2014). Following the News? Reception of Uncivil Partisan Media and the Use of Incivility in Political Expression. *Political Communication*, 31(4), 564–583. <https://doi.org/10.1080/10584609.2013.852640>

Gibson, C. M. (2006). *Citizens at the center: A new approach to civic engagement*. <https://www.casefoundation.org/resource/citizens-center/>

Giddens, A. (2013). *Beyond left and right: The future of radical politics*. Polity Press.

Gil de Zúñiga, H., & Cheng, Z. (2021). Origin and evolution of the News Finds Me perception: Review of theory and effects. *Profesional de la información*, 30(3). <https://doi.org/10.3145/epi.2021.may.21>

Gil de Zúñiga, H., Weeks, B., & Ardèvol-Abreu, A. (2017). Effects of the News-Finds-Me Perception in Communication: Social Media Use Implications for News Seeking and Learning About Politics. *Journal Of Computer-Mediated Communication*, 22(3), 105–123. <https://doi.org/https://doi.org/10.1111/jcc4.12185>

Gilbert, D. (2024, July 16). Supporters believe 'hand of God' saved Trump. *Wired*. <https://www.wired.com/story/supporters-believe-hand-of-god-saved-trump/>

Gilbert, E., Karahalios, K., & Sandvig, C. (2010). The Network in the Garden: Designing Social Media for Rural Life. *American Behavioral Scientist*, 53(9), 1367–1388.

Gill, J., Johnson, P., & Clark, M. (2010). *Research Methods for Managers* (4th ed.). SAGE Publications.

Goldfarb, M. (2001). All Journalism is Local: Reporting on the Middle East: How the U.S. and European Media Cover the Same Events Differently. *Harvard International Journal of Press/Politics*, *6*(3), 110–115. <https://doi.org/10.1177/108118001129172251>

Golgowski, N. (2022, July 24). Rep. Marjorie Taylor Greene says GOP 'should be Christian Nationalists' party. *HuffPost*. <https://www.huffpost.com/entry/marjorie-taylor-greene-christian-nationalism-republican-party_n_62dd70bde4b081f3a9007344>

Good, J. E. (2009). The Cultivation, Mainstreaming, and Cognitive Processing of Environmentalists Watching Television. *Environmental Communication*, *3*(3), 279–297. <https://doi.org/10.1080/17524030903229746>

Goodin, R. E. (2018). If Deliberation Is Everything, Maybe It's Nothing. In A. Bachtiger, J. S. Dryzek, J. Mansbridge, & M. Warren (Eds.), *The Oxford Handbook of Deliberative Democracy* (1st ed., pp. 883–899). Oxford University Press.

Gorski, P. S., & Perry, S. L. (2022). *The Flag and the Cross: White Christian Nationalism and the Threat to American Democracy*. Oxford University Press.

Gottfried, J. (2021, July 1). Republicans less likely to trust their main news source if they see it as 'mainstream'; Democrats more likely. *Pew Research Center*. <https://www.pewresearch.org/fact-tank/2021/07/01/republicans-less-likely-to-trust-their-main-news-source-if-they-see-it-as-mainstream-democrats-more-likely/>

Gottfried, J., Walker, M., & Mitchell, A. (2020, August 31). Partisans remain sharply divided in many views toward the news media; stark differences between Trump's strongest supporters, critics. *Pew Research Center*. <https://www.pewresearch.org/journalism/2020/08/31/partisans-remain-sharply-divided-in-many-views-toward-the-news-media-stark-differences-between-trumps-strongest-supporters-critics/>

Gowen, A. (2022, July 24). 'The stakes could not be higher': Kansas abortion vote set for Aug. 2. *The Washington Post*. <https://www.washingtonpost.com/nation/2022/07/25/kansas-abortion-constitutional-amendment/>

Grabenstein, H. (2024, August 22). WATCH: Walz says 'mind your own damn business' when it comes to reproductive freedom. *PBS News*. <https://www.pbs.org/newshour/politics/watch-walz-says-mind-your-own-damn-business-when-it-comes-to-reproductive-freedom>

Greenberg, J. (2022, June 16). Most Republicans still falsely believe Trump's stolen election claims. Here are some reason why. *Poynter*. <https://www.poynter.org/fact-checking/2022/70-percent-republicans-falsely-believe-stolen-election-trump/>

Greifeneder, R., Jaffe, M. E., Newman, E. J., & Schwarz, N. (Eds.). (2021). *The psychology of fake news: Accepting, sharing and correcting misinformation*. Routledge. <https://doi.org/10.4324/9780429295379>.

Groshek, J. (2011). Media, Instability, and Democracy: Examining the Granger-Causal Relationships of 122 Countries From 1946 to 2003. *Journal Of Communication*, 61(6), 1161–1182. <https://doi.org/https://doi.org/10.1111/j.1460-2466.2011.01594.x>

Groshek, J., & Koc-Michalska, K. (2017). Helping populism win? Social media use, filter bubbles, and support for populist presidential candidates in the 2016 US election campaign. *Information, Communication & Society*, 20(9), 1389–1407. <https://doi.org/10.1080/1369118X.2017.1329334>

Gross, N., & Simmons, S. (2014). The social and political views of American professors. *Sociological Forum*, 29(1), 40–64.

Guess, A. M., Nagler, J., & Tucker, J. (2020). Less than you think: Prevalence and predictors of fake news dissemination on Facebook. *Science Advances*, 5(1). <https://doi.org/10.1126/sciadv.aau4586>

Gutman, D. (2023, September 20). Embattled WA library wins lawsuit, won't shut down after book-ban fight. *The Seattle Times*. <https://www.seattletimes.com/seattle-news/embattled-wa-library-wins-lawsuit-wont-shut-down-after-fight-over-books/>

Gutmann, A., & Thompson, D. F. (2018). Reflections on Deliberative Democracy. In A. Bachtiger, J. S. Dryzek, J. Mansbridge, & M. Warren (Eds.), *The Oxford Handbook of Deliberative Democracy* (1st ed., pp. 900–912). Oxford University Press.

Gutsche, R. E. (2019). The State and Future of Television News Studies: Theoretical Perspectives, Methodological Problems, and Practice. *Journalism Practice*, 13(9), 1034–1041. <https://doi.org/10.1080/17512786.2019.1644965>

Habermas, J. (1991). *The Structural Transformation of the Public Sphere: An Inquiry into a Category of Bourgeois Society* (T. Burger & F. Lawrence, Trans.). MIT Press.

Habermas, J. (1994). Three normative models of democracy. *Constellations*, 1(1), 1–10. <https://doi.org/doi:10.1111/j.1467-8675.1994.tb00001.x>

Habermas, J., Lennox, S., & Lennox, F. (1974). The Public Sphere: An Encyclopedia Article (1964). *New German Critique*(3), 49–55. <https://doi.org/10.2307/487737>

Hajjar, L. (2020). Reactionary Politics and the Rule of Law. *Hague Journal on the Rule of Law*, 12(1), 215–221. <https://doi.org/10.1007/s40803-020-00136-0>

Hameleers, M., & van der Meer, T. (2020). Fight or flight? Attributing responsibility in response to mixed congruent and incongruent partisan news in selective exposure media environments. *Information, Communication & Society*, 23(9), 1327–1352. <https://doi.org/10.1080/1369118X.2019.1566394>

Han, J., & Federico, C. M. (2018). The Polarizing Effect of News Framing: Comparing the Mediating Roles of Motivated Reasoning, Self-stereotyping, and Intergroup Animus. *Journal Of Communication*, 68(4), 685–711. <https://doi.org/10.1093/joc/jqy025>

Hanlon, J. (2023, September 19). Proposition to close Columbia County Library is unconstitutional, court commissioner rules. *The Spokesman-Review*. <https://www.spokesman.com/stories/2023/sep/19/proposition-to-close-columbia-county-library-is-un/>

Haridakis, P. M., & Whitmore, E. H. (2006). Understanding Electronic Media Audiences: The Pioneering Research of Alan M. Rubin. *Journal Of Broadcasting & Electronic Media*, 50(4), 766–774. <https://doi.org/10.1207/s15506878jobem5004_13>

Harmon, M. D., Fontenot, M., Geidner, N., & Mazumdar, A. (2019). Affluenza Revisited: Casting Doubt on Cultivation Effects. *Journal Of Broadcasting & Electronic Media*, 63(2), 268–284. <https://doi.org/10.1080/08838151.2019.1622338>

Harte, D., Williams, A., & Turner, J. (2017). Reciprocity and The Hyperlocal Journalist. *Journalism Practice*, 11(2–3), 160–176. <https://doi.org/10.1080/17512786.2016.1219963>

Harwell, D., Boorstein, M., & Dawsey, J. (2024, July 16). Trump's close call in assassination attempt fuels talk he was 'chosen' by God. *The Washington Post*. <https://www.washingtonpost.com/nation/2024/07/16/trump-religion-messiah/>

Healy, J. (2021, January 11). These are the 5 people who died in the Capitol Riot. *The New York Times*. <https://www.nytimes.com/2021/01/11/us/who-died-in-capitol-building-attack.html>

Heath, R. L., & Waymer, D. (2014). Terrorism: Social capital, social construction, and constructive society? *Public Relations Inquiry*, 3(2), 227–244. <https://doi.org/10.1177/2046147x14529683>

Heath, W., & Lowrey, W. (2021). Social capital and conflict avoidance in campus news. *Newspaper Research Journal*, 42(4), 449–468. <https://doi.org/10.1177/07395329211047960>

Hemmer, N. (2016). *Messengers of the Right: Conservative Media and the Transformation of American Politics*. University of Pennsylvania Press.

Henneman, A., Franzen-Castle, L., Colgrove, K., & Wells, C. (2015). Who Says Online Newsletters Are a Dying Breed? How an Email Newsletter Can Grow Your Nutrition Education Outreach. *Journal of Nutrition Education & Behavior*, 47, 20.

Hershewe, T., & Smith, A. (2025). When Politics Override Place: How Political Affiliation Supersedes Rural Identity. *American Politics Research*, *53*(1), 17–27. <https://doi.org/10.1177/1532673x241282286>

Hess, K. (2015). Making Connections. *Journalism Studies*, *16*(4), 482–496. <https://doi.org/10.1080/1461670X.2014.922293>

Hesse, C. (2017). Survey: Questionnaire. In M. Allen (Ed.), *The SAGE Encyclopedia of Communication Research Methods* (pp. 1717–1718). SAGE Publications, Inc.

Hobbs, A. (2024, July 14). Why many leaders are suggesting Trump is ordained by God after the assassination attempt. *Texas Monthly*. <https://www.texasmonthly.com/news-politics/trump-assassination-texas-christians/>

Hofstetter, C. R., & Gianos, C. L. (1997). Political talk radio: Actions speak louder than words. *Journal Of Broadcasting & Electronic Media*, *41*(4), 501. <https://doi.org/10.1080/08838159709364423>

Hollander, B. A. (1997). Fuel to the Fire: Talk Radio and the Gamson Hypothesis. *Political Communication*, *14*(3), 355–369. <https://doi.org/10.1080/105846097199371>

Homolar, A., & Scholz, R. (2019). The power of Trump-speak: populist crisis narratives and ontological security. *Cambridge Review of International Affairs*, *32*(3), 344–364. <https://doi.org/10.1080/09557571.2019.1575796>

Hopmann, D. N., Shehata, A., & Strömbäck, J. (2015). Contagious Media Effects: How Media Use and Exposure to Game-Framed News Influence Media Trust. *Mass Communication & Society*, *18*(6), 776–798. <https://doi.org/10.1080/15205436.2015.1022190>

Horten, G. (2002). *Radio Goes to War: The Cultural Politics of Propaganda During World War II*. University of California Press.

Howley, K. (2007). Community Media and the Public Sphere. International Communication Association Annual Meeting,

Hudson, A. (2020). Bowling Alone at Twenty. *National Affairs*. <https://www.nationalaffairs.com/publications/detail/bowling-alone-at-twenty>

Huntsberger, M. W. (2020). Community media in the United States: Fostering pluralism and inclusivity in challenging times. *Interactions: Studies in Communication & Culture*, *11*(2), 191–205. <https://doi.org/10.1386/iscc_00018_1>

Ingram, J., & Bladt, C. (2024, July 22). Misinformation and conspiracy theories swirl in wake of Trump assassination attempt. *CBS News*. <https://www.cbsnews.com/news/trump-rally-shooting-misinformation-conspiracy-theories/>

Ingram, M. (2021, March 11). What should we do about the algorithmic amplification of disinformation? *Columbia Journalism Review*. <https://www.cjr.org/the_media_today/what-should-we-do-about-the-algorithmic-amplification-of-disinformation.php>

Innes, H., & Innes, M. (2021). De-platforming disinformation: conspiracy theories and their control. *Information, Communication & Society*, 1–19. <https://doi.org/10.1080/1369118X.2021.1994631>

Institute for Strategic Dialogue. (2020). *Anatomy of a Disinformation Empire: Investigating NaturalNews*. <https://www.isdglobal.org/wp-content/uploads/2021/10/20211013-ISDG-NaturalNews-Briefing.pdf>

Iyengar, S., Lelkes, Y., Levendusky, M., Malhotra, N., & Westwood, S. J. (2019). The Origins and Consequences of Affective Polarization in the United States. *Annual Review of Political Science*, 22(1), 129–146. <https://doi.org/10.1146/annurev-polisci-051117-073034>

Jacobs, N., & Munis, B. K. (2023). Place-Based Resentment in Contemporary U.S. Elections: The Individual Sources of America's Urban-Rural Divide. *Political Research Quarterly*, 76(3), 1102–1118. <https://doi.org/10.1177/10659129221124864>

Jain, P. (2021). The COVID-19 Pandemic and Positive Psychology: The Role of News and Trust in News on Mental Health and Well-Being. *Journal of Health Communication*, 26(5), 317–327. <https://doi.org/10.1080/10810730.2021.1946219>

Jangdal, L. (2019). Local Democracy and the Media. *NORDICOM Review*, 40(s2), 69–83. <https://doi.org/10.2478/nor-2019-0027>

Jenkins, J., & Nielsen, R. K. (2020). Proximity, Public Service, and Popularity: A Comparative Study of How Local Journalists View Quality News. *Journalism Studies*, 21(2), 236–253. <https://doi.org/10.1080/1461670X.2019.1636704>

Jin, B., & Kim, S. (2014). Telethon Viewing, Social Capital, and Community Participation in South Korea. *Communication Quarterly*, 62(3), 253–268. <https://doi.org/10.1080/01463373.2014.911762>

Jingnan, H., Hagen, L., & Yousef, O. (2024, July 14). Conspiracy theories surge following the assassination attempt on Trump. *NPR*. <https://www.npr.org/2024/07/14/nx-s1-5039234/examining-how-narratives-about-the-trump-assassination-attempt-are-resonating>

Johnson, K. M., & Scala, D. J. (2020). The Rural-Urban Continuum of Polarization: Understanding the Geography of the 2018 Midterms. *The Forum*, 18(4), 607–626. <https://doi.org/doi:10.1515/for-2020-2102>

Johnson, T., & Kaye, B. (2013). Putting out Fire with Gasoline: Testing the Gamson Hypothesis on Media Reliance and Political Activity. *Journal Of Broadcasting & Electronic Media*, 57(4), 456–481. <https://doi.org/10.1080/08838151.2013.845825>

Jones, D. A. (1998). Political Talk Radio: The Limbaugh Effect on Primary Voters. *Political Communication*, 15(3), 367–381. <https://doi.org/10.1080/105846098198948>

Jones, J. P. (2012). THE 'NEW' NEWS AS NO 'NEWS': US CABLE NEWS CHANNELS AS BRANDED POLITICAL ENTERTAINMENT TELEVISION. *Media International Australia*(144), 146–155. <https://doi.org/10.1177/1329878X1214400119>

Jones, S. L., & Butman, R. E. (2012). *Modern Psychotherapies: A Comprehensive Christian Appraisal*. InterVarsity Press.

Joseph, C. (2024, July 18). For many Republicans, Trump's near miss signals 'God is involved'. *The Christian Science Monitor*. <https://www.csmonitor.com/USA/Politics/2024/0718/trump-assassination-survival-republicans-christian-nationalism>

Jurkowitz, M., Mitchell, A., Shearer, E., & Walker, M. (2020). *U.S. media polarization and the 2020 election: A nation divided*. Pew Research Center. <https://www.pewresearch.org/journalism/wp-content/uploads/sites/8/2020/01/PJ_2020.01.24_Media-Polarization_FINAL.pdf>

Kaczynski, A. (2022, October 3). Minnesota GOP nominee for governor claimed kids are using litter boxes in schools—it's an internet hoax. *CNN*. <https://www.cnn.com/2022/10/03/politics/scott-jennings-minnesota-schools-cat-litter-box/index.html>

Kalogeropoulos, A., Suiter, J., Udris, L., & Eisenegger, M. (2019). News Media Trust and News Consumption: Factors Related to Trust in News in 35 Countries. *International Journal of Communication (19328036), 13*, 3672–3693.

Kansas Department of Agriculture. (2023). *Division of Conservation (DOC)*. State of Kansas. <https://agriculture.ks.gov/divisions-programs/division-of-conservation>

Kansas Farm Bureau. (n.d.). *About Kansas Farm Bureau*. Kansas Farm Bureau. Retrieved Dec. 5, 2022 from <https://www.kfb.org/about>

Kansas Sampler Foundation. (2019). *Meet Our Team*. Kansas Sampler Foundation. <https://kansassampler.org/who-we-are>

Kansas Secretary of State. (2023). *Elections Statistics Data*. State of Kansas. Retrieved from <https://sos.ks.gov/elections/elections-statistics-data.html>

Karlsen, R., & Aalberg, T. (2021). Social Media and Trust in News: An Experimental Study of the Effect of Facebook on News Story Credibility. *Digital Journalism*, 1–17. <https://doi.org/10.1080/21670811.2021.1945938>

Karlsson, M., & Rowe, E. H. (2019). Local Journalism when the Journalists Leave Town: Probing the news gap that hyperlocal media are supposed to fill. *NORDICOM Review, 40*, 15–29. <https://doi.org/10.2478/nor-2019-0025>

Katz, B., & Nowak, J. (2018). *The new localism: How cities can thrive in the age of populism*. Brookings Institution Press.

Katz, E., Blumler, J. G., & Gurevitch, M. (1973). USES AND GRATIFICATIONS RESEARCH. *Public Opinion Quarterly, 37*(4), 509. <https://doi.org/10.1086/268109>

Kent, K., & Davis, D. (2006, 2006 2006 Annual Meeting). Framing Theory and Research: Implications for the Practice of Journalism.

Kiesler, S., Siegel, J., & McGuire, T. W. (1984). Social psychological aspects of computer-mediated communication. *American Psychologist*, *39*(10), 1123–1134.

Kiger, M. E., & Varpio, L. (2020). Thematic analysis of qualitative data: AMEE Guide No. 131. *Medical Teacher*, *42*(8), 846–854. <https://doi.org/10.1080/0142159X.2020.1755030>

Killenberg, G. M., & Dardenne, R. (1997). Instruction in news reporting as community-focused journalism. *Journalism & Mass Communication Educator*, *52*(1), 52–58. <https://doi.org/10.1177/107769589705200106>

Kim, E. T. (2023, April 20). When the culture wars come for the public library. *The New Yorker*. <https://www.newyorker.com/news/dispatch/when-the-culture-wars-come-for-the-public-library>

Kim, Y.-C., & Ball-Rokeach, S. J. (2006a). Civic Engagement From a Communication Infrastructure Perspective. *Communication Theory*, *16*(2), 173–197. <https://doi.org/10.1111/j.1468-2885.2006.00267.x>

Kim, Y.-C., & Ball-Rokeach, S. J. (2006b). Community Storytelling Network, Neighborhood Context, and Civic Engagement: A Multilevel Approach. *Human Communication Research*, *32*, 411–439. <https://doi.org/10.1111/j.1468-2958.2006.00282.x>

Klein, E. (2025, February 18). A democrat who is thinking differently. *The Ezra Klein Show*. <https://www.nytimes.com/2025/02/18/opinion/ezra-klein-podcast-jake-auchincloss.html>

Klepper, D., & Swenson, A. (2024, July 14). Minutes after Trump shooting, misinformation started flying. Here are the facts. *Associated Press*. <https://apnews.com/article/trump-assassination-biden-tiktok-misinformation-fact-check-4b7ab8e21c00aa6ef47f25ec76984fe6>

Knobloch-Westerwick, S., Mothes, C., Johnson, B. K., Westerwick, A., & Donsbach, W. (2015). Political Online Information Searching in Germany and the United States: Confirmation Bias, Source Credibility, and Attitude Impacts. *Journal Of Communication*, *65*(3), 489–511. <https://doi.org/10.1111/jcom.12154>

Kolotouchkina, O., Gonzálvez Vallés, J. E., & Alonso Mosquera, M. d. H. (2021). Fostering Key Professional Skills and Social Activism Through Experiential Learning Projects in Communication and Advertising Education. *Journalism & Mass Communication Educator*, *76*(1), 46–64. <https://doi.org/10.1177/1077695820919633>

Konieczna, M., & Robinson, S. (2014). Emerging news non-profits: A case study for rebuilding community trust? *Journalism*, *15*(8), 968–986. <https://doi.org/10.1177/1464884913505997>

Kopytowska, M. (2015). Ideology of 'Here and Now'. *Critical Discourse Studies*, *12*(3), 347–365. <https://doi.org/10.1080/17405904.2015.1013485>

Korhonen, V. (2024, July 5). U.S. religious identity of Republicans and Democrats 2023. *Statista*. <https://www.statista.com/statistics/1411981/us-religious-identity-of-republicans-and-democrats-2023/>

Kron, G. (2014). Animal Husbandry. In G. L. Campbell (Ed.), *The Oxford Handbook of Animals in Classical Thought and Life*. Oxford University Press. <https://doi.org/10.1093/oxfordhb/9780199589425.001.0001>

Kruse, L. M., Norris, D. R., & Flinchum, J. R. (2018). Social Media as a Public Sphere? Politics on Social Media. *The Sociological Quarterly*, *59*(1), 62–84. <https://doi.org/10.1080/00380253.2017.1383143>

Ksiazek, T. B., Kim, S. J., & Malthouse, E. C. (2019). Television News Repertoires, Exposure Diversity, and Voting Behavior in the 2016 U.S. Election. *Journalism & Mass Communication Quarterly*, *96*(4), 1120–1144. <https://doi.org/10.1177/1077699018815892>

Kubin, E., & von Sikorski, C. (2021). The role of (social) media in political polarization: a systematic review. *Annals of the International Communication Association*, *45*(3), 188–206. <https://doi.org/10.1080/23808985.2021.1976070>

Kusisto, L., & Barrett, J. (2022, August 3). Kansas votes to protect abortion rights in state constitution: Abortion now expected to remain legal and accessible in the state. *The Wall Street Journal*. <https://www.wsj.com/articles/kansas-abortion-vote-results-11659440554>

Lamberth, E. B., & Aucoin, J. (1993). Understanding Communities: The Journalist as Leader. *Journalism Educator*, *48*(1), 12–19. <https://doi.org/10.1177/107769589304800102>

Langbert, M. (2018). *Homogeneous: The political affiliations of elite liberal arts college faculty*. *Academic Questions*, *31*(2), 186–197. National Association of Scholars. Retrieved from <https://www.nas.org/academic-questions/31/2/homogenous_the_political_affiliations_of_elite_liberal_arts_college_faculty>

Laor, T. (2022). Radio on demand: New habits of consuming radio content. *Global Media & Communication*, *18*(1), 25–48. <https://doi.org/10.1177/17427665211073868>

Lazarsfeld, P. F. (1940). *Radio and the Printed Page: An Introduction to the Study of Radio and Its Role in the Communication of Ideas*. Duell, Sloan, and Pearce.

Leary, A. (2024, July 20). Trump says he 'took a bullet for democracy' in first rally since assassination attempt. *The Wall Street Journal*. <https://www.wsj.com/politics/elections/trump-hosts-first-rally-since-narrowly-surviving-assassination-attempt-i-shouldnt-be-here-59656b2d>

Lee, F. F. (2012). REMEDIATING PRIOR TALK AND CONSTRUCTING PUBLIC DIALOGUE. *Journalism Studies*, *13*(4), 583–599. <https://doi.org/10.1080/1461670X.2012.662399>

Lee, G., & Cappella, J. N. (2001). The Effects of Political Talk Radio On Political Attitude Formation: Exposure Versus Knowledge. *Political Communication*, *18*(4), 369–394. <https://doi.org/10.1080/10584600152647092>

Lee, J., Ott, T., & Deavours, D. (2021). Combating misinformation in risk: Emotional appeal in false beliefs. In R. Luttrell, L. Xiao, & J. Glass (Eds.), *Democracy in the Disinformation Age: Influence and Activism in American Politics* (pp. 165–181). Routledge.

Lee, K. M. (2020). Theistnormativity and the Negation of American Atheists in Presidential Inaugural Addresses. *Rhetoric and Public Affairs*, *23*(2), 255–291. <https://doi.org/10.14321/rhetpublaffa.23.2.0255>

Lee, K. M. (2022). "In God We Trust?": Christian Nationalists' Establishment and Use of Theistnormative Legislation. *Rhetoric Society Quarterly*, *52*(5), 417–432. <https://doi.org/10.1080/02773945.2022.2062435>

Lee, S. (2017). Media Freedom and Social Capital. *Journal of Media Economics*, *30*(1), 3–18. <https://doi.org/10.1080/08997764.2017.1282492>

Leung, L. (2009). User-generated content on the internet: an examination of gratifications, civic engagement and psychological empowerment. *New Media & Society*, *11*(8), 1327–1347. <https://doi.org/10.1177/1461444809341264>

Leupold, A., Klinger, U., & Jarren, O. (2018). IMAGINING THE CITY: How local journalism depicts social cohesion. *Journalism Studies*, *19*(7), 960–982. <https://doi.org/10.1080/1461670X.2016.1245111>

Lewandowsky, S., Ecker, U. K. H., Seifert, C. M., Schwarz, N., & Cook, J. (2012). Misinformation and its correction: Continued influence and successful debiasing. *Psychological Science in the Public Interest*, *13*(3), 106–131. <https://doi.org/10.1177/1529100612451018>

Lewis, R. (2020). "This Is What the News Won't Show You": YouTube Creators and the Reactionary Politics of Micro-celebrity. *Television & New Media*, *21*(2), 201–217. <https://doi.org/10.1177/1527476419879919>

Lewis, S. C. (2020). Lack of trust in the news media, institutional weakness, and relational journalism as a potential way forward. *Journalism*, *21*(3), 345–348. <https://doi.org/10.1177/1464884918807597>

Lewis, S. C., Holton, A. E., & Coddington, M. (2014). Reciprocal journalism: A concept of mutual exchange between journalists and audiences. *Journalism Practice*, 8(2), 1–13. <https://doi.org/10.1080/17512786.2013.859840>

Lin, J., & Lunz Trujillo, K. (2023). Urban-Rural Residency, Place Identity, and Affective Polarization in the United States. *OSF Preprints*, 0(0), 1–25. <https://doi.org/10.31219/osf.io/97a3x>

Lin, J., & Lunz Trujillo, K. (2024). Are rural attitudes just Republican? *Political Science Research and Methods*, 12(3), 675–684. <https://doi.org/10.1017/psrm.2023.48>

Lin, N. (2002). *Social capital: A theory of social structure and action*. Cambridge University Press.

Liu, J., & McLeod, D. M. (2021). Pathways to news commenting and the removal of the comment system on news websites. *Journalism*, 22(4), 867–881. <https://doi.org/10.1177/1464884919849954>

Lonsdorf, K., Dorning, C., Isackson, A., Kelly, M. L., & Chang, A. (2022, January 5). A timeline of the Jan. 6 Capitol attack—including when and how Trump responded. *NPR*. <https://www.npr.org/2022/01/05/1069977469/a-timeline-of-how-the-jan-6-attack-unfolded-including-who-said-what-and-when>

Loury, G. (2020). Relations before transactions: A personal plea. In D. Allen & R. Somanathan (Eds.), *Difference without domination: Pursuing justice in diverse democracies*. The University of Chicago Press.

Lowrey, W. (2012). The challenge of measuring community journalism. In B. Reader & J. A. Hatcher (Eds.), *Foundations of Community Journalism* (pp. 87–103). SAGE Publications, Inc.

Lowrey, W., Brozana, A., & Mackay, J. B. (2008). Toward a measure of community journalism. *Mass Communication and Society*, 11(3), 275–299. <https://doi.org/10.1080/15205430701668105>

Lunz Trujillo, K. (2024). Feeling Out of Place: Who Are the Non-Rural Rural Identifiers, and Are They Unique Politically? *Political Behavior*, 46(4), 2215–2239. <https://doi.org/10.1007/s11109-024-09915-z>

Lunz Trujillo, K., & Crowley, Z. (2022). Symbolic versus material concerns of rural consciousness in the United States. *Political Geography*, 96, 102658. <https://doi.org/10.1016/j.polgeo.2022.102658>

Luppicini, R. (2007). Review of computer mediated communication research for education. *Instructional Science*, 35(2), 141–185. <https://doi.org/10.1007/s11251-006-9001-6>

Lyons, J., & Utych, S. M. (2023). You're Not From Here!: The Consequences of Urban and Rural Identities. *Political Behavior*, 45(1), 75–101. <https://doi.org/10.1007/s11109-021-09680-3>

Macdonald, I. (2021). Picturing Haitian Earthquake Survivors: Graphic Reportage as an Ethical Strategy for Representing Vulnerable Sources. *Journalism Practice*, 1–21. <https://doi.org/10.1080/17512786.2021.1904790>

MacKay, J., & LaRoche, C. D. (2018). Why Is There No Reactionary International Theory?: THEORY NOTE. *International Studies Quarterly*, 62(2), 234–244.

Maguire, M., & Delahunt, B. (2017). Doing a Thematic Analysis: A Practical, Step-by-Step Guide for Learning and Teaching Scholars. *All Ireland Journal of Teaching and Learning in Higher Education*, 9(3), 1–14. <https://ojs.aishe.org/index.php/aishe-j/article/view/335>

Mahl, D., Zeng, J., & Schäfer, M. S. (2021). From "Nasa Lies" to "Reptilian Eyes": Mapping Communication About 10 Conspiracy Theories, Their Communities, and Main Propagators on Twitter. *Social Media + Society*, 7(2), 20563051211017482. <https://doi.org/10.1177/20563051211017482>

Maras, S. (2006). Social Capital Theory, Television, and Participation. *Continuum: Journal Of Media & Cultural Studies*, 20(1), 87–109. <https://doi.org/10.1080/10304310500475855>

Maresh-Fuehrer, M. M., & Gurney, D. (2021). Infowars and the crisis of political disinformation on social media. In R. Luttrell, L. Xiao, & J. Glass (Eds.), *Democracy in the Disinformation Age: Influence and Activism in American Politics* (pp. 147–164). Routledge.

Matei, S. (2003). The impact of state-level social capital on emergence of virtual communities. *Conference Papers—International Communication Association.*, 1–32.

Matsa, K. E., & Naseer, S. (2021, November 8). News Platform Fact Sheet. *Pew Research Center*. <https://www.pewresearch.org/journalism/fact-sheet/news-platform-fact-sheet/>

Matthews, J. C. (2022). College students' perspectives of bias in their news consumption habits. *Journal of Media Literacy Education*, 14(3), 39–52. <https://doi.org/10.23860/JMLE-2022-14-3-4>

McCombs, M. E., & Shaw, D. L. (1972). The Agenda-Setting Function of Mass Media. *The Public Opinion Quarterly*, 36(2), 176–187. <http://www.jstor.org/stable/2747787>

McLeod, J. M., & Daily, K. (1996). Community integration, local media use, and democratic processes. *Communication Research*, 23(2), 179. <https://doi.org/10.1177/009365096023002002>

McLuhan, M. (2003). *Understanding Me: Lectures and Interviews* (S. McLuhan & D. Staines, Eds.). MIT Press.

McQuail, D. (1984). With the Benefit of Hindsight: Reflections on Uses and Gratifications Research. *Critical Studies in Mass Communication*, *1*(2), 177. <https://doi.org/10.1080/15295038409360028>

McQuail, D. (2010). *McQuail's Mass Communication Theory* (6 ed.). Sage Publications Ltd.

McQuail, D., Blumler, J. G., & Brown, J. R. (1972). The television audience: A revised perspective. In D. McQuail (Ed.), *Sociology of Mass Communications: Selected Readings* (pp. 135–165). Penguin.

Megerian, C. (2024). Biden's disastrous debate performance offers lessons for Harris and warnings for Trump. *Associated Press*. <https://apnews.com/article/joe-biden-donald-trump-debate-d62e8e7281fff34be8925adc9b4e6dc2>

Melotte, S. (2023, July 18). A rural western North Carolina county will keep its public library in the regional system, but not without debate. *The Daily Yonder*. <https://dailyyonder.com/a-rural-western-north-carolina-county-will-keep-its-public-library-in-the-regional-system-but-not-without-debate/2023/07/18/>

Merritt, D. (1997). *Public Journalism and Public Life: Why Telling the News Is Not Enough* (2nd ed.). Routledge.

Mertens, D. M. (2010). Transformative Mixed Methods Research. *Qualitative Inquiry*, *16*(6), 469–474. <https://doi.org/10.1177/1077800410364612>

Mettler, S., & Brown, T. (2022). The Growing Rural-Urban Political Divide and Democratic Vulnerability. *The ANNALS of the American Academy of Political and Social Science*, *699*(1), 130–142. <https://doi.org/10.1177/00027162211070061>

Meyer, H. K., & Daniels, G. L. (2012). Community journalism in an online world. In B. Reader & J. A. Hatcher (Eds.), *Foundations of Community Journalism* (pp. 199–217). SAGE Publications, Inc.

Michel, L., & Herbeck, D. (2001). *American Terrorist: Timothy McVeigh and the Tragedy at Oklahoma City*. HarperCollins.

Miller, Z., Long, C., & Superville, D. (2024, July 21). Biden drops out of 2024 race after disastrous debate inflamed age concenrs. VP Harris gets his nod. *Associated Press*. <https://apnews.com/article/biden-drops-out-2024-election-ddffde72838370032bdcff946cfc2ce6>

Morgan, M., Shanahan, J., & Signorielli, N. (2015). Yesterday's New Cultivation, Tomorrow. *Mass Communication & Society*, *18*(5), 674–699. <https://doi.org/10.1080/15205436.2015.1072725>

Morgan, S. (2018). Fake news, disinformation, manipulation and online tactics to undermine democracy. *Journal of Cyber Policy*, *3*(1), 39–43. <https://doi.org/10.1080/23738871.2018.1462395>

Morphew, C. C., & Hartley, M. (2006). Mission Statements: A Thematic Analysis of Rhetoric Across Institutional Type. *Journal of Higher Education*, 77(3), 456–471. <https://doi.org/10.1353/jhe.2006.0025>

Mosharafa, E. (2015). All you Need to Know About: The Cultivation Theory.

Moskalenko, S., & and McCauley, C. (2009). Measuring Political Mobilization: The Distinction Between Activism and Radicalism. *Terrorism and Political Violence*, 21(2), 239–260. <https://doi.org/10.1080/09546550902765508>

Mou, Y., & Lin, C. A. (2017). The impact of online social capital on social trust and risk perception. *Asian Journal of Communication*, 27(6), 563–581. <https://doi.org/10.1080/01292986.2017.1371198>

Moyer-Gusé, E., Giles, H., & Linz, D. (2008). Communication Studies, Overview. In L. Kurtz (Ed.), *Encyclopedia of Violence, Peace, & Conflict* (2nd ed., pp. 368–379). Academic Press. <https://doi.org/10.1016/B978-012373985-8.00032-5>

Muirhead, R., & Rosenblum, N. L. (2019). *A Lot of People are Saying: The New Conspiracism and the Assault on Democracy*. Princeton University Press.

Munis, B. K. (2022). Us Over Here Versus Them Over There … Literally: Measuring Place Resentment in American Politics. *Political Behavior*, 44(3), 1057–1078. <https://doi.org/10.1007/s11109-020-09641-2>

Muscat, T. (2018). NURTURING AUTHORITY: Reassessing the social role of local television news. *Journalism Practice*, 12(2), 220–235. <https://doi.org/10.1080/17512786.2017.1377630>

Mutz, D. C. (2006). *Hearing the other side: Deliberative versus participatory democracy*. Cambridge University Press.

Mwesige, P. G. (2009). The democratic functions and dysfunctions of political talk radio: the case of Uganda. *Journal of African Media Studies*, 1(2), 221–245. <https://doi.org/10.1386/jams.1.2.221_1>

National Press Office. (2024). *Update on the FBI investigation of the attempted assassination of former President Donald Trump* <https://www.fbi.gov/news/press-releases/update-on-the-fbi-investigation-of-the-attempted-assassination-of-former-president-donald-trump>

Nechushtai, E., & Lewis, S. C. (2019). What kind of news gatekeepers do we want machines to be? Filter bubbles, fragmentation, and the normative dimensions of algorithmic recommendations. *Computers in Human Behavior*, 90, 298–307. <https://doi.org/10.1016/j.chb.2018.07.043>

Nemerever, Z., & Rogers, M. (2021). Measuring the Rural Continuum in Political Science. *Political Analysis*, 29(3), 267–286. <https://doi.org/10.1017/pan.2020.47>

Nevzat, R. (2018). *Reviving cultivation theory for social media* The Asian Conference on Media, Communication & Film, Tokyo, Japan. <http://papers.iafor.org/wp-content/uploads/papers/mediasia2018/MediAsia2018_42554.pdf>

Newman, N. (2020). The Resurgence and Importance of Email Newsletters. *Reuters Institute Digital News Report*.

Newman, N., Fletcher, R., Schulz, A., Andi, S., Robertson, C. T., & Nielsen, R. K. (2021). *Reuters Institute Digital News Report*. Reuters Institute for the Study of Journalism. <https://doi.org/10.60625/risj-7khr-zj06>

Newport, F. (2023, September 1). The politics of religion. *Gallup*. <https://news.gallup.com/opinion/polling-matters/510464/politics-religion.aspx>

Niekamp, R. (2009). Community Correspondent: One Broadcaster's Attempt at Citizen Journalism. *Southwestern Mass Communication Journal*, 24(2), 45–53.

Nielsen. (2019). *Tops of 2019: Radio*. The Nielsen Company (US) LLC. <https://www.nielsen.com/insights/2019/tops-of-2019-radio/>

Noelle-Neumann, E. (1974). The Spiral of Silence A Theory of Public Opinion. *Journal Of Communication*, 24(2), 43–51. <https://doi.org/10.1111/j.1460-2466.1974.tb00367.x>

Norander, S., & Galanes, G. (2014). "Bridging the Gap": Difference, Dialogue, and Community Organizing. *Journal of Applied Communication Research*, 42(4), 345–365. <https://doi.org/10.1080/00909882.2014.911939>

Noriega, C. A., & Iribarren, J. (2014). Studying Hate Speech on Commercial Talk Radio. *Journal of Radio & Audio Media*, 21(2), 193–195. <https://doi.org/10.1080/19376529.2014.950137>

Nowell, L. S., Norris, J. M., White, D. E., & Moules, N. J. (2017). Thematic Analysis: Striving to Meet the Trustworthiness Criteria. *International Journal of Qualitative Methods*, 16(1), 1–13. <https://doi.org/10.1177/1609406917733847>

NPR Staff. (2021, February 9). The Jan. 6 attack: The cases behind the biggest criminal investigation in U.S. history. *National Public Radio*. <https://www.npr.org/2021/02/09/965472049/the-capitol-siege-the-arrested-and-their-stories>

Nygren, G. (2019). Local Media Ecologies. *NORDICOM Review*, 40(s2), 51–67. <https://doi.org/10.2478/nor-2019-0026>

Nygren, G., Leckner, S., & Tenor, C. (2018). Hyperlocals and legacy media: Media ecologies in transition. *NORDICOM Review*, 39(1), 33–49.

Ollstein, A. M. (2022, August 3). Kansas landslide fuels abortion rights movement's next fights. *Politico*. <https://www.politico.com/news/2022/08/03/kansas-abortion-rights-roe-v-wade-00049710>

Olmstead, M. (2022, August 5). "Christian Nationalism" used to be taboo. Now it's all the rage. *Slate*. <https://slate.com/news-and-politics/2022/08/christian-nationalist-identity-marjorie-taylor-greene.html>

Olmsted, E. (2024, July 15). MAGA Republicans claim Trump's shooting is proof he was chosen by God. *The New Republic*. <https://newrepublic.com/post/183824/maga-republicans-cult-mode-trump-shooting-rnc>

Olsen, R. K., & Solvoll, M. K. (2018). Bouncing off the Paywall—Understanding Misalignments Between Local Newspaper Value Propositions and Audience Responses. *JMM: The International Journal on Media Management*, 20(3), 174–192. <https://doi.org/10.1080/14241277.2018.1529672>

Olson, M. K., Vos, S. C., & Sutton, J. (2020). Threat and Efficacy in Television News: Reporting on an Emerging Infectious Disease. *Western Journal of Communication*, 84(5), 623–640. <https://doi.org/10.1080/10570314.2020.1755721>

Padgett, J., Dunaway, J. L., & Darr, J. P. (2019). As Seen on TV? How Gatekeeping Makes the U.S. House Seem More Extreme. *Journal Of Communication*, 69(6), 696–719. <https://doi.org/10.1093/joc/jqz039>

Palinkas, L. A., Horwitz, S. M., Green, C. A., Wisdom, J. P., Duan, N., & Hoagwood, K. (2015). Purposeful Sampling for Qualitative Data Collection and Analysis in Mixed Method Implementation Research. *Administration and Policy in Mental Health and Mental Health Services Research*, 42(5), 533–544. <https://doi.org/10.1007/s10488-013-0528-y>

Pang, N., & Ng, J. (2017). Misinformation in a riot: a two-step flow view. *Online Information Review*, 41(4), 438–453. <https://doi.org/10.1108/OIR-09-2015-0297>

Pariser, E. (2011). *The filter bubble: What the Internet is hiding from you*. Penguin Books.

Park, S., Fisher, C., Flew, T., & Dulleck, U. (2020). Global Mistrust in News: The Impact of Social Media on Trust. *JMM: The International Journal on Media Management*, 22(2), 83–96. <https://doi.org/10.1080/14241277.2020.1799794>

Parker, C. S., & Barreto, M. (2013). *Change They Can't Believe In: The Tea Party and Reactionary Politics in America*. Princeton University Press.

Parker, C. S., & Lavine, H. (2024). Status threat: The core of reactionary politics. *Political Psychology*, 0(0), 1–25. <https://doi.org/10.1111/pops.12983>

Pass, S. (2004). *Parallel Paths to Constructivism: Jean Piaget and Lev Vygotsky*. Information Age Publishing.

Paul, K. (2015). Stakeholder theory, meet communications theory: Media systems dependency and community infrastructure theory, with an application to

California's cannabis/marijuana industry. *Journal of Business Ethics, 129*(3), 705–720.

Pauly, J. J., & Eckert, M. (2002). The myth of 'the local' in American journalism. *Journalism & Mass Communication Quarterly, 79*(2), 310–326. <https://doi.org/10.1177/107769900207900204>

Pearson, G. D. H., & Knobloch-Westerwick, S. (2019). Is the Confirmation Bias Bubble Larger Online? Pre-Election Confirmation Bias in Selective Exposure to Online versus Print Political Information. *Mass Communication & Society, 22*(4), 466–486. <https://doi.org/10.1080/15205436.2019.1599956>

Perks, L. G., & Turner, J. S. (2019). Podcasts and Productivity: A Qualitative Uses and Gratifications Study. *Mass Communication & Society, 22*(1), 96–116. <https://doi.org/10.1080/15205436.2018.1490434>

Perks, L. G., Turner, J. S., & Tollison, A. C. (2019). Podcast Uses and Gratifications Scale Development. *Journal Of Broadcasting & Electronic Media, 63*(4), 617–634. <https://doi.org/10.1080/08838151.2019.1688817>

Perreault, M. F. (2021). Journalism Beyond the Command Post: Local Journalists as Strategic Citizen Stakeholders in Natural Disaster Recovery. *Journalism Studies, 22*(10), 1279–1297. <https://doi.org/10.1080/1461670X.2021.1950565>

Peterson-Salahuddin, C. (2021). Opening the gates: defining a model of intersectional journalism. *Critical Studies In Media Communication, 38*(5), 391–407. <https://doi.org/10.1080/15295036.2021.1968014>

Pew Research Center. (2014). *Religious Landscape Study: Adults in Kansas*. The Pew Charitable Trusts. <https://www.pewresearch.org/religion/religious-landscape-study/state/kansas/>

Pew Research Center. (2019a). *For local news, Americans embrace digital but still want strong community connection*. The Pew Charitable Trusts. <https://www.pewresearch.org/journalism/wp-content/uploads/sites/8/2019/03/PJ_2019.03.26_Local-News_FINAL.pdf>

Pew Research Center. (2019b). The Growing Partisan Divide in Views of Higher Education. Retrieved from <https://www.pewresearch.org/social-trends/2019/08/19/the-growing-partisan-divide-in-views-of-higher-education-2/>

Pew Research Center. (2021a). *Americans see broad responsibilities for government; little change since 2019*. The Pew Charitable Trusts. <https://www.pewresearch.org/politics/2021/05/17/americans-see-broad-responsibilities-for-government-little-change-since-2019/>

Pew Research Center. (2021b). *Audio and Podcasting Fact Sheet*. The Pew Charitable Trusts. <https://www.pewresearch.org/journalism/fact-sheet/audio-and-podcasting/>

Pipal, C., Song, H., & Boomgaarden, H. G. (2022). If You Have Choices, Why Not Choose (and Share) All of Them? A Multiverse Approach to Understanding News Engagement on Social Media. *Digital Journalism*, 1–21. <https://doi.org/10.1080/21670811.2022.2036623>

Plessy v. Ferguson, 163 U.S. 537 (1896). <https://supreme.justia.com/cases/federal/us/163/537/#tab-opinion-1917400>

Ponder, J. D., & Haridakis, P. (2015). Selectively Social Politics: The Differing Roles of Media Use on Political Discussion. *Mass Communication & Society*, *18*(3), 281–302. <https://doi.org/10.1080/15205436.2014.940977>

Post, C. (2009). Reputational politics and the symbolic accretion of John Brown in Kansas. *Historical Geography*, *37*(2), 92–113.

Potter, W. J. (2014). A Critical Analysis of Cultivation Theory. *Journal Of Communication*, *64*(6), 1015–1036. <https://doi.org/10.1111/jcom.12128>

Potter, W. J. (2016). *Media Literacy* (8th ed.). SAGE Publications, Inc.

Prochazka, F., & Schweiger, W. (2019). How to Measure Generalized Trust in News Media? An Adaptation and Test of Scales. *Communication Methods & Measures*, *13*(1), 26–42. <https://doi.org/10.1080/19312458.2018.1506021>

Putnam, R. D. (2001). *Bowling alone: The collapse and revival of American community*. Simon & Schuster.

Putnam, R. D., Campbell, D. E., & Garrett, S. R. (2010). *American grace: How religion divides and unites us*. Simon & Schuster.

Ramirez, I., & McCarthy, M. (2024, July 14). Republicans embrace 'divine intervention' for Trump's near-miss martyrdom. *Politico*. <https://www.politico.com/news/2024/07/14/trump-shooting-republicans-god-intervention-00168108>

Reber, B. H., & Chang, Y. (2000). Assessing cultivation theory and public health model for crime reporting. *Newspaper Research Journal*, *21*(4), 99. <https://doi.org/10.1177/073953290002100407>

Recuero, R., Zago, G., & Soares, F. (2019). Using Social Network Analysis and Social Capital to Identify User Roles on Polarized Political Conversations on Twitter. *Social Media + Society*, *5*(2), 2056305119848745. <https://doi.org/10.1177/2056305119848745>

Reid, T., Slattery, G., & Coster, H. (2024, July 14). After assassination attempt, Trump and Biden seek calm, unity. *Reuters*. <https://www.reuters.com/world/us/trump-shooting-raises-questions-about-security-lapses-2024-07-14/>

RFD-TV. (n.d.). *About Us*. Rural Media Group, Inc. <https://www.rfdtv.com/about-us>

Richards, I. (2013). Beyond city limits: Regional journalism and social capital. *Journalism*, *14*(5), 627–642. <https://doi.org/10.1177/1464884912453280>

Robinson, R. S. (2014). Purposive Sampling. In A. C. Michalos (Ed.), *Encyclopedia of Quality of Life and Well-Being Research* (pp. 5243–5245). Springer Netherlands. <https://doi.org/10.1007/978-94-007-0753-5_2337>

Robinson, S. (2017). Teaching journalism for better community: A deweyan approach. *Journalism and Mass Communication Quarterly*, *94*(1), 303–317. <https://doi.org/10.1177/1077699016681986>

Romiszowski, A., & Mason, R. (2013). Computer-mediated communication. In *Handbook of research on educational communications and technology* (pp. 402–436). Routledge.

Ross, M. W., Essien, E. J., & Torres, I. (2006). Conspiracy Beliefs About the Origin of HIV/AIDS in Four Racial/Ethnic Groups. *JAIDS Journal of Acquired Immune Deficiency Syndromes*, *41*(3).

Rotolo, M., Smith, G. A., & Evans, J. (2024). *8 in 10 Americans say religion is losing influence in public life: Few see Biden or Trump as especially religious.* Pew Research Center. <https://www.pewresearch.org/wp-content/uploads/sites/20/2024/03/PR_2024.3.15_religion-public-life_REPORT.pdf>

Rubin, A. M., & Haridakis, P. M. (2001). Mass communication research at the dawn of the 21st century. *Annals of the International Communication Association*, *24*(1), 73–98.

Rubin, O., Mallin, A., & Steakin, W. (2022). By the numbers: How the Jan. 6 investigation is shaping up 1 year later. *ABC News*. <https://abcnews.go.com/US/numbers-jan-investigation-shaping-year/story?id=82057743>

Ruggiero, T. E. (2000). Uses and Gratifications Theory in the 21st Century. *Mass Communication and Society*, *3*(1), 3–37. <https://doi.org/10.1207/S15327825MCS0301_02>

Saldaña, M., & Vu, H. T. (2022). You Are Fake News! Factors Impacting Journalists' Debunking Behaviors on Social Media. *Digital Journalism*, *10*(5), 823–842. <https://doi.org/10.1080/21670811.2021.2004554>

Sargent, G. (2018). *An Uncivil War: Taking Back Our Democracy in an Age of Trumpian Disinformation and Thunderdome Politics*. Custom House.

Sass, E. (2016). People Prefer Social Media To Face-to-Face Communication. *Mediapost*, para. <https://www.mediapost.com/publications/article/278620/people-prefer-social-media-to-face-to-face-communi.html>

Scala, D. J., & Johnson, K. M. (2017). Political Polarization along the Rural-Urban Continuum? The Geography of the Presidential Vote, 2000–2016. *The ANNALS of the American Academy of Political and Social Science*, *672*(1), 162–184. <https://doi.org/10.1177/0002716217712696>

Scala, D. J., Johnson, K. M., & Rogers, L. T. (2015). Red rural, blue rural? Presidential voting patterns in a changing rural America. *Political Geography*, 48, 108–118. <https://doi.org/10.1016/j.polgeo.2015.02.003>

Schaller, T., & Waldman, P. (2024). *White Rural Rage: The Threat to American Democracy*. Random House.

Schermele, Z. (2022, August 4). A cultural power struggle at an Iowa library casts a 'dark cloud' over a small town. *NBC News*. <https://www.nbcnews.com/nbc-out/out-news/small-town-library-shut-say-culture-wars-closed-rcna39816>

Schmid, A. P. (2013). Radicalisation, de-radicalisation, counter-radicalisation: A conceptual discussion and literature review. *ICCT research paper*, 97(1), 22.

Schoewe, W. H., Horr, W. H., Burt, C. E., & Wooster, L. D. (1937). Symposium on the Geology, Flora, and Fauna of "Rock City," a Proposed National Monument in Ottawa County, Kansas. *Transactions of the Kansas Academy of Science (1903-)*, 40, 179–191. <https://doi.org/10.2307/3625405>

Schwartz, A. B. (2015). *Broadcast Hysteria: Orson Welles's War of the Worlds and the Art of Fake News*. Farrar, Straus and Giroux.

Searles, K., & Smith, G. (2016). Who's the Boss? Setting the Agenda in a Fragmented Media Environment. *International Journal of Communication (19328036)*, 10, 2074–2095.

Severin, W. J., & Tankard, J. W. (2000). *Communication theories: Origins, methods, and uses in the mass media* (5th ed.). Pearson College Division.

Shearer, E. (2021, January 12). More than eight-in-ten Americans get news from digital devices. *Pew Research Center*. <https://www.pewresearch.org/fact-tank/2021/01/12/more-than-eight-in-ten-americans-get-news-from-digital-devices/>

Sherry, J. L. (2006). Flow and Media Enjoyment. *Communication Theory*, 14(4), 328–347. <https://doi.org/10.1111/j.1468-2885.2004.tb00318.x>

Shoemaker, P. J., Vos, T. P., & Reese, S. D. (2009). Journalists as gatekeepers. In *The handbook of journalism studies* (pp. 93–107). Routledge.

Shrader, J. (2013). Folly of Outrage: Talk Radio's Unethical and Damaging Business Model. *Journal Of Mass Media Ethics*, 28(4), 289–292. <https://doi.org/10.1080/08900523.2013.837291>

Shrum, L. J. (2017). Cultivation Theory: Effects and Underlying Processes. In *The International Encyclopedia of Media Effects* (pp. 1–12). <https://doi.org/https://doi.org/10.1002/9781118783764.wbieme0040>

Sienkiewicz, M., & Marx, N. (2022). *That's not funny: How the Right makes comedy work for them*. University of California Press.

Siisiainen, M. (2003). Two concepts of social capital: Bourdieu vs. Putnam. *International journal of contemporary sociology*, 40(2), 183–204.

Skoric, M. M., Zhu, Q., Goh, D., & Pang, N. (2016). Social media and citizen engagement: A meta-analytic review. *New Media & Society*, *18*(9), 1817–1839. <https://doi.org/10.1177/1461444815616221>

Smethers, J. S., Bressers, B., & Mwangi, S. C. (2017). Friendships sustain volunteer newspaper for 21 years. *Newspaper Research Journal*, *38*(3), 379–391. <https://doi.org/10.1177/0739532917722984>

Smethers, J. S., Mwangi, S. C., & Bressers, B. (2021). Signal interruption in Baldwin City: Filling a communication vacuum in a small town "news desert." *Newspaper Research Journal*, *42*(3), 379–396. <https://doi.org/10.1177/07395329211030687>

Smith, C. C. (2018). Identity(ies) explored: How journalists' self-conceptions influence small-town news. *Journalism Practice*, *13*(5), 524–536. <https://doi.org/10.1080/17512786.2018.1544849>

Smith, C. C., & Schiffman, J. R. (2018). Remaining close to home: Small daily newspapers provide (mostly) hyperlocal election news during 2016 elections. *Newspaper Research Journal*, *39*(4), 420–432. <https://doi.org/10.1177/0739532918806873>

Smith, G. A., Gecewicz, C., Schiller, A., & Nolan, H. (2019). *Americans have positive views about religion's role in society, but want it out of politics: Most say religion is losing influence in American life*. Pew Research Center. <https://www.pewresearch.org/wp-content/uploads/sites/20/2019/11/PF_11.15.19_trust.in_.religion_FULL.REPORT.pdf>

Smith, G. A., Rotolo, M., & Tevington, P. (2022). *45% of Americans say U.S. should be a 'Christian Nation'*. Pew Research Center. <https://www.pewresearch.org/religion/2022/10/27/45-of-americans-say-u-s-should-be-a-christian-nation/>

Smith, M. (2022, July 24). "Everybody is dug in": Kansans fiercely debate the first post-Roe vote on abortion. *The New York Times*. <https://www.nytimes.com/2022/07/24/us/kansas-abortion-vote.html>

Smith, M., & Glueck, K. (2022, August 2). Kansas votes to preserve abortion rights protections in its constitution. *The New York Times*. <https://www.nytimes.com/2022/08/02/us/kansas-abortion-rights-vote.html>

Smith, S. (2021, January 12). Kansas Republicans target 2022 primary for abortion amendment. *Kansas Reflector*. <https://kansasreflector.com/2021/01/12/kansas-republicans-target-2022-primary-for-abortion-amendment/>

Smith, S., & Becker, L. O. S. (2022, August 2). Kansas voters defeat abortion amendment in unexpected landslide. *Kansas Reflector*. <https://kansasreflector.com/2022/08/02/kansas-voters-defeat-abortion-amendment-in-unexpected-landslide-1/>

Snyder v. Phelps, 562 U.S. 443 (2011). <https://supreme.justia.com/cases/federal/us/562/443/#tab-opinion-1963459>

Sobieraj, S., & Berry, J. (2011). From Incivility to Outrage: Political Discourse in Blogs, Talk Radio, and Cable News. *Political Communication*, 28(1), 19–41. <https://doi.org/10.1080/10584609.2010.542360>

Song, H., Gil de Zúñiga, H., & Boomgaarden, H. G. (2020). Social Media News Use and Political Cynicism: Differential Pathways Through "News Finds Me" Perception. *Mass Communication and Society*, 23(1), 47–70. <https://doi.org/10.1080/15205436.2019.1651867>

St. John III, B., Johnson, K., & Nah, S. (2013). Patch.com: The challenge of connective community journalism in the digital sphere. *Journalism Practice*, 8(2), 197–212. <https://doi.org/10.1080/17512786.2013.859835>

Stamps, D. (2021). It's All Relative: The Dual Role of Media Consumption and Media Literacy among Black Audiences. *Southern Communication Journal*, 86(3), 231–243. <https://doi.org/10.1080/1041794X.2021.1905053>

Stanford, L. (2022, November 29). Litter boxes in schools: How a disruptive and demeaning hoax frustrated school leaders. *Education Week*. <https://www.edweek.org/leadership/litter-boxes-in-schools-how-a-disruptive-and-demeaning-hoax-frustrated-school-leaders/2022/11>

State Library of Kansas. (n.d.). *City Data* <https://kslib.info/426/City-Data>

Steele, B. J., & Homolar, A. (2019). Ontological insecurities and the politics of contemporary populism. *Cambridge Review of International Affairs*, 32(3), 214–221. <https://doi.org/10.1080/09557571.2019.1596612>

Stephens, P. (2013). "Reading at It": Gertrude Stein, Information Overload, and the Makings of Americanitis. *Twentieth Century Literature*, 59(1), 126–156. <http://www.jstor.org/stable/24247113>

Stiegler, Z. (2014). Michael Savage and the Political Transformation of Shock Radio. *Journal of Radio & Audio Media*, 21(2), 230–246. <https://doi.org/10.1080/19376529.2014.950147>

Stites, T. (2018, June 1). New data tracks how fast news deserts are spreading. *Poynter*. <https://www.poynter.org/reporting-editing/2018/new-data-tracks-how-fast-news-deserts-are-spreading/>

Strömbäck, J., Tsfati, Y., Boomgaarden, H., Damstra, A., Lindgren, E., Vliegenthart, R., & Lindholm, T. (2020). News media trust and its impact on media use: toward a framework for future research. *Annals of the International Communication Association*, 44(2), 139–156. <https://doi.org/10.1080/23808985.2020.1755338>

Sullivan, M. (2020). *Ghosting the news: Local journalism and the crisis of American democracy*. Columbia Global Reports.

Swart, J., & Broersma, M. (2022). The Trust Gap: Young People's Tactics for Assessing the Reliability of Political News. *The International Journal of Press/Politics*, 27(2), 396–416. <https://doi.org/10.1177/19401612211006696>

Talisse, R. (2020 December 22). America's political divide will be very hard to heal. *The Conversation*, para. <https://theconversation.com/amp/can-joe-biden-heal-the-united-states-political-experts-disagree-150519>

Talisse, R. B. (2021). *Sustaining Democracy: What We Owe to the Other Side*. Oxford University Press.

Terry, G., & Hayfield, N. (2021). Conceptual foundations of thematic analysis. In *Essentials of thematic analysis*. (pp. 3–14). American Psychological Association. <https://doi.org/10.1037/0000238-001>

The Associated Press-NORC Center for Public Affairs Research. (2018). *The Role of Religion in Politics*. University of Chicago. <https://apnorc.org/projects/the-role-of-religion-in-politics/>

Thompson, J. (2021). Watching Together: Local Media and Rural Civic Engagement. *Rural Sociology*, 86(4), 938–967. <https://doi.org/https://doi.org/10.1111/ruso.12383>

Thomson, T. J., Angus, D., Dootson, P., Hurcombe, E., & Smith, A. (2022). Visual Mis/disinformation in Journalism and Public Communications: Current Verification Practices, Challenges, and Future Opportunities. *Journalism Practice*, 16(5), 938–962. <https://doi.org/10.1080/17512786.2020.1832139>

Thornton, K. (2022a, December 6). The Divided Dial: Episode 4—From the Extreme to the Mainstream In *On the Media*. WNYC Studios. <https://www.wnycstudios.org/podcasts/otm/episodes/divided-dial-episode-4->

Thornton, K. (2022b, November 15). The Divided Dial: Episode 1—The True Believers In *On the Media*. WNYC Studios. <https://www.wnycstudios.org/podcasts/otm/episodes/divided-dial-episode-1-true-believers>

Toff, B., Palmer, R., & Nielsen, R. K. (2023). *Avoiding the News: Reluctant Audiences for Journalism*. Columbia University Press.

Tornoe, R. (2017). Creating a "Customer-Engagement Funnel": Why email newsletters continue to succeed for newspapers. *Editor & Publisher*, 150(11), 24–25.

Torres-Lugo, C., Yang, K.-C., & Menczer, F. (2020). The Manufacture of Partisan Echo Chambers by Follow Train Abuse on Twitter. *arXiv preprint arXiv:2010.13691*.

Towers, W. M. (1985). Weekday and Sunday Readership Seen Through Uses and Gratifications. *Newspaper Research Journal*, 6(3), 20–32. <https://doi.org/10.1177/073953298500600303>

Turkle, S. (2012). *Alone Together: Why we expect more from technology and less from each other*. Basic Books.

U.S. Census Bureau. (2010a). *Census Regions and Divisions of the United States*. U.S. Department of Commerce's Economics and Statistics Administration. <https://www.census.gov/geographies/reference-maps/2010/geo/2010-census-regions-and-divisions-of-the-united-states.html>

U.S. Census Bureau. (2010b). *State Area Measurements and Internal Point Coordinates*. U.S. Department of Commerce's Economics and Statistics Administration Retrieved from <https://www.census.gov/geographies/reference-files/2010/geo/state-area.html>

U.S. Census Bureau. (2021a). *City and Town Population Totals: 2020–2021*. U.S. Department of Commerce's Economics and Statistics Administration Retrieved from <https://www.census.gov/data/tables/time-series/demo/popest/2020s-total-cities-and-towns.html>

U.S. Census Bureau. (2021b). *County Population Totals: 2020–2021*. U.S. Department of Commerce's Economics and Statistics Administration Retrieved from <https://www.census.gov/data/tables/time-series/demo/popest/2020s-counties-total.html>

U.S. Census Bureau. (2022a). *American Community Survey 5-Year Data (2009–2021)*. U.S. Department of Commerce's Economics and Statistics Administration. Retrieved from <https://www.census.gov/data/developers/data-sets/acs-5year.html>

U.S. Census Bureau. (2022b). *QuickFacts: Kansas*. U.S. Department of Commerce's Economics and Statistics Administration. Retrieved from <https://www.census.gov/quickfacts/KS>

U.S. Census Bureau. (2023). *Urban and Rural: State-level Urban and Rural Information for the 2020 Census and 2010 Census*. U.S. Department of Commerce's Economics and Statistics Administration. Retrieved from <https://www.census.gov/programs-surveys/geography/guidance/geo-areas/urban-rural.html>

U.S. Energy Information Administration. (2022). *Kansas: State Profile and Energy Estimates*. United States Department of Energy. Retrieved from <https://www.eia.gov/state/analysis.php?sid=KS>

Ullah, R. (2018). ROLE OF FM RADIOS IN NEWS AND INFORMATION: A STUDY OF FM RADIOS IN PESHAWAR, KHYBER PAKTUNKHWA. *International Journal of Communication Research*, 8(2), 144–152.

Union of Concerned Scientists. (2021, April 14). Bigger Farms, Bigger Problems: Farmland consolidation is harming US rural communities—and better policies can help. *UCSUSA.org*. <https://www.ucsusa.org/resources/bigger-farms-bigger-problems>

USDA. (n.d.). *Co-ops: A Key part of rural America*. U.S. Department of Agriculture. <https://www.usda.gov/topics/rural/co-ops-key-part-fabric-rural-america>

Usher, N. (2018). RE-THINKING TRUST IN THE NEWS: A material approach through "Objects of Journalism". *Journalism Studies*, 19(4), 564–578. <https://doi.org/10.1080/1461670X.2017.1375391>

Usher, N. (2019). Putting "Place" in the Center of Journalism Research: A Way Forward to Understand Challenges to Trust and Knowledge in News. *Journalism & communication monographs.*, 21(2), 84. <https://doi.org/10.1177/1522637919848362>

Valkenburg, P. M., Peter, J., & Walther, J. B. (2016). Media effects: Theory and research. *Annual review of psychology*, 67(1), 315–338.

Value Them Both. (n.d.). *The Amendment*. The Value Them Both Coalition. <https://valuethemboth.com/the-amendment/>

Vaughn, S. L. (Ed.). (2008). *Encyclopedia of American Journalism*. Routledge.

Vincent, C. S., & Gismondi, A. (2021). Fake news, reality apathy, and the erosion of trust and authenticity in American politics. In R. Luttrell, L. Xiao, & J. Glass (Eds.), *Democracy in the Disinformation Age: Influence and Activism in American Politics* (pp. 79–98). Routledge.

Vivian, B. (2023). *Campus misinformation: The real threat to free speech in American higher education*. Oxford University Press.

Vogts, T. R. (2023). U.S. Student Media Associations' Mission Statements Provide Discursive Leadership in Support of Civic Culture. *Journalism & Mass Communication Educator*, 78(3), 317–342. <https://doi.org/10.1177/10776958231170319>

Vraga, E. K., & Tully, M. (2021). News literacy, social media behaviors, and skepticism toward information on social media. *Information, Communication & Society*, 24(2), 150–166. <https://doi.org/10.1080/1369118X.2020.1761859>

Vu, H. T., & Saldaña, M. (2021). Chillin' Effects of Fake News: Changes in Practices Related to Accountability and Transparency in American Newsrooms Under the Influence of Misinformation and Accusations Against the News Media. *Journalism & Mass Communication Quarterly*, 98(3), 769–789. <https://doi.org/10.1177/1077699020984781>

Walker, B., & Haider-Markel, D. P. (2024). Fear and Loathing: How Demographic Change Affects Support for Christian Nationalism. *Public Opinion Quarterly*, 88(2), 382–407. <https://doi.org/10.1093/poq/nfae005>

Walker, S., Mercea, D., & Bastos, M. (2019). The disinformation landscape and the lockdown of social platforms. *Information, Communication & Society*, 22(11), 1531–1543. <https://doi.org/10.1080/1369118X.2019.1648536>

Watson, K. (2024, July 15). Trump picks Sen. JD Vance as VP running mate for 2024 election. *CBS News*. <https://www.cbsnews.com/news/trump-vp-pick-jd-vance/>

Weaver, B. (2013). The Phantom Public Airwaves: Applying Walter Lippmann's Vision to Talk Radio. *Journal Of Mass Media Ethics*, 28(4), 297–299. <https://doi.org/10.1080/08900523.2013.837294>

Weaver, D. A. (2017). The Participatory Roots of Selective Exposure: Baby Boomers, Political Protest, and Talk Radio. *International Journal of Communication (19328036)*, 11, 383–407. <https://search.ebscohost.com/login.aspx?direct=true&db=ufh&AN=126812878&site=ehost-live>

Wei, F.-Y. (2009). Birthdays Then and Now: Applying Uses and Gratifications Theory to Analyze the Media Progression Cycle. *Communication Teacher*, 23(1), 23–27. <https://doi.org/10.1080/17404620802592940>

Weinger, M. (2013, June 6). Distributor: Rush doing 'very well'. *Politico*. <https://www.politico.com/story/2013/06/distributor-rush-limbaugh-doing-very-well-092355>

Weiss, J. (2020). *The cultivation theory and reality television: An old theory with a modern twist* (Publication Number 3) Arcadia University]. Capstone Showcase. <https://scholarworks.arcadia.edu/showcase/2020/media_communication/3/>

Weiyan, L. (2015). A historical overview of Uses and Gratifications Theory. *Cross-Cultural Communication*, 11(9), 71–78. <https://doi.org/10.3968/7415>

Welch, S., & Comer, J. (1988). *Quantitative Methods for Public Administration: Techniques and Applications*. Dorsey Press.

Wendling, M. (2024, September 18). Springfield grapples with false pet-eating rumours—and real problems. *BBC News*. <https://www.bbc.com/news/articles/c1l4g6g5d97o>

Wenzel, A. (2019). To Verify or to Disengage: Coping with "Fake News" and Ambiguity. *International Journal of Communication (19328036)*, 13, 1977–1995.

Wenzel, A. (2020). Red state, purple town: Polarized communities and local journalism in rural and small-town Kentucky. *Journalism*, 21(4), 557–573. <https://doi.org/10.1177/1464884918783949>

Wenzel, A. D., Ford, S., & Nechushtai, E. (2020). Report for America, Report about Communities: Local News Capacity and Community Trust. *Journalism Studies*, 21(3), 287–305. <https://doi.org/10.1080/1461670X.2019.1641428>

Westlund, O., & Ekström, M. (2021). Critical Moments of Coordination in Newswork. *Journalism Practice*, 15(6), 728–746. <https://doi.org/10.1080/17512786.2021.1903970>

Westwood, S. J., Iyengar, S., Walgrave, S., Leonisio, R., Miller, L., & Strijbis, O. (2018). The tie that divides: Cross-national evidence of the primacy of partyism. *European Journal of Political Research*, 57(2), 333–354. <https://doi.org/10.1111/1475-6765.12228>

White, A. (2022). Overcoming 'confirmation bias' and the persistence of conspiratorial types of thinking. *Continuum: Journal Of Media & Cultural Studies*, 36(3), 364–376. <https://doi.org/10.1080/10304312.2021.1992352>

White, A. (2022). Misinformation and disinformation in the digital age: A systematic review of definitions and trends. *New Media & Society*, 24(3), 345–365. https://doi.org/10.1177/14614448211012313

Whitehead, A. L. (2022, September 26). 3 threats Christian Nationalism poses to the United States. *Time*. <https://time.com/6214724/christian-nationalism-threats-united-states/>

Whitehead, A. L., Schnabel, L., & Perry, S. L. (2018). Gun Control in the Crosshairs: Christian Nationalism and Opposition to Stricter Gun Laws. *Socius*, 4, 2378023118790189. <https://doi.org/10.1177/2378023118790189>

Whitehurst, L. (2022, October 12). Oath Keepers jury hears about massive weapon cache on Jan. 6. *The Associated Press*. <https://apnews.com/article/capitol-siege-florida-virginia-conspiracy-government-and-politics-6ac80882e8cf61af36be6c46252ac24c>

Whitney, D. C., & Becker, L. B. (1982). 'Keeping the Gates' for Gatekeepers: The Effects of Wire News. *Journalism Quarterly*, 59(1), 60–65. <https://doi.org/10.1177/107769908205900109>

Wieland, M., & Kleinen-von Königslöw, K. (2020). Conceptualizing different forms of news processing following incidental news contact: A triple-path model. *Journalism*, 21(8), 1049–1066. <https://doi.org/10.1177/1464884920915353>

Wimmer, R. D., & Dominick, J. R. (2014). *Mass media research: an introduction* (10th ed.). Wadsworth Cengage Learning.

Woolley, J., & Peters, G. (n.d.). *Statistics: Elections Data Archive* <https://www.presidency.ucsb.edu/statistics/elections>

Wuthnow, R. (2012). *Red State Religion: Faith and Politics in America's Heartland*. Princeton University Press.

Wuthnow, R. (2015). *In the Blood: Understanding America's Farm Families*. Princeton University Press.

Wuthnow, R. (2019). *The Left Behind: Decline and Rage in Small-Town America* (2nd ed.). Princeton University Press.

Xiao, L. (2021). Fighting disinformation in social media: An online persuasion perspective. In R. Luttrell, L. Xiao, & J. Glass (Eds.), *Democracy in the Disinformation Age: Influence and Activism in American Politics* (pp. 201–220). Routledge.

Yamamoto, M., Ran, W., & Xu, S. (2021). How You Watch Television News Matters: A Panel Analysis of Second Screening and Political Learning from the News. *Journal Of Broadcasting & Electronic Media*, 65(3), 377–396. <https://doi.org/10.1080/08838151.2021.1957894>

Yang, F., & Hanasono, L. K. (2021). Coping with Racial Discrimination with Collective Power: How Does Bonding and Bridging Social Capital Help Online and Offline? *Howard Journal of Communications*, 32(3), 274–293. <https://doi.org/10.1080/10646175.2021.1910882>

Yanich, D. (2020). *Buying Reality: Political Ads, Money, and Local Television News*. Fordham University Press.

Yilek, C., Cordes, N., Navarro, A., Cavazos, N., Woodall, H., Jiang, W., & O'Keefe, E. (2024, August 6). Kamala Harris picks Minnesota Governor Tim Walz as her VP running mate. *CBS News*. <https://www.cbsnews.com/news/tim-walz-vp-kamala-harris-running-mate-2024/>

Young, D. G. (2021). *Irony and Outrage: The Polarized Landscape of Rage, Fear, and Laughter in the United States*. Oxford University Press.

Zhang, W., & Seltzer, T. (2010). Another Piece of the Puzzle: Advancing Social Capital Theory by Examining the Effect of Political Party Relationship Quality on Political and Civic Participation. *International Journal Of Strategic Communication*, 4(3), 155–170. <https://doi.org/10.1080/15531180903415954>

Zimmermann, F., & Kohring, M. (2020). Mistrust, Disinforming News, and Vote Choice: A Panel Survey on the Origins and Consequences of Believing Disinformation in the 2017 German Parliamentary Election. *Political Communication*, 37(2), 215–237. <https://doi.org/10.1080/10584609.2019.1686095>

APPENDIX 1

Sample Survey Questions

DEMOGRAPHICS

How old are you?
- 18–29
- 30–49
- 50–64
- 65+

What gender do you identify as?
- Male
- Female
- Trans Male/Trans Man
- Trans Female/Trans Woman
- Genderqueer/Gender Nonconforming
- Different Identity

What sex were you assigned at birth, such as on an original birth certificate?
- Male
- Female

Do you consider yourself Hispanic/Latino or not Hispanic/Latino?
- Hispanic/Latino
- Not Hispanic/Latino

APPENDIX 1

Which of the following racial designations best describes you? More than one choice is acceptable.
- American Indian or Alaska Native
- Asian
- Black or African American
- Native Hawaiian or Other Pacific Islander
- White
- Two or more races
- Non-Resident Alien (of any race or ethnicity)
- Race unknown

What is your sexual orientation?
- Heterosexual or straight
- Gay
- Lesbian
- Bisexual
- Not listed above (please specify): _____

What is your relationship status?
- Single
- Married
- Divorced
- Dating
- Long-term committed relationship, unmarried
- Other: _____

Where do you live in Kansas?
- Allen County
- Anderson County
- Atchison County
- Barber County
- Barton County
- Bourbon County
- Brown County
- Butler County
- Chase County
- Chautauqua County
- Cherokee County
- Cheyenne County

- Clark County
- Clay County
- Cloud County
- Coffey County
- Comanche County
- Cowley County
- Crawford County
- Decatur County
- Dickinson County
- Doniphan County
- Douglas County
- Edwards County
- Elk County
- Ellis County
- Ellsworth County
- Finney County
- Ford County
- Franklin County
- Geary County
- Gove County
- Graham County
- Grant County
- Gray County
- Greeley County
- Greenwood County
- Hamilton County
- Harper County
- Harvey County
- Haskell County
- Hodgeman County
- Jackson County
- Jefferson County
- Jewell County
- Johnson County
- Kearny County
- Kingman County
- Kiowa County
- Labette County
- Lane County

- Leavenworth County
- Lincoln County
- Linn County
- Logan County
- Lyon County
- Marion County
- Marshall County
- McPherson County
- Meade County
- Miami County
- Mitchell County
- Montgomery County
- Morris County
- Morton County
- Nemaha County
- Neosho County
- Ness County
- Norton County
- Osage County
- Osborne County
- Ottawa County
- Pawnee County
- Phillips County
- Pottawatomie County
- Pratt County
- Rawlins County
- Reno County
- Republic County
- Rice County
- Riley County
- Rooks County
- Rush County
- Russell County
- Saline County
- Scott County
- Sedgwick County
- Seward County
- Shawnee County

- Sheridan County
- Sherman County
- Smith County
- Stafford County
- Stanton County
- Stevens County
- Sumner County
- Thomas County
- Trego County
- Wabaunsee County
- Wallace County
- Washington County
- Wichita County
- Wilson County
- Woodson County
- Wyandotte County
- I don't live in Kansas. I live in _____.

What is the highest level of education have you completed?
- Less than high school diploma or equivalent
- High school diploma or equivalent
- Technical Certificate
- Some college coursework, but no degree
- Associate degree
- Bachelor's Degree
- Master's Degree
- Doctoral Degree

What political party do you align with?
- Republican Party
- Democratic Party
- Libertarian Party
- Green Party
- Alliance Party
- Independent
- Unaffiliated
- Other: _____

APPENDIX 1

What religious beliefs do you align with?
- Christianity
  - Protestant
  - Catholic
  - Mormon
  - Orthodox Christian
- Unaffiliated
- Atheist
- Agnostic
- Jewish
- Muslim
- Hindu
- Buddhist
- Other: _____

What is your general income level?
- Less than $20,000
- $20,000 to $49,999
- $45,000 to $139,999
- $140,000 to $149,999
- $150,000 to $199,999
- $200,000+

What best describes your current employment status?
- Unemployed, looking for work
- Unemployed, not looking for work
- Part-Time Employment (1–39 hours per week), hourly wage
- Part-Time Employment (1–39 hours per week), salaried wage
- Full-Time Employment (40+ hours per week), hourly wage
- Full-Time Employment (40+ hours per week), salaried wage
- Self-Employed
- Retired
- Disable, unable to work

What best describes your current, primary occupation?
- Oil and natural gas occupations
- Wind and solar power occupations
- Farming and ranching occupations

- Wildlife, fishing and forestry occupations
- Computer and technology occupations
- Education occupations (teacher, administrator, paraprofessional, librarian, etc.)
- Law enforcement occupations (police, sheriff, etc.)
- Health and medical occupations (CNA, nursing, physical therapist, etc.)
- Emergency services occupations (dispatcher, EMT, firefighter, etc.)
- Retail occupations
- Manufacturing occupations
- Automotive sales occupations
- Automotive repair occupations
- Legal services occupations (lawyer, judge, attorney, paralegal, law clerk, etc.)
- Governmental occupations (city administrator, county clerk, mayor, etc.)
- Architecture and engineering occupations
- Farm sales/repairs occupations (equipment dealer, etc.)
- Insurance occupations
- Real estate occupations (agent, broker, etc.)
- Accounting occupations
- Banking occupations (teller, branch president, etc.)
- Construction and extraction occupations
- Community and social service occupations
- Plumbing, heating and air occupations
- Electrician occupations
- Not Applicable
- Other: _____

How did you come to participate in this survey?
- Via Social Media
- Direct Mail or Email
- Personal Recruit by the Researcher
- Other: _____

MEDIA USE QUESTIONS

On a scale of 1 to 5 with 1 being "never" and 5 being "hourly," how often do you consume news and information from media outlets?

Never 1 2 3 4 5 *Hourly*

APPENDIX 1

Where do you get the most of your news and information?
- FM Radio
- AM Radio
- Local/Antenna Television
- Cable/Satellite Television
- Streaming Television
- Daily Newspapers
- Weekly Newspapers
- Monthly Magazines
- Quarterly Magazines
- News Outlet Websites
- Social Media

Of the following options, which cable television news outlet do you feel is the most reliable?
- CNN
- Fox News
- MSNBC
- Newsmax TV
- NewsNation
- Blaze TV
- Free Speech TV
- RFD-TV
- CNBC
- Bloomberg Television
- Newsy
- Fox Business Network
- One America News Network (OANN)
- InfoWars
- BBC World News

Of the following options, which cable television news outlet do (or would) you watch the most?
- CNN
- Fox News
- MSNBC
- Newsmax TV
- NewsNation
- Blaze TV

SAMPLE SURVEY QUESTIONS

- Free Speech TV
- RFD-TV
- CNBC
- Bloomberg Television
- Newsy
- Fox Business Network
- One America News Network (OANN)
- InfoWars
- BBC World News

Do you regularly watch local news broadcasts from local affiliates/channels of CBS, ABC, NBC, or PBS?
- Yes
- No
- Sometimes

What social media platforms do you use? Check all that apply.
- Facebook
- Twitter
- Instagram
- TikTok
- Snapchat
- Pinterest
- YouTube
- Reddit
- LinkedIn
- WhatsApp
- Other: _____
- None of the Above

On a scale of 1 to 5 with 1 being "never" and 5 being "hourly," how often do you look at social media?

   Never 1 2 3 4 5 *Hourly*

What social media platform do you use the most?
- Facebook
- Twitter
- Instagram

- TikTok
- Snapchat
- Pinterest
- YouTube
- Reddit
- LinkedIn
- WhatsApp
- Other: _____
- None of the Above

When on social media, what is your primary purpose for using the platform?
- Posting/creating content
- Selling items
- Marketing purposes (self-promotion or business promotion)
- Building and/or maintaining relationships
- Consuming news and information
- Entertainment
- General communication
- Other: _____

On a scale of 1 to 5 with 1 being "never" and 5 being "often," how often do you consume news and information on social media?

Never 1 2 3 4 5 *Often*

Regardless of the medium (print product, radio or television broadcast, or social media), what type of news and information do you seek out the most?
- Local news/information
- State news/information
- National news/information
- Professional sports news/information
- Political news/information
- Entertainment news/information
- Weather news/information
- Business/stock news/information
- Agricultural (farming, livestock, etc.) news/information
- Energy sector (oil, gas, solar, wind, etc.) news/information
- Other: _____

On a scale of 1 to 5 with 1 being "none at all" and 5 being "extremely," how often does the news reported by the media feel important to your everyday life?

None At All 1 2 3 4 5 *Extremely*

On a scale of 1 to 5 with 1 being "never" and 5 being "all the time," how often do you think the news media misses the important stories?

Never 1 2 3 4 5 *All The Time*

On a scale of 1 to 5 with 1 being "all the time" and 5 being "never," how often do you see local journalists or reporters in your community talking to community members?

All The Time 1 2 3 4 5 *Never*

On a scale of 1 to 5 with 1 being "all the time" and 5 being "never," how often do you see local journalists or reporters in your community covering community events?

All The Time 1 2 3 4 5 *Never*

Do you wish local journalists or reporters would work with the community (develop story ideas, contribute content of articles or photos, take part in focus groups, etc.) to provide more news of local importance?
- Yes
- No
- Maybe
- I Don't Know

If given the opportunity to work with local journalists or reporters (develop story ideas, contribute content of articles or photos, take part in focus groups, etc.) to provide more news of local importance, would you do so?
- Yes
- No
- Maybe
- I Don't Know

APPENDIX 1

NEWS TRUST & MIS/DISINFORMATION QUESTIONS

On a scale of 1 to 5 with 1 being "extremely" and 5 being "none," how would you rank your trust in the news media and journalists in general?

Extremely 1 2 3 4 5 *None*

On a scale of 1 to 5 with 1 being "none" and 5 being "extremely," how would you rank your trust in the national news media and journalists?

None 1 2 3 4 5 *Extremely*

On a scale of 1 to 5 with 1 being "extremely" and 5 being "none," how would you rank your trust in the local news media and journalists?

Extremely 1 2 3 4 5 *None*

On a scale of 1 to 5 with 1 being "an extreme amount" and 5 being "none," how much misinformation or disinformation is present on social media?

An Extreme Amount 1 2 3 4 5 *None*

On a scale of 1 to 5 with 1 being "an extreme amount" and 5 being "none," how much misinformation or disinformation is present on the television?

An Extreme Amount 1 2 3 4 5 *None*

On a scale of 1 to 5 with 1 being "none" and 5 being "an extreme amount," how much misinformation or disinformation is present on the radio?

None 1 2 3 4 5 *An Extreme Amount*

On a scale of 1 to 5 with 1 being "none" and 5 being "an extreme amount," how much misinformation or disinformation is present in printed news products such as newspapers and magazines?

None 1 2 3 4 5 *An Extreme Amount*

SAMPLE SURVEY QUESTIONS

On a scale of 1 to 5 with 1 being "strongly disagree" and 5 being "strongly agree," rank how much you agree with the following statement: "The press is the enemy of the people."

Strongly Disagree 1 2 3 4 5 *Strongly Agree*

Of the following options, which cable television news outlet do you feel spreads the most misinformation or disinformation?
- CNN
- Fox News
- MSNBC
- Newsmax TV
- NewsNation
- Blaze TV
- Free Speech TV
- RFD-TV
- CNBC
- Bloomberg Television
- Newsy
- Fox Business Network
- One America News Network (OANN)
- InfoWars
- BBC World News

Of the following options, which cable television news outlet do you feel spreads the least misinformation or disinformation?
- CNN
- Fox News
- MSNBC
- Newsmax TV
- NewsNation
- Blaze TV
- Free Speech TV
- RFD-TV
- CNBC
- Bloomberg Television

APPENDIX 1

- Newsy
- Fox Business Network
- One America News Network (OANN)
- InfoWars
- BBC World News

On a scale of 1 to 5 with 1 being "none whatsoever" and 5 being "extremely so," do you feel that misinformation and disinformation are a problem in society?

None Whatsoever 1 2 3 4 5 *Extremely So*

Using a scale of 1 to 5 with 1 being "strongly disagree" and 5 being "strongly agree," rank your reaction to the following statement: "Aliens are real. They landed in Roswell, New Mexico, and Area 51 contains evidence that the government is hiding from us."

Strongly Disagree 1 2 3 4 5 *Strongly Agree*

Using a scale of 1 to 5 with 1 being "strongly disagree" and 5 being "strongly agree," rank your reaction to the following statement: "No one has ever landed on the moon. The moon landing was faked and filmed on a soundstage in Hollywood."

Strongly Disagree 1 2 3 4 5 *Strongly Agree*

Using a scale of 1 to 5 with 1 being "strongly agree" and 5 being "strongly disagree," rank your reaction to the following statement: "Lee Harvey Oswald did not act alone in President John F. Kennedy's assassination."

Strongly Agree 1 2 3 4 5 *Strongly Disagree*

Using a scale of 1 to 5 with 1 being "strongly agree" and 5 being "strongly disagree," rank your reaction to the following statement: "President Barack Obama was not born in the United States."

Strongly Agree 1 2 3 4 5 *Strongly Disagree*

Using a scale of 1 to 5 with 1 being "strongly disagree" and 5 being "strongly agree," rank your reaction to the following statement: "Donald Trump won the 2020 United States presidential election."

Strongly Disagree 1 2 3 4 5 *Strongly Agree*

Using a scale of 1 to 5 with 1 being "strongly agree" and 5 being "strongly disagree," rank your reaction to the following statement: "Birds aren't real. They are surveillance drones for the United States government."

Strongly Agree 1 2 3 4 5 *Strongly Disagree*

On a scale of 1 to 5 with 1 being "not at all" and 5 being "extremely," how important do you feel journalism is to society?

Not At All 1 2 3 4 5 *Extremely*

On a scale of 1 to 5 with 1 being "not at all" and 5 being "extremely," how relevant do you feel national journalism is to your daily life?

Not At All 1 2 3 4 5 *Extremely*

On a scale of 1 to 5 with 1 being "not at all" and 5 being "extremely," how relevant do you feel local/community journalism is to your daily life?

Not At All 1 2 3 4 5 *Extremely*

SOCIAL & CIVIC ENGAGEMENT QUESTIONS

How frequently do you vote?
- In every election, both national and local
- Only in national elections
- Only in local elections
- Only in presidential election years
- Most of the time
- Some of the time
- Only when an issue important to me is on the ballot
- Never

APPENDIX 1

Have you ever run for an elected office (board of education, county commission, city council, state legislature, etc.)?
· Yes
· No

Have you ever held an elected office (board of education, county commission, city council, state legislature, etc.)?
· Yes
· No

Who did you vote for in the 2012 Presidential Election?
 · Mitt Romney and Paul Ryan (Republican Party)
 · Barack Obama and Joe Biden (Democratic Party)
 · Gary Johnson and Jim Gray (Libertarian Party)
 · Jill Stein and Cheri Honkala (Green Party)
 · Virgil Goode and Jim Clymer (Constitution Party)
 · Rocky Anderson and Luis J. Rodriguez (Justice Party)
 · Other: _____
 · Did not vote

Who did you vote for in the 2016 Presidential Election?
 · Donald Trump and Mike Pence (Republican Party)
 · Hillary Clinton and Time Kaine (Democratic Party)
 · Gary Johnson and Bill Weld (Libertarian Party)
 · Jill Stein and Ajamu Baraka (Green Party)
 · Darrell Castle and Scott Bradley (Constitution Party)
 · Evan McMullin and Mindy Finn (Independent Ticket)
 · Other: _____
 · Did not vote

Who did you vote for in the 2020 Presidential Election?
 · Donald Trump and Mike Pence (Republican Party)
 · Joe Biden and Kamala Harris (Democratic Party)
 · Jo Jorgensen and Spike Cohen (Libertarian Party)
 · Howie Hawkins and Angela Walker (Green Party)
 · Don Blankenship and William Mohr (Constitution Party)
 · Other: _____
 · Did not vote

SAMPLE SURVEY QUESTIONS

Did you vote "yes" or "no" on the Kansas Constitutional Amendment referred to as "Value Them Both" that sought to overturn the Kansas Supreme Court's ruling that abortion was legal because of ideas of bodily autonomy?
- Yes
- No
- Did not vote

On a scale of 1 to 5 with 1 being "none" and 5 being "extreme," how would you rank your level of trust in politicians?

None 1 2 3 4 5 *Extreme*

On a scale of 1 to 5 with 1 being "extreme" and 5 being "none," how would you describe your level of trust in the government?

Extreme 1 2 3 4 5 *None*

On a scale of 1 to 5 with 1 being "none" and 5 being "extreme," how would you score your satisfaction with democracy as a method of self-governance?

None 1 2 3 4 5 *Extreme*

On a scale of 1 to 5 with 1 being "a lot" and 5 being "none," how would you describe your level of trust toward your neighbors?

A Lot 1 2 3 4 5 *None*

On a scale of 1 to 5 with 1 being "none" and 5 being "extreme," how would you rank the importance of religion in your life?

None 1 2 3 4 5 *Extreme*

On a scale of 1 to 5 with 1 being "a lot" and 5 being "none," how would you describe the impact of your religious views on your political views?

A Lot 1 2 3 4 5 *None*

APPENDIX 1

CLOSING QUESTIONS

What questions regarding news use, community journalism, media trust, and mis/disinformation did this survey not ask that it should have? What else would you like to discuss that wasn't covered?

Would you be interested and willing to be interviewed about the topics of this survey and more? Interviews would be conducted via the phone, video conferencing, or in person depending upon preference and availability.

· Yes
· No

APPENDIX 2

Sample Interview Questions

1. How do you prefer to be referred to?
2. How old are you?
3. What gender do you identify as?
4. Where do you live?
5. What level of education have you completed?
6. Do you align with a particular political party? If so, which one and why?
7. How do your political beliefs impact your views on politics, society and the world?
8. Do you align with a particular religious belief? If so, which one and why?
9. How do your religious beliefs impact your views on politics, society and the world?
10. Are you involved in any community organizations? If so, which one(s) and why?
11. What is your profession?
12. How long have you been doing this type of work?
13. What does an average day look like for you in your line of work?
14. What made you want to pursue it?
15. What is the hardest part of the job, and what is the most rewarding aspect?
16. Do you do any other jobs/work that you don't consider to be part of your primary profession but contribute to your overall income and activities?
17. What technologies do you use in order to accomplish your daily duties?
18. What technologies do you use on a daily basis that may or may not contribute to your profession?
19. Do you listen to the radio? If so, where? What type of programming do you listen to the most and why?
20. Do you use social media? If so, what platforms do you use the most and why?

21. Do you listen to the radio or use social media during the times you are working at your job? If so, explain how such uses work within the confines of your duties?
22. How often do you consume news?
23. What types of news stories do you prefer to consume (e.g., politics, sports, weather, crime, economy, general, et cetera)?
24. Do you read newspapers or magazines? If so, what types of outlets do you consume?
25. Do you listen to news or talk radio? If so, what programs do you gravitate toward?
26. Do you get news from social media? If so, how much of the news you consume comes from social media, and what platform provides you with the most news and information?
27. How often do you share news you consume with family and friends, whether it came from social media or not, and how do you share it (via social media, in conversation, or something else)?
28. How open-minded would you describe yourself? Do you change your mind easily or stay firm in your stance in most situations? Please explain.
29. What impact does the news you consume have on your beliefs, opinions and perspectives of the world in terms of politics, society and other aspects of daily life?
30. How do you describe the news media? Why?
31. Describe your level of trust with the news media. Are there certain outlets you trust more than others? If so, what are they and why do you turn to them more often as trusted sources of information?
32. Are you more likely to trust local news outlets or national news outlets? Why?
33. How often do you believe the news media is accurate?
34. How often do you believe the news media is inaccurate?
35. Do you believe disinformation is a problem in society? Why or why not?
36. Who seems to be the most likely to spread disinformation? Please explain.
37. Have you ever spread disinformation via interpersonal communication or social media? Please explain.
38. Do you think the news media spreads misinformation? Why or why not?
39. Have you ever spread misinformation via interpersonal communication or social media? Please explain.
40. Have you ever believed a certain piece of information and found out later that it was inaccurate? Please explain.
41. Have you ever believed a certain piece of information and continued to believe it despite evidence suggesting it was inaccurate? Please explain.

42. When you encounter information you know is false, do you take steps to correct it or ignore it? Please explain.
43. How likely are you to believe a piece of information if it is relayed to you (via the news media or social media) if it comes from an outlet or individual you believe to be trustworthy or otherwise contain expertise in the subject matter? Please explain.
44. What causes you to not believe a source of information? Please explain.
45. Do you tend to believe, what others might classify as, conspiracy theories in general or any conspiracy theories in particular? Please explain.
46. Are you involved in your community? Please explain.
47. How important is being involved in the community to you? Please explain.
48. How involved in politics are you? Please explain.
49. Do you put political signs on your property? Please explain.
50. Do you share political messages or opinions on social media? Please explain.
51. Are you more likely to vote in local elections, state elections, or national elections?
52. Do you feel you are most informed about local politics, state politics, or national politics? Please explain.
53. What type of news and information do you consume to be informed about politics?
54. How would you describe your level of trust in politicians?
55. How would you describe your level of trust in the government?
56. How would you describe the importance of journalism?
57. How would you describe the importance of community journalism?
58. If given the opportunity to contribute to news coverage of your community, how would you do so and what types of news would you push to see more of?
59. Is there anything else you would like to add on this topic that we haven't covered?

Index

A
ABC: 37, 48, 58, 111, 118
   ABC News: 48, 111
Aalberg: 45, 59, 105
Abdullah: 68, 95
Abernathy: 11, 32, 91, 95
Abraham: 26, 34, 46, 49, 57, 66, 74, 78, 85
Abramowitz: 13, 95
Abramsky: 64, 95
Ackermann: 82, 95
Activism: 2, 105, 106, 108, 115, 116
Ad: 3, 9, 18, 20, 21, 23, 24, 29, 33, 36, 38, 40, 41, 42, 43, 45, 48, 53, 54, 55, 56, 57, 59, 61, 75, 85, 86, 87, 88, 95, 97, 99, 102, 105, 106, 110, 111, 114, 115, 116
   Ad Fontes Media: 43, 88, 95
Aehl: 60, 74, 92, 98
Affective: 104, 107
   Affective Polarization: 104, 107
African: 15, 98, 109, 117
   African Media Studies: 98, 109
Agenda: 95, 108, 112
Agriculture: 21, 25, 99, 100, 105, 114
Algorithms: 3, 84
Alkazemi: 69, 77, 82, 95
All: 16, 20, 31, 32, 48, 62, 87, 95, 97, 102, 103, 107, 108, 111, 113, 117, 119, 121
   All The Time: 119
Allam: 31, 95
Allen: 20, 103, 107, 117
Almgren: 36, 95
Along: 49, 72, 82
Also: 9, 15, 24, 26, 27, 28, 34, 49, 50, 54, 65, 66, 75, 81, 85, 91, 92
Amazon: 23, 37
American: 3, 6, 8, 9, 10, 11, 12, 13, 14, 15, 16, 17, 19, 20, 29, 30, 32, 35, 36, 39, 43, 52, 54, 65, 72, 77, 81, 82, 95, 96, 97, 99, 102, 103, 105, 106, 108, 109, 110, 111, 112, 113, 114, 115, 116, 117
   American Academy: 108, 112
   American Democracy: 102, 112
   American Politics: 96, 97, 103, 106, 108, 109, 115, 116

Americans: 8, 10, 11, 12, 15, 16, 17, 29, 30, 32, 35, 36, 65, 81, 82, 95, 96, 99, 110, 111, 112, 113
An: 3, 5, 8, 9, 12, 19, 22, 34, 43, 46, 47, 48, 49, 51, 56, 58, 61, 63, 74, 76, 78, 80, 94, 95, 96, 97, 98, 100, 101, 103, 104, 105, 106, 107, 108, 109, 110, 111, 113, 114, 115, 116, 117, 118, 119, 120, 121
   An Extreme Amount: 119, 120
   An Extreme Amount On: 119, 120
And: 12, 34, 47, 48, 49, 51, 56, 61, 63, 74, 76, 78, 80, 100, 109, 117, 121
Annals: 106, 111, 113
Annenberg: 8, 9, 95
   Annenberg Public Policy Center: 8, 9, 95
Applied: 98, 109
   Applied Communication Research: 98, 109
April: 80, 88, 105, 114
Arachchi: 4, 83, 84, 95
Are: 79, 97, 100, 103, 107, 111, 114, 120, 122, 123
As: 2, 3, 4, 5, 6, 9, 11, 13, 15, 17, 18, 21, 23, 24, 27, 28, 30, 31, 32, 33, 34, 35, 37, 38, 39, 42, 44, 45, 54, 57, 59, 61, 64, 67, 69, 70, 71, 72, 73, 74, 75, 78, 80, 81, 82, 83, 85, 86, 87, 88, 89, 91, 93, 94, 96, 99, 101, 104, 105, 106, 108, 109, 110, 111, 113, 115, 116, 117
   As Dahlgren: 31, 73
   As Vaughn: 35
Assessing: 111, 113
Associated: 72, 105, 108, 113, 116
   Associated Press: 72, 105, 108, 113, 116
Attention: 30, 96, 99
Aucoin: 81, 106
Audio: 96, 109, 110, 113
   Audio Media: 96, 109, 113
Aug: 5, 19, 95, 101, 102, 106, 109, 112, 113, 116
August: 5, 95, 101, 102, 106, 109, 112, 113, 116
Automotive: 118
Auxier: 3, 12

B
BBC: 37, 40, 41, 46, 48, 50, 58, 115, 118, 120

INDEX

BBC News: 48, 115
BBC World News: 37, 50, 58, 118, 120
Bachtiger: 96, 102, 103
Ball: 18, 32, 88, 93, 95, 105
Ballotpedia: 18, 95
Balter: 20, 97
Banks: 42, 95
Baran: 32, 95
Barney: 26, 47, 57, 66, 76, 88
Barreto: 2, 110
Barrett: 20, 75, 106
Bart: 21, 26, 47, 51, 61, 66, 87, 91, 95, 117
Bartelme: 91, 95
Bartels: 21, 95
Based: 2, 23, 32, 41, 42, 50, 56, 60, 94, 98, 104
Basic: 99, 114
    Basic Books: 99, 114
Batsell: 31, 92, 95
Bauer: 60, 96
Beauvais: 68, 96
Beck: 12, 20, 29, 36, 53, 75, 96, 113, 116
Becker: 12, 20, 36, 75, 96, 113, 116
Beckers: 36, 96
Belair: 31, 38, 96
Ben: 1, 42, 46, 69, 70, 86, 96, 108
    Ben Shapiro: 42, 46
Benkler: 86, 96
Bennett: 1, 69, 96
Berger: 22, 81, 82, 96
Bergillos: 36, 96
Berry: 8, 54, 62, 87, 96, 113
Beyond: 100, 101, 110, 111
Biden: 5, 6, 9, 19, 33, 41, 46, 108, 111, 121
Bilandzic: 45, 96
Birnbauer: 92, 96
Bladt: 5, 104
Block: 9, 96
Blumler: 70, 105, 108
Board: 20, 24, 97
Bobkowski: 12, 81, 96
Bodrozic: 92, 97
Boomgaarden: 110, 113
Borger: 92, 97
Borter: 4, 97
Boyd: 53, 97

Braun: 25, 97
Breitbart: 41, 46
Brennen: 25, 97
Bressers: 12, 32, 38, 92, 93, 97, 112
Briggs: 31, 97
Bringula: 83, 97
Brinkley: 8
Broersma: 45, 59, 90, 113
Brooks: 14, 97
Brounstein: 91, 97
Brouwer: 20, 97
Brown: 10, 20, 97, 108, 111, 117
Brummette: 8, 97
Bruner: 20, 97
Bucy: 68, 97
Burchardt: 91, 97
Burke: 73, 97
Burr: 82, 98
Business: 13, 98, 110, 112, 118, 120
    Business Insider: 13, 98
Busselle: 45, 96
But: 4, 16, 35, 48, 58, 61, 88, 94, 105, 117
Butman: 94, 105

C

CBS: 5, 34, 37, 48, 58, 104, 115, 116, 118
    CBS News: 5, 48, 104, 115, 116
CIT: 31, 32, 93, 106
CNN: 37, 40, 41, 43, 46, 48, 50, 58, 105, 118, 120
    CNN Fox News MSNBC Newsmax TV NewsNation Blaze TV Free Speech TV RFD: 118, 120
COVID: 1, 79, 80, 89, 95, 98, 100, 104
California: 6, 104, 110, 112
    California Press: 104, 112
Callanan: 85, 98
Cambridge: 99, 104, 107, 109, 113
    Cambridge Review: 104, 113
    Cambridge University Press: 99, 107, 109
Campbell: 34, 35, 52, 53, 54, 98, 106, 111
Canton: 43
Capitol: 1, 4, 6, 7, 9, 10, 62, 73, 100, 103, 107
Cappella: 54, 106
Carey: 12, 98
Carney: 8, 98

INDEX

Carrion: 90, 98
Carson: 73, 74, 98
Carter: 2
Catalini: 52, 98
Catholic: 65, 66, 72, 80, 117
Census: 9, 10, 18, 19, 21, 24, 114
    Census Bureau: 9, 10, 18, 19, 21, 24, 114
Centre: 100
Chakraborty: 67, 98
Chalmers: 26, 42, 49, 57, 65, 76, 78
Chang: 45, 96, 99, 107, 110, 111, 115
Chapp: 60, 74, 92, 98
Cheng: 31, 102
Chicago: 99, 107, 113
    Chicago Press: 99, 107
Chimuanya: 66, 89, 98
Christ: 5, 6, 21, 24, 25, 26, 27, 28, 29, 61, 63, 64, 65, 66, 72, 73, 97, 99, 102, 105, 106, 109, 113, 115, 116, 117
Christian: 5, 6, 21, 24, 25, 26, 27, 28, 29, 61, 64, 65, 66, 72, 73, 97, 99, 102, 105, 106, 109, 113, 115, 116, 117
    Christian Nationalism: 5, 6, 72, 73, 97, 99, 102, 109, 115, 116
    Christian Nationalists: 72, 73, 102, 106
Christianity: 24, 25, 26, 64, 65, 72, 117
Christians: 21, 66
Cineas: 64, 98
Citizens: 99, 101
Civic: 80, 92, 95, 96, 99, 101, 105, 114, 115, 116
    Civic Engagement: 96, 101, 105, 114
Clancy: 26, 49, 50
Clarke: 25, 97
Claussen: 92, 98
Cletus: 26, 34, 47, 58, 71, 90
Collier: 31, 98
Collins: 5, 86, 98, 108
Columbia: 96, 103, 104, 113, 114
    Columbia University Press: 96, 114
Combined: 17, 71
Comer: 23, 115
Commerce: 114
Communication: 7, 31, 70, 71, 87, 93, 96, 97, 98, 99, 101, 102, 103, 104, 105, 106, 107, 108, 109, 110, 111, 112, 113, 114, 115, 116

Communication Infrastructure Theory: 31, 93
Communication Research: 96, 98, 103, 105, 108, 109, 114
Communication Theory: 96, 105, 108, 112
Communications: 87, 96, 98, 108, 114, 116
Communities: 66, 74, 98, 106, 107, 115
Community: 12, 29, 60, 96, 97, 98, 100, 104, 105, 107, 108, 109, 114, 115, 118
    Community Journalism: 107, 108
Computer: 71, 98, 101, 102, 109, 111, 117
Concerned: 30, 100, 114
    Concerned Scientists: 30, 100, 114
Connaughton: 25, 98
Consequences: 104, 107, 116
Conservative: 8, 9, 13, 14, 18, 19, 54, 97, 101, 103
Conservatives: 8, 9, 19, 54, 101
Considering: 9, 17, 83, 86
Conspiracy: 89, 104, 107, 111
Constitution: 12, 20, 72, 95, 100, 121
    Constitution Party: 121
Continuum: 104, 107, 109, 112, 115
Conway: 56, 98
Cook: 100, 106
Coping: 115, 116
Craig: 34, 35, 98
Cramer: 10, 43, 52, 71, 91, 98
Crary: 30, 99
Creating: 73, 114
Creswell: 25, 29, 99
Crisp: 52, 99
Crockett: 22, 99
Cross: 99, 102, 115, 116
Croteau: 34, 99
Croucher: 56, 99
Crowley: 10, 107
Cultivation: 44, 56, 93, 95, 96, 98, 101, 102, 103, 108, 111, 112
    Cultivation Process: 96, 101
    Cultivation Theory: 44, 56, 93, 98, 108, 111, 112
Cultural: 99, 104, 107, 115, 116
    Cultural Studies: 107, 116
Culture: 45, 98, 99, 104, 115
Currid: 10, 99

INDEX

D
DEI: 1, 3
Dahlgren: 31, 73, 99
Daily: 32, 39, 42, 108, 118
Damasceno: 55, 99
Daniels: 93, 108
Dardenne: 81, 105
Darr: 7, 9, 32, 60, 74, 91, 92, 99, 110, 121
Davis: 12, 32, 73, 93, 95, 99, 105
Dayton: 64
DeRose: 6, 99
Debing: 36, 99
Dec: 6, 23, 32, 35, 81, 100, 101, 105, 113, 114, 116, 117
December: 35, 81, 113, 114
Delahunt: 25, 107
Deliberation: 96, 99, 102
Deliberative: 95, 96, 100, 101, 102, 103, 109
    Deliberative Democracy: 95, 96, 100, 101, 102, 103
Democracy: 6, 16, 54, 73, 95, 96, 98, 100, 101, 102, 103, 104, 106, 108, 109, 111, 112, 113, 115, 116
Democrat: 3, 8, 10, 11, 18, 21, 24, 25, 27, 28, 29, 45, 46, 52, 56, 72, 75, 77, 80, 102, 106, 108, 117, 121
Democratic: 24, 28, 45, 46, 52, 72, 75, 77, 108, 117, 121
    Democratic Party: 24, 28, 46, 75, 117, 121
Democrats: 3, 8, 10, 11, 18, 21, 25, 28, 29, 56, 72, 80, 102, 106
Department: 21, 25, 99, 100, 101, 105, 114
Despite: 6, 32, 36, 37, 39, 50, 58, 63, 68, 69, 73, 75
Dickey: 5, 99
Did: 121
Difference: 107, 109
Digital: 81, 97, 98, 101, 105, 109, 111
    Digital Age: 98
    Digital Journalism: 97, 101, 105, 111
Dingemans: 71, 99
Disinformation: 29, 96, 100, 104, 106, 108, 111, 115, 116
    Disinformation Age: 106, 108, 115, 116
Diversion: 70, 86
Dize: 52, 99
Dobbs: 19, 99
Docherty: 94, 99
Doherty: 72, 99
Doing: 2, 90, 93, 99, 107
Dominick: 22, 116
Don: 2, 4, 8, 10, 13, 21, 46, 52, 53, 95, 98, 105, 109, 117, 119, 120, 121
Donald: 2, 4, 8, 10, 13, 21, 46, 52, 53, 98, 109, 120, 121
    Donald Trump: 2, 8, 10, 13, 21, 46, 52, 53, 98, 109, 120, 121
Dori: 26, 49, 51, 53, 55, 57, 58, 61, 76, 77, 79, 99
Doris: 26, 49, 51, 55, 57, 58, 61, 76, 77, 79
Dreisbach: 6, 99
Druckman: 8, 100
Dryzek: 96, 100, 102, 103
Due: 39, 45, 67, 106
Dulleck: 100, 110
Dunaway: 98, 99, 110
Dzur: 93, 100

E
Echo: 100, 101, 114
    Echo Chambers: 100, 101, 114
Ecker: 38, 55, 100, 106, 110
Eckert: 38, 110
Economic: 23, 79, 100, 106, 114
    Economic Research Service: 23, 100
Economics: 106, 114
Eddie: 27, 46, 66, 76, 77, 79, 89
Eddington: 57, 100
Edgar: 68, 100
Edna: 27, 37, 51, 57, 78, 89
Education: 12, 20, 97, 101, 103, 105, 107, 108, 110, 113, 117
Effect: 31, 83, 85, 95, 96, 99, 101, 102, 103, 104, 105, 106, 112, 115, 116
Effects: 85, 96, 99, 101, 102, 103, 104, 106, 112, 115, 116
Elections: 97, 104, 105, 116
Electronic: 96, 98, 103, 104, 110, 116
    Electronic Media: 96, 98, 103, 104, 110, 116
Encyclopedia: 103, 109, 111, 112, 114
Energy: 21, 114, 118
    Energy Information Administration: 21, 114

Engaged: 92, 95
Episode: 114
Etelson: 72, 100
European: 3, 12, 96, 100, 102, 115
    European Commission: 3, 12, 100
Eventually: 12, 35, 63
Everybody: 51, 113
Everyone: 50, 65
Everything: 51, 72, 102
Examining: 102, 116
Exposure: 85, 95, 96, 104, 106, 110, 115
Extreme: 89, 110, 114, 119, 120, 121, 122
    Extreme On: 121, 122
Extremely: 119, 120, 121
    Extremely On: 119, 121

F

Fabiansson: 44, 100
Facebook: 22, 33, 39, 40, 41, 56, 77, 79, 89, 99, 101, 102, 105, 118
    Facebook Twitter Instagram TikTok Snapchat Pinterest YouTube Reddit LinkedIn WhatsApp Other: 118
Fairclough: 25, 100
Fairness: 37, 53
    Fairness Doctrine: 37, 53
Fake: 8, 97, 108, 111, 112, 115
    Fake News: 97, 111, 112, 115
Farming: 51, 100, 117
Farrell: 74, 100
Fear: 98, 115, 116
February: 53, 97, 101, 105, 109
Federico: 8, 103
Ferguson: 20, 30, 100, 111
Fertig: 5, 100
Finds: 4, 15, 31, 56, 59, 82, 83, 84, 85, 88, 90, 95, 102, 113
Finlayson: 73, 100
Finneman: 8, 22, 60, 92, 100
Fire: 34, 98, 104
First: 9, 12, 20, 63, 72, 90, 95, 101
    First Amendment: 9, 12, 20, 63, 72, 95
Fish: 14, 90, 92, 100, 110
Fisher: 90, 92, 100, 110
Flatt: 64, 101
Flaxman: 11, 54, 101

Flew: 100, 110
Florida: 9, 64
Folkenflik: 53, 101
Following: 3, 101
For: 2, 3, 4, 6, 7, 8, 13, 15, 16, 18, 19, 20, 21, 24, 25, 26, 29, 31, 32, 33, 34, 35, 36, 37, 39, 40, 42, 44, 45, 47, 49, 50, 51, 52, 53, 54, 55, 60, 61, 62, 64, 65, 66, 67, 72, 75, 77, 78, 79, 80, 82, 85, 88, 91, 92, 96, 97, 99, 102, 104, 105, 106, 110, 114, 115, 116, 117
    For Kent: 51, 52
Foundations: 95, 107, 108
Fox: 5, 7, 37, 40, 41, 46, 47, 48, 50, 58, 82, 88, 91, 96, 118, 120
    Fox News: 5, 7, 37, 40, 41, 46, 47, 48, 50, 58, 82, 88, 91, 96, 118, 120
Frank: 8, 17, 21, 34, 53, 71, 101, 117
Fraser: 11, 12, 101
Frenkel: 89, 101
Frounfelker: 2, 101
Fuck: 19
    Fuck Biden: 19
Fuehrer: 60, 107
Full: 117
Future: 95, 100, 103, 114

G

GOP: 64, 102, 105
Gadarian: 44, 101
Gagnon: 31, 38, 96
Galanes: 25, 109
Gamson: 104
    Gamson Hypothesis: 104
Gary: 121
    Gary Johnson: 121
Gastil: 12, 54, 67, 69, 83, 94, 101
Gaultney: 7, 8, 60, 90, 101
Gearhart: 60, 101
Gelman: 21, 101
Geological: 18, 101
    Geological Survey: 18, 101
George: 46, 79
    George Soros: 46, 79
Gerbner: 44, 45, 56, 57, 85, 98, 101
Gervais: 54, 56, 101

INDEX

Ghost: 98, 113
   Ghost Newspapers: 98
Gianos: 69, 104
Gibson: 12, 101
Giddens: 68, 81, 101
Gil: 4, 5, 23, 31, 69, 83, 101, 102, 108, 113
Gilbert: 5, 69, 102
Gill: 23, 102
Gismondi: 54, 60, 86, 115
Glass: 106, 108, 115, 116
Glueck: 20, 75, 113
God: 5, 6, 7, 18, 20, 63, 65, 66, 72, 89, 97, 100, 102, 103, 104, 105, 106, 109
Goldfarb: 38, 102
Golgowski: 73, 102
Good: 43, 73, 74, 85, 96, 102, 121
Goodin: 73, 74, 102
Gottfried: 11, 102
Gowen: 19, 75, 102
Grabe: 68, 77, 97, 102
Grabenstein: 77, 102
Gratifications: 70, 86, 108, 110, 111, 114, 115
   Gratifications Theory: 70, 86, 111, 115
Green: 9, 34, 72, 97, 102, 110, 117, 121
   Green Party: 117, 121
Greenberg: 9, 102
Greifeneder: 8, 102
Groshek: 1, 60, 81, 102
Gross: 13, 44, 56, 57, 85, 101, 102
Guess: 84, 102
Guo: 90, 102
Gurney: 60, 107
Gutman: 64, 73, 103
Gutmann: 73, 103
Gutsche: 36, 37, 103

H

Habermas: 11, 54, 73, 100, 103
Hacohen: 53, 99
Haider: 72, 115
Haitian: 52, 99, 107
Haitians: 52
Hajjar: 2, 103
Halkett: 10, 99
Hameleers: 41, 42, 85, 88, 103

Han: 8, 19, 53, 64, 67, 71, 94, 96, 101, 102, 103, 106, 111, 116
Hanasono: 67, 71, 94, 116
Hanlon: 64, 103
Haridakis: 44, 71, 82, 86, 103, 111
Harmon: 85, 103
HarperCollins: 98, 108
Harris: 3, 5, 33, 46, 52, 108, 116, 121
Harte: 91, 103
Hartley: 25, 108
Harwell: 5, 103
Hatcher: 107, 108
Have: 110, 121, 123
Hayfield: 25, 113
Health: 19, 42, 95, 99, 104, 110, 118
   Health Organization: 19, 99
Healy: 6, 103
Heath: 4, 83, 84, 103
Helen: 27, 37, 40, 41, 46, 50, 55, 65, 76, 78, 92
Hemmer: 8, 54, 87, 103
Henneman: 31, 103
Herbeck: 45, 108
Here: 1, 4, 59, 73, 84, 89, 100, 102, 105, 106, 107, 109
Herman: 27, 41, 42, 51, 61, 65, 76, 88
Hershewe: 10, 103
Hess: 20, 22, 69, 97, 103
Hesse: 22, 103
Higher: 12, 16, 107, 108, 110
   Higher Education: 12, 107, 108, 110
His: 5, 8, 20, 27, 28, 53, 96, 111, 117
Hispanic: 117
Hitt: 99
Hobbs: 5, 103
Hofstetter: 69, 104
Hollander: 62, 104
Homolar: 21, 104, 113
Hopmann: 47, 104
Horten: 35, 104
How: 3, 6, 8, 9, 10, 13, 14, 18, 30, 34, 35, 36, 37, 38, 40, 42, 44, 50, 51, 55, 63, 64, 65, 66, 67, 68, 70, 72, 74, 76, 77, 78, 81, 83, 84, 85, 86, 88, 90, 92, 96, 97, 98, 99, 100, 101, 102, 103, 104, 105, 106, 110, 111, 112, 113, 115, 116, 118, 121, 122, 123, 124

However: 3, 6, 8, 9, 10, 13, 14, 18, 30, 34, 35, 36, 37, 40, 42, 44, 50, 51, 55, 63, 64, 66, 67, 68, 70, 72, 74, 76, 77, 78, 81, 83, 84, 85, 86, 88, 90, 92
Howley: 38, 104
Hoynes: 34, 99
Hudson: 68, 104
Huntsberger: 39, 104

I
Igwebuike: 66, 89, 98
Image: 97, 101
　　Image Bite Politics: 97
In: 1, 2, 3, 4, 5, 6, 7, 8, 10, 11, 12, 13, 14, 15, 16, 17, 18, 19, 21, 23, 24, 25, 26, 27, 28, 29, 30, 31, 32, 33, 34, 35, 36, 37, 39, 40, 41, 42, 45, 47, 50, 51, 52, 53, 55, 56, 57, 58, 59, 60, 61, 62, 64, 65, 67, 68, 69, 70, 71, 72, 73, 74, 75, 77, 78, 80, 82, 84, 85, 87, 88, 89, 90, 91, 92, 93, 94, 95, 96, 97, 98, 99, 100, 101, 102, 103, 104, 105, 106, 107, 108, 109, 110, 111, 112, 113, 114, 115, 116, 117, 118, 120, 121, 122
　　In God We Trust: 72, 106
Inc: 36, 57, 88, 97, 98, 99, 100, 101, 103, 107, 108, 111, 113
Independent: 24, 28, 117, 121
Individuals: 7, 45, 47, 82, 90, 98
Influence: 12, 104, 106, 108, 115, 116
InfoWars: 42, 118, 120
　　InfoWars BBC World News Of: 118, 120
Information: 21, 30, 32, 73, 97, 98, 99, 101, 102, 103, 104, 105, 110, 113, 114, 115
Ingram: 5, 60, 104
Innes: 60, 89, 104
Innovation: 95, 101
Instagram: 33, 40, 41, 56, 118
Instead: 37, 90, 92
Institute: 33, 41, 42, 56, 59, 65, 95, 97, 104, 109
Interactions: 41, 104
Interestingly: 40, 41
International: 99, 102, 104, 105, 106, 107, 108, 109, 110, 111, 112, 113, 114, 115, 116
　　International Affairs: 104, 113

International Communication Association: 104, 106, 108, 111, 113
International Journal: 99, 102, 105, 109, 110, 112, 113, 114, 115, 116
Internet: 5, 7, 31, 42, 51, 91, 99, 110
Interstate: 18, 19, 80
Interviews: 96, 108, 122
Iowa: 64, 112
Iribarren: 54, 109
Iyengar: 7, 104, 115

J
JMM: 110
Jackson: 19, 99, 117
　　Jackson Women: 19, 99
Jacobs: 10, 104
Jain: 55, 104
Jan: 1, 4, 6, 9, 23, 39, 62, 96, 103, 104, 107, 109, 111, 112, 113, 116
Jangdal: 39, 104
January: 1, 4, 9, 62, 96, 103, 107, 112, 113
Jasper: 27, 34, 49, 51, 57, 76, 78, 79, 85
Jean: 13, 98, 110
　　Jean Carroll: 13, 98
Jenkins: 91, 104
Jill: 41, 121
　　Jill Stein: 41, 121
Jin: 5, 56, 71, 104
Jingnan: 5, 104
Joe: 5, 6, 9, 41, 121
　　Joe Biden: 5, 6, 9, 41, 121
John: 7, 8, 10, 17, 20, 38, 39, 62, 78, 79, 90, 98, 102, 104, 105, 111, 112, 113, 117, 120, 121
　　John Brown: 20, 111
　　John III: 38, 113
Johnson: 7, 10, 62, 90, 102, 104, 105, 112, 113, 117, 121
Jones: 5, 37, 53, 54, 94, 98, 104, 105
Joseph: 5, 55, 105
Journal: 40, 41, 43, 46, 60, 95, 96, 97, 98, 99, 100, 101, 102, 103, 104, 105, 106, 107, 108, 109, 110, 111, 112, 113, 114, 115, 116
　　Journal Of Broadcasting: 96, 98, 103, 104, 110, 116

Journal Of Communication: 96, 99, 101, 102, 103, 105, 109, 110, 111
Journal Of Computer: 98, 102
Journal Of Mass Media Ethics: 112, 115
Journal Of Media: 107
Journalism: 43, 95, 96, 97, 98, 100, 101, 102, 103, 104, 105, 106, 107, 108, 109, 110, 111, 112, 113, 114, 115, 116
    Journalism Practice: 95, 96, 97, 100, 101, 103, 107, 109, 112, 113, 114, 115
    Journalism Studies: 100, 103, 104, 106, 110, 114, 115
Journalists: 60, 100, 104, 105, 110, 111, 112
July: 4, 5, 17, 19, 64, 97, 99, 100, 102, 103, 104, 105, 106, 108, 109, 111, 113, 115
Junction: 45
    Junction City: 45
June: 19, 62, 64, 102, 113, 115
Jurkowitz: 43, 88, 105

K
Kaczynski: 89, 105
Kalogeropoulos: 47, 59, 90, 92, 105
Kamala: 3, 5, 46, 52, 116, 121
    Kamala Harris: 3, 5, 46, 52, 116, 121
Kansans: 17, 21, 22, 23, 24, 33, 34, 41, 46, 56, 59, 64, 65, 75, 82, 83, 84, 85, 90, 91, 94, 113
Kansas: 3, 4, 8, 17, 18, 19, 20, 21, 22, 23, 24, 25, 26, 27, 28, 29, 35, 37, 43, 45, 50, 51, 59, 61, 62, 64, 66, 67, 72, 75, 77, 80, 81, 87, 88, 89, 91, 92, 93, 95, 99, 100, 101, 102, 105, 106, 109, 110, 111, 112, 113, 114, 117, 121
    Kansas Department: 25, 105
    Kansas Farm Bureau: 22, 23, 105
    Kansas Reflector: 113
    Kansas Sampler Foundation: 23, 105
    Kansas Secretary: 24, 105
    Kansas State University: 23
    Kansas Supreme Court: 19, 75, 121
Karlsen: 45, 59, 105
Karlsson: 38, 105
Katz: 70, 91, 105
Kaveh: 44, 95
Kaye: 7, 62, 104

Keith: 12, 54, 67, 69, 83, 94, 101
Kennedy: 41, 78, 79, 120
Kent: 12, 27, 41, 42, 51, 52, 55, 58, 79, 80, 105, 115
Key: 71, 95, 105, 114
Kiesler: 71, 105
Kiger: 25, 105
Killenberg: 81, 105
Kim: 32, 56, 64, 71, 93, 104, 105, 106
Klaus: 46, 79
    Klaus Schwab: 46, 79
Klein: 31, 92, 105, 116
Kleinen: 31, 116
Klepper: 5, 105
Knobloch: 11, 41, 42, 83, 84, 85, 88, 105, 110
Koc: 60, 102
Kohring: 90, 116
Kolotouchkina: 77, 105
Konieczna: 92, 106
Kopytowska: 36, 106
Korhonen: 72, 106
Kron: 94, 106
Kruse: 73, 106
Ksiazek: 37, 106
Kubin: 86, 106
Kusisto: 20, 75, 106

L
LGBTQ: 64
LaRoche: 2, 107
Lamberth: 81, 106
Langbert: 13, 106
Laor: 86, 106
Latino: 117
Lavine: 2, 110
Law: 95, 101, 103, 116, 118
Lazarsfeld: 86, 106
Learning: 102, 105, 107, 116
Leary: 6, 106
Lee: 11, 45, 54, 60, 67, 72, 78, 88, 100, 106, 120
    Lee Harvey Oswald: 78, 120
Lennox: 103
Less: 12, 102, 117
Let: 49, 95
Leung: 82, 106

INDEX

Leupold: 12, 32, 39, 106
Levendusky: 100, 104
Lewandowsky: 84, 100, 106
Lewis: 3, 7, 11, 39, 92, 93, 96, 107, 109
Libertarian: 24, 25, 28, 117, 121
   Libertarian Party: 25, 117, 121
Liberty: 5, 64, 99
Life: 19, 102, 106, 108, 111
Like: 2, 7, 25, 33, 35, 43, 47, 51, 79, 81, 87, 101
Likewise: 2, 25, 33, 35, 43, 47, 51, 79, 81
Limbaugh: 8, 18, 53, 54, 101, 104
Lin: 10, 40, 67, 68, 94, 98, 107, 108, 113, 117, 118
Liu: 31, 107
Living: 101
Local: 38, 48, 69, 95, 98, 99, 100, 102, 104, 105, 109, 110, 113, 114, 115, 116, 118
   Local Media: 95, 109, 114
   Local News: 95, 98, 99, 109, 115
Locally: 48, 100
Lonsdorf: 6, 107
Lot: 109, 122
Loury: 67, 107
Lowrey: 4, 38, 83, 84, 93, 103, 107
Luckily: 45, 92
Luckmann: 82, 96
Lugo: 7, 54, 114
Lunz: 10, 107
   Lunz Trujillo: 10, 107
Luppicini: 71, 107
Luttrell: 106, 107, 115, 116
Lyons: 10, 107

M

MAGA: 72, 109
   MAGA Republicans: 72, 109
MFT: 4, 15, 56, 59, 84, 85, 90
MIT: 99, 103, 108
   MIT Press: 99, 103, 108
MSNBC: 8, 37, 50, 58, 91, 118, 120
MacKay: 2, 107
Macdonald: 36, 107
Maguire: 25, 107
Mahl: 89, 107
Mak: 6, 97, 99, 100, 103, 110, 113
Managi: 4, 83, 84, 95

Mansbridge: 96, 102, 103
Maras: 67, 68, 69, 107
March: 19, 23, 99, 104
Maresh: 60, 107
Marine: 9, 20
Marjorie: 72, 102
   Marjorie Taylor Greene: 72, 102
Markel: 72, 115
Martin: 98
Marvin: 27, 32, 33, 42, 50, 55, 58, 61, 78, 83
Marx: 7, 112
Mason: 71, 111
Mass: 95, 96, 97, 98, 104, 105, 106, 107, 108, 109, 110, 111, 112, 113, 115, 116
   Mass Communication: 96, 97, 98, 104, 105, 106, 107, 108, 109, 110, 111, 113, 115
   Mass Communication Educator: 96, 105, 106, 115
   Mass Communication Quarterly: 96, 97, 106, 110, 111, 115
Matei: 68, 81, 108
Matsa: 30, 36, 108
Matter: 20, 95, 96, 97, 101, 116
Matthews: 90, 108
Maude: 28, 42, 48, 55, 57, 61, 66, 79
May: 7, 17, 61, 79, 98, 99, 101, 102, 119
Maybe: 7, 17, 61, 79, 102, 119
McCarthy: 5, 111
McCauley: 2, 108
McCombs: 12, 108
McLeod: 31, 39, 107, 108
McLuhan: 30, 108
McQuail: 70, 71, 86, 108
Measuring: 101, 108, 109
Media: 1, 6, 7, 9, 29, 33, 41, 43, 51, 56, 59, 62, 65, 70, 71, 74, 85, 86, 87, 88, 90, 92, 95, 96, 97, 98, 99, 100, 101, 102, 103, 104, 105, 106, 107, 108, 109, 110, 111, 112, 113, 114, 115, 116, 118
   Media Effects: 85, 101, 104, 112
   Media Institute: 33, 41, 56, 59, 65
   Media Literacy: 101, 108, 111, 113
   Media Literacy Education: 101, 108
   Media Management: 110
Mediated: 71, 98, 102

INDEX

Mediated Communication: 71, 98, 102
Meer: 41, 42, 85, 88, 103
Meet: 22, 95, 104, 105, 109
Megerian: 46, 108
Melotte: 64, 108
Meltwater: 22, 33, 41, 56, 59, 65
Mental: 104, 110
    Mental Health: 104, 110
Merritt: 93, 108
Mertens: 29, 108
Mettler: 10, 97, 108
Meyer: 93, 108
Michael: 53, 54, 70, 113
    Michael Savage: 53, 54, 113
Michalska: 60, 102
Michel: 45, 108
Midwest: 8, 9, 10, 11, 17, 22, 71
Midwesterners: 10, 22
Mike: 5, 42, 121
    Mike Pence: 121
Miller: 5, 12, 96, 108, 115
Mind: 53, 77, 95, 121
Minutes: 56, 105
Misinformation: 4, 6, 8, 15, 16, 51, 52, 54, 55, 56, 59, 77, 82, 83, 84, 85, 86, 87, 88, 90, 96, 104, 106, 110, 115, 116
    Misinformation Finds Them: 4, 15, 56, 59, 82, 83, 84, 85, 88, 90
Missouri: 18, 64
Mitchell: 102, 105, 117
Moe: 28, 50, 58, 74, 76, 101
Monroe: 28, 37, 42, 43, 74, 76, 77
Montgomery: 28, 34, 42, 61, 65, 90, 117
Moreover: 65, 70
Morgan: 12, 85, 101, 108
Morphew: 25, 108
Mosharafa: 44, 85, 108
Moskalenko: 2, 108
Mou: 67, 94, 108, 109
Moyer: 93, 108
Muirhead: 89, 109
Munis: 10, 104, 109
Murphy: 28, 47, 48, 50, 57, 61, 74, 80, 90
Muscat: 12, 109
Mutz: 67, 109
Mwangi: 97, 112

Mwesige: 54, 109

N

NBC: 8, 34, 37, 50, 58, 91, 112, 118, 120
NFM: 4, 31, 83, 84
NORC: 72, 113
    NORC Center: 72, 113
NORDICOM: 104, 105, 109
    NORDICOM Review: 104, 105, 109
NPR: 6, 9, 34, 35, 40, 41, 46, 48, 96, 99, 100, 101, 104, 107, 109
    NPR Staff: 9, 109
Naseer: 30, 36, 108
National: 4, 5, 6, 11, 13, 29, 34, 62, 72, 73, 97, 99, 102, 104, 106, 109, 112, 115, 116, 118
    National Association: 13, 106
    National Press Office: 4, 109
Nechushtai: 7, 11, 109, 115
Ned: 28, 47, 51, 55, 75, 76, 86, 88
Nelson: 28, 57, 61, 66, 80, 96
Nemerever: 21, 109
Neumann: 14, 77, 109
Nevzat: 56, 109
New: 4, 5, 7, 29, 30, 31, 32, 33, 35, 37, 40, 41, 42, 43, 45, 46, 47, 48, 50, 52, 58, 72, 82, 83, 88, 89, 91, 95, 96, 97, 98, 99, 100, 101, 102, 103, 104, 105, 106, 107, 108, 109, 110, 111, 112, 113, 114, 115, 116, 118, 120
    New Media: 106, 107, 112, 116
    New York Times: 32, 33, 43, 48, 101, 103, 113
Newman: 30, 31, 48, 102, 109
News: 4, 5, 7, 29, 30, 31, 35, 37, 40, 41, 42, 45, 46, 47, 48, 50, 52, 58, 82, 83, 88, 89, 91, 95, 96, 97, 98, 99, 100, 101, 102, 103, 104, 105, 106, 107, 108, 109, 110, 111, 112, 113, 114, 115, 116, 118, 120
    News Deserts: 89, 97, 98
    News Finds Me: 4, 83, 102, 113
    News Media: 97, 98, 105, 111, 115
Newsmax: 5, 37, 41, 58, 118, 120
Newspaper: 98, 99, 100, 101, 103, 109, 111, 112, 114, 118
    Newspaper Research Journal: 98, 100, 101, 103, 111, 112, 114
Newsy: 37, 50, 118, 120

Niekamp: 36, 109
Nielsen: 52, 91, 104, 109, 114
Noelle: 14, 77, 109
Non: 41, 107, 116, 117, 118, 119, 120, 121, 122
None: 41, 118, 119, 120, 121, 122
    None On: 119, 121, 122
Norander: 25, 109
Noriega: 54, 109
Norris: 106, 109
North: 3, 9, 11, 64, 108
    North Carolina: 3, 64, 108
Northeast: 9, 11
Not: 5, 18, 53, 86, 102, 107, 108, 110, 117, 118, 120, 121
    Not At All: 121
November: 12, 108, 113, 114
Now: 7, 25, 86, 91, 105, 106, 109, 115
Nowak: 91, 105
Nowell: 25, 109
Numerous: 13, 29
Nygren: 32, 39, 93, 109

O
OANN: 50, 118, 120
Oath: 9, 116
    Oath Keepers: 9, 116
Ochs: 9
October: 105, 116
Ohio: 5, 9, 52, 98
Oklahoma: 45, 108
    Oklahoma City: 45, 108
Ollstein: 20, 75, 109
Olmstead: 73, 109
Olmsted: 5, 109
Olsen: 29, 109
Olson: 36, 110
Olsson: 36, 95
One: 6, 7, 8, 10, 16, 18, 22, 41, 50, 53, 57, 58, 60, 85, 87, 90, 109, 118, 120
    One America News: 41, 50, 58, 118, 120
Only: 35, 37, 64, 78, 121
Origin: 102, 104, 111, 112, 116
Origins: 104, 112, 116
Others: 5, 47, 53
Our: 55, 70, 80, 99, 100, 105, 111
Outrage: 112, 113, 116

Outside: 22, 58, 68, 78
Overall: 40, 50
Oxford: 95, 96, 97, 100, 102, 103, 106, 113, 115, 116
    Oxford University Press: 95, 96, 97, 100, 102, 103, 106, 113, 115, 116

P
Padgett: 7, 9, 110
Palinkas: 25, 110
Pang: 29, 110, 112
Pariser: 84, 110
Park: 2, 4, 59, 90, 100, 101, 110
Parker: 2, 110
Part: 8, 21, 24, 25, 26, 28, 29, 46, 57, 71, 72, 75, 95, 96, 99, 100, 101, 102, 104, 107, 110, 114, 115, 116, 117, 121
Pass: 82, 110
Pathways: 30, 82, 98, 107, 113
Patty: 28, 37, 51, 66, 78, 87, 88
Paulussen: 92, 97
Pauly: 38, 110
Pearson: 11, 41, 42, 83, 84, 85, 88, 110, 112
Penguin: 96, 108, 110
Pennsylvania: 4, 5, 95, 103
Perception: 31, 83, 95, 96, 98, 99, 100, 102, 113
Perhaps: 7, 17, 29, 44
Perks: 87, 110
Perreault: 38, 110
Perry: 73, 99, 102, 116
Personal: 70, 86, 96, 118
    Personal Identity: 70, 86
    Personal Relationships: 70, 86
Perspectives: 97, 101, 103
Peters: 10, 18, 36, 110, 116
Peterson: 36, 110
Pew: 9, 15, 21, 31, 36, 99, 102, 105, 108, 110, 111, 112, 113
    Pew Research Center: 9, 15, 21, 31, 36, 99, 102, 105, 108, 110, 111, 112, 113
Phelps: 20, 97, 113
Pipal: 7, 110
Place: 103, 104, 107, 109, 114
Plandemic: 89, 101
Please: 123

Plessy: 20, 111
Podcasts: 43, 87, 110
Polarization: 6, 59, 60, 87, 99, 104, 107, 112
Political: 9, 12, 26, 27, 28, 29, 33, 62, 71, 76, 87, 88, 95, 96, 98, 99, 101, 103, 104, 105, 106, 107, 108, 109, 110, 111, 112, 113, 115, 116, 118
  Political Behavior: 107, 109
  Political Communication: 99, 101, 104, 106, 113, 116
  Political Geography: 107, 112
  Political Science: 95, 101, 104, 107, 109
  Political Talk Radio: 96, 99, 104, 106
Politically: 26, 27, 28, 107
Politico: 5, 100, 109, 111, 115
Politics: 57, 76, 80, 96, 97, 98, 99, 100, 102, 103, 104, 106, 107, 108, 109, 110, 111, 113, 115, 116
Ponder: 82, 111
Post: 20, 43, 48, 95, 98, 102, 103, 110, 111, 118
Poth: 25, 99
Potter: 81, 90, 111
Poynter: 102, 113
Practical: 97, 107
  Practical Guide: 97
Practice: 95, 96, 97, 100, 101, 103, 105, 107, 109, 112, 113, 114, 115
President: 2, 4, 5, 6, 7, 9, 10, 13, 23, 34, 46, 52, 53, 60, 78, 79, 95, 106, 109, 112, 120, 121
  President Biden: 5, 46
  President Donald Trump: 2, 10, 13, 52, 53, 109
  President Joe Biden: 5, 6, 9
  President John: 78, 79, 120
  President Trump: 2, 4, 5, 6, 7, 9
Presidential: 53, 60, 95, 106, 112, 121
  Presidential Election: 121
Press: 4, 72, 95, 96, 97, 98, 99, 100, 101, 102, 103, 104, 105, 106, 107, 108, 109, 110, 112, 113, 114, 115, 116
Princeton: 96, 109, 110, 116
  Princeton University Press: 96, 109, 110, 116
Prochazka: 46, 111

Professors: 14
Protestants: 72
Public: 8, 9, 64, 72, 93, 95, 96, 97, 98, 99, 100, 101, 102, 103, 104, 105, 106, 107, 108, 109, 111, 113, 114, 115
  Public Affairs: 72, 96, 97, 106, 113
  Public Affairs Research: 72, 113
  Public Opinion Quarterly: 100, 101, 105, 108, 115
  Public Sphere: 99, 101, 103, 104, 106
Put: 4, 12, 45, 66, 67, 68, 69, 71, 72, 81, 83, 84, 85, 92, 94, 104, 111, 112, 114
Putnam: 4, 12, 45, 66, 67, 68, 69, 71, 83, 84, 85, 94, 111, 112
Putting: 92, 104, 114

Q

Qualitative: 97, 99, 108, 109, 110
Quarterly: 95, 96, 97, 100, 101, 104, 105, 106, 107, 108, 110, 111, 115, 116, 118
  Quarterly Journal: 95, 101
Quimby: 29, 47, 50, 51, 55, 78, 81

R

RFD: 38, 50, 111, 118, 120
RFDTV: 38, 111
Race: 98, 117
Radicalism: 1, 2, 64, 97, 108
Radicalization: 1, 96, 101
Radio: 34, 35, 52, 53, 96, 98, 99, 104, 106, 109, 112, 113, 115, 118
Rage: 112, 116
Ramirez: 5, 111
Rather: 31, 36, 72, 82, 88, 92
Reactionary: 98, 103, 107, 110
  Reactionary Politics: 98, 103, 107, 110
Reader: 107, 108, 114
Reagan: 37, 53
Reber: 45, 111
Reciprocity: 96, 103
Recuero: 60, 111
Red: 9, 112, 115, 116, 118
Reflections: 103, 108
Regardless: 5, 7, 12, 18, 38, 48, 53, 66, 77, 86, 89, 92, 118
Reid: 4, 111

Reitz: 20, 97
Relatedly: 24, 37, 40, 58, 75
Religion: 29, 89, 95, 99, 113, 116
Rep: 4, 5, 6, 8, 9, 10, 11, 15, 18, 21, 24, 25, 26, 27, 28, 29, 52, 53, 56, 65, 72, 75, 89, 95, 97, 98, 102, 105, 106, 107, 109, 110, 111, 113, 115, 117, 121
Report: 95, 97, 102, 107, 109, 110, 113, 115
Reporting: 97, 102, 110
Republican: 4, 6, 8, 9, 10, 11, 15, 18, 21, 24, 25, 26, 27, 28, 29, 52, 53, 56, 65, 72, 75, 89, 98, 102, 105, 106, 107, 109, 111, 113, 117, 121
  Republican Party: 24, 26, 72, 75, 117, 121
Republicans: 6, 8, 9, 10, 11, 15, 25, 26, 27, 28, 56, 72, 102, 105, 106, 109, 111, 113
Respondents: 24, 50, 83
Retrieved: 98, 100, 101, 105, 106, 110, 114
Reuters: 40, 97, 109, 111
  Reuters Institute Digital News Report: 109
Review: 24, 97, 100, 102, 103, 104, 105, 107, 109, 110, 113
Reviving: 100, 109
Rhetoric: 97, 106, 108
Richards: 94, 111
Ridder: 8, 55, 99
Right: 95, 99, 100, 103, 112
Rivard: 5, 100
Roadside: 18, 80, 88
  Roadside Sign: 18, 80, 88
Robinson: 25, 81, 92, 106, 111
Rock: 19, 112, 121
  Rock City: 19, 112
Roe: 19, 113
Rogers: 21, 109, 112
Rokeach: 32, 93, 105
Romiszowski: 71, 111
Roosevelt: 34
Rosenberger: 85, 98
Rosenblum: 89, 109
Ross: 89, 111
Rotolo: 72, 111, 113
Routledge: 97, 98, 100, 102, 106, 108, 111, 112, 115, 116
Rowe: 38, 105
Rubin: 6, 44, 103, 111
Ruggiero: 71, 111

Rule: 103
Rural: 1, 4, 9, 17, 21, 22, 29, 43, 97, 98, 99, 100, 101, 102, 103, 104, 107, 108, 109, 111, 112, 114
Rush: 8, 18, 53, 99, 101, 115, 117
  Rush Limbaugh: 8, 18, 53, 101
Ryder: 45

S
SAGE: 97, 99, 102, 103, 107, 108, 111
  SAGE Publications: 97, 99, 102, 103, 107, 108, 111
STN: 32, 93
Salahuddin: 36, 110
Salina: 18, 19, 35
Sarah: 29, 33, 47, 48, 50, 55, 74, 87
Sargent: 82, 111
Sass: 69, 112
Scala: 10, 104, 112
Schaller: 30, 45, 73, 112
Schermele: 64, 112
Schiffman: 38, 112
Schmid: 2, 100, 112
Schoewe: 19, 112
Scholars: 13, 106, 107
Scholz: 21, 104
Schuster: 111
Schwartz: 35, 112
Schwarz: 102, 106
Schweiger: 46, 111
Science: 95, 98, 101, 102, 104, 105, 107, 108, 109, 112
Sean: 8, 53
  Sean Hannity: 8, 53
Searles: 30, 112
Secret: 4, 24, 105
  Secret Service: 4
Selective: 85, 110, 111, 115
  Selective Exposure: 85, 110, 115
Self: 85, 103, 117
Seltzer: 83, 116
Sen: 5, 97, 115
Sept: 6, 44, 52, 69, 79, 95, 98, 99, 103, 109, 115, 116
September: 44, 52, 69, 79, 95, 98, 99, 103, 109, 115, 116

INDEX

Serving: 11, 45
Seven: 24, 66, 78
Several: 40, 42, 58, 77, 88, 90
Severin: 70, 112
Shaw: 12, 108, 117
She: 3, 27, 28, 29, 30, 31, 36, 39, 48, 51, 55, 61, 70, 76, 78, 79, 85, 91, 100, 101, 104, 105, 108, 110, 112, 117
Shearer: 30, 31, 36, 105, 112
Sherri: 29, 39, 51, 55, 61, 76, 78, 79, 85, 91
Sherry: 70, 112
Shoemaker: 12, 112
Shrader: 54, 56, 62, 87, 112
Shrum: 56, 112
Sienkiewicz: 7, 112
Signorielli: 101, 108
Siisiainen: 12, 112
Sikorski: 86, 106
Similarly: 23, 25, 29, 30, 31, 33, 34, 37, 41, 42, 46, 49, 61, 64, 65, 77, 79, 86, 87, 89
Simmons: 13, 102
Simon: 111
Skoric: 12, 112
Small: 22, 112, 116
Smethers: 29, 32, 92, 93, 94, 97, 112
Smith: 10, 19, 20, 30, 38, 72, 75, 103, 111, 112, 113, 114, 117
Snapchat: 40, 118
Snyder: 20, 97, 113
Sobieraj: 8, 54, 62, 113
Social: 8, 33, 41, 45, 56, 59, 60, 65, 67, 68, 92, 94, 95, 96, 98, 99, 100, 101, 102, 103, 104, 105, 106, 107, 108, 110, 111, 112, 113, 116, 118
   Social Capital: 98, 99, 101, 104, 106, 107, 111, 116
   Social Media: 33, 41, 56, 59, 65, 95, 96, 99, 100, 102, 105, 106, 107, 110, 111, 112, 113, 118
   Social Media Mentions: 33, 41, 56, 59, 65
   Social Science: 108, 112
Society: 45, 82, 95, 96, 99, 100, 102, 103, 104, 106, 107, 108, 110, 111, 112, 113, 115, 116
Sociology: 99, 101, 108, 114
Solvoll: 29, 109
Sometimes: 7, 50, 52, 101, 118

Song: 31, 82, 110, 113
Source: 18, 19, 33, 41, 53, 56, 59, 65, 80, 88, 104, 105, 107
South: 6, 9, 10, 11, 104, 109, 113
Specifically: 25, 33, 37, 70
Springfield: 52, 115
Stamps: 57, 113
Stanford: 89, 113
State: 3, 6, 8, 10, 11, 12, 18, 19, 20, 21, 23, 24, 30, 31, 44, 45, 48, 53, 60, 61, 72, 74, 75, 86, 90, 95, 98, 99, 100, 101, 103, 104, 105, 107, 108, 113, 114, 115, 116, 118, 120
   State Library: 18, 113
Statistics: 105, 114, 116
   Statistics Administration: 114
   Statistics Administration Retrieved: 114
Stephens: 30, 113
Sterling: 23, 64, 95
   Sterling College: 23
Stiegler: 54, 113
Stites: 91, 113
Strategic: 42, 104, 110, 116
   Strategic Dialogue: 42, 104
Strategies: 99, 101
Strongly: 120
   Strongly Agree: 120
   Strongly Agree Using: 120
   Strongly Disagree: 120
   Strongly Disagree Using: 120
Stryker: 56, 98
Studies: 39, 95, 96, 98, 100, 103, 104, 106, 107, 108, 109, 110, 114, 115, 116
Suiter: 100, 105
Sullivan: 34, 91, 113
Sunday: 35, 100, 114
Supreme: 8, 19, 20, 75, 97, 121
   Supreme Court: 8, 19, 20, 75, 97, 121
Surveillance: 70, 86
Survey: 18, 22, 50, 101, 103, 114, 116
Sustainability: 95
Swart: 45, 59, 90, 113
Swenson: 5, 105

T

TV: 8, 37, 38, 44, 50, 51, 57, 58, 110, 111, 118, 120

INDEX

TV CNBC Bloomberg Television Newsy Fox Business Network One America News Network: 118, 120
Take: 18, 19, 54
Talisse: 81, 113
Talk: 42, 52, 96, 99, 101, 104, 106, 109, 112, 113, 115
    Talk Radio: 96, 99, 104, 106, 109, 112, 113, 115
Tankard: 70, 112
Teaching: 107, 111
Television: 36, 37, 86, 96, 99, 100, 101, 102, 103, 106, 107, 110, 116, 118, 120
    Television News: 96, 99, 103, 106, 110, 116, 118, 120
Terrorism: 97, 101, 103, 108
Terry: 25, 113
Thank: 20, 30, 37, 62, 97
    Thank God: 20, 97
Thanks: 30, 37, 62
The: 1, 2, 3, 4, 6, 7, 8, 9, 10, 11, 12, 13, 14, 15, 16, 17, 18, 19, 20, 21, 22, 23, 24, 25, 26, 27, 28, 29, 30, 31, 32, 33, 34, 35, 36, 37, 38, 39, 40, 41, 42, 43, 44, 45, 46, 48, 49, 50, 51, 52, 53, 54, 56, 57, 58, 59, 60, 61, 62, 63, 64, 65, 68, 69, 70, 71, 72, 73, 74, 75, 76, 77, 78, 80, 81, 82, 83, 84, 85, 86, 87, 88, 89, 90, 91, 92, 93, 94, 95, 96, 97, 98, 99, 100, 101, 102, 103, 104, 105, 106, 107, 108, 109, 110, 111, 112, 113, 114, 115, 116, 119, 120, 121
    The ANNALS: 108, 112
    The Associated Press: 72, 113, 116
    The Conversation: 96, 99, 113
    The Divided Dial: 87, 114
    The Effects: 106, 116
    The Forum: 97, 104
    The International Journal: 110, 113
    The New York Times: 32, 33, 101, 103, 113
    The Oxford Handbook: 96, 102, 103, 106
    The Pew Charitable Trusts: 110
    The Role: 104, 113
    The State: 95, 103
    The Wall Street Journal: 40, 106
    The Washington Post: 102, 103

Their: 13, 50, 69, 82, 96, 107
Them: 4, 15, 19, 25, 56, 59, 82, 83, 84, 85, 88, 90, 95, 97, 99, 105, 107, 108, 109, 111, 114, 121
Thematic: 25, 97, 105, 107, 108, 109
    Thematic Analysis: 97, 107, 108, 109
Theory: 31, 44, 56, 70, 86, 93, 95, 96, 98, 100, 105, 107, 108, 109, 111, 112, 114, 115, 116
Therefore: 4, 11, 20, 21, 30, 31, 39, 43, 57, 59, 69, 80, 87, 88, 92, 94
They: 6, 8, 11, 15, 24, 25, 26, 31, 37, 50, 51, 52, 53, 56, 58, 61, 62, 63, 73, 76, 82, 88, 89, 99, 107, 110, 120
Thomas: 4, 8, 60, 100, 117
Thompson: 12, 73, 103, 114
Thomson: 86, 114
Thornton: 87, 114
Though: 2, 4, 6, 17, 32, 33, 35, 43, 51, 62, 70, 71, 74, 89, 92, 106
Threat: 97, 100, 102, 110, 112
Three: 74, 103
Through: 2, 10, 11, 25, 45, 53, 54, 73, 83, 91, 105, 113, 114
Thus: 1, 89
Tim: 5, 32, 33, 41, 43, 45, 48, 77, 98, 101, 103, 108, 113, 116, 117, 119, 121
    Tim Walz: 5, 77, 116
Time: 32, 33, 41, 43, 48, 98, 101, 103, 113, 116, 117, 119, 121
    Time Employment: 117
Timothy: 45, 108
    Timothy McVeigh: 45, 108
Toff: 31, 82, 114
Too: 74, 93
Topeka: 20, 48, 95, 97
Tornoe: 31, 114
Torres: 7, 54, 111, 114
Total: 33, 41, 56, 59, 65, 114
    Total Social Media Mentions: 41, 56, 59, 65
Toward: 41, 96, 97, 107
Towers: 70, 114
Trump: 2, 3, 4, 5, 6, 7, 8, 9, 10, 12, 13, 15, 16, 18, 19, 21, 33, 41, 46, 52, 53, 60, 65, 72, 80, 96, 97, 98, 99, 100, 102, 103, 104, 105, 106, 107, 108, 109, 111, 115, 120, 121

201

Trust: 32, 59, 72, 99, 100, 101, 104, 105, 106, 109, 110, 111, 113, 114, 115
Tully: 85, 115
Turkle: 69, 73, 114
Turner: 87, 103, 110
Tweet: 87
Twenty: 101, 104
Twitter: 5, 22, 40, 52, 97, 107, 111, 114, 118
Two: 5, 42, 112, 117

U

USDA: 52, 114
Ullah: 87, 114
Understanding: 11, 17, 21, 98, 103, 104, 106, 108, 109, 111, 116
Undoubtedly: 21, 52, 72
Unemployed: 117
Unfortunately: 64, 69, 74, 90
Union: 30, 53, 100, 114
United: 3, 6, 8, 10, 11, 12, 18, 19, 20, 30, 31, 44, 60, 61, 72, 74, 75, 86, 98, 101, 104, 105, 107, 114, 116, 120
    United States: 3, 6, 8, 10, 11, 12, 18, 19, 20, 30, 31, 44, 60, 61, 72, 74, 75, 86, 98, 101, 104, 105, 107, 114, 116, 120
Universities: 14, 15
University: 13, 23, 95, 96, 97, 98, 99, 100, 102, 103, 104, 106, 107, 109, 110, 112, 113, 114, 115, 116
Urban: 97, 104, 107, 108, 112, 114
    Urban Continuum: 104, 112
Use: 31, 70, 86, 99, 101, 102, 104, 106, 108, 110, 111, 113, 114, 115
Uses: 70, 86, 108, 110, 111, 114, 115
Usher: 11, 32, 47, 90, 91, 93, 114
Using: 9, 32, 56, 65, 68, 82, 96, 97, 111, 120
Usually: 39, 77
Utych: 10, 107

V

Valkenburg: 70, 114
Value: 19, 109, 114, 121
    Value Them Both: 19, 114, 121
Van: 5, 71, 99, 115
    Van Ingen: 71, 99
Varpio: 25, 105

Vaughn: 34, 35, 37, 53, 54, 114
Vice: 5, 23, 52
    Vice President Kamala Harris: 5, 52
Views: 62, 99, 110
Vincent: 54, 60, 86, 115
Visual: 97, 114
    Visual Framing: 97
Vivian: 15, 115
Vogts: 1, 18, 19, 80, 81, 88, 115
Vos: 110, 112
Vote: 18, 19, 101, 104, 112, 116
    Vote No: 19
    Vote Trump: 18
    Vote Yes: 19
Vox: 96, 98, 99
Vraga: 85, 100, 115

W

WBC: 20
WNYC: 114
    WNYC Studios: 114
Waldman: 30, 45, 73, 112
Walker: 59, 72, 98, 102, 105, 115, 121
Wall: 40, 41, 46, 106, 117
    Wall Street Journal: 40, 41, 46, 106
War: 20, 34, 35, 42, 55, 96, 102, 103, 104, 111, 112, 118, 120
Warren: 96, 102, 103
Watson: 5, 115
Waymer: 83, 103
Weaver: 41, 42, 53, 54, 70, 85, 115
Webster: 13, 95
Wei: 56, 70, 85, 86, 115
Weinger: 56, 115
Weiss: 85, 115
Weiyan: 86, 115
Welch: 23, 115
Well: 42, 43, 76, 78, 79, 99, 103, 104, 111, 112
Wendling: 52, 115
Wenzel: 18, 90, 91, 93, 115
West: 9, 11, 20, 29, 41, 42, 72, 83, 84, 85, 88, 97, 104, 105, 110, 115
Westboro: 20, 97
    Westboro Baptist Church: 20, 97
Western: 97, 110
    Western Journal: 97, 110

Westerwick: 11, 41, 42, 83, 84, 85, 88, 105, 110
Westlund: 29, 115
Westwood: 72, 104, 115
What: 1, 18, 20, 30, 51, 61, 93, 95, 96, 97, 99, 101, 104, 107, 109, 110, 113, 116, 117, 118, 120, 122, 123
White: 6, 7, 20, 24, 45, 61, 72, 73, 83, 97, 102, 109, 112, 115, 116, 117
    White Christian: 61, 73, 97, 102
    White Christian Nationalism: 73, 97, 102
Whitehead: 72, 73, 116
Whitehurst: 6, 116
Whitmore: 71, 82, 86, 103
Whitney: 12, 116
Who: 97, 100, 103, 107, 112, 121, 123
Why: 97, 98, 99, 103, 107, 108, 110, 114, 123
Wichita: 18, 35, 37, 93, 117
    Wichita Eagle: 93
Wieland: 31, 116
Wimmer: 22, 116
Within: 6, 31, 71, 101
Without: 5, 47, 52, 68, 73, 83
Woolley: 9, 18, 116
World: 33, 34, 35, 37, 50, 55, 58, 79, 104, 112, 118, 120
    World War II: 35, 55, 104

Worlds: 34, 112
Wuthnow: 11, 18, 21, 26, 64, 66, 71, 72, 75, 77, 116

X
Xiao: 86, 106, 107, 115, 116

Y
Yahoo: 40, 42
Yamamoto: 37, 116
Yang: 67, 71, 94, 114, 116
Yanich: 86, 88, 90, 116
Yeah: 57, 88
Yes: 19, 66, 77, 100, 108, 118, 119, 121, 122
    Yes No Maybe: 119
Yet: 9, 10, 37, 39, 41, 67
Yilek: 5, 116
You: 1, 37, 40, 51, 52, 53, 54, 62, 80, 87, 88, 98, 99, 100, 103, 104, 107, 110, 111, 113, 116, 118
YouTube: 40, 52, 107, 118
Young: 37, 53, 54, 62, 87, 100, 113, 116
    Young People: 100, 113

Z
Zhang: 83, 116
Zimmermann: 90, 116

General Editors
Mitchell S. McKinney and Mary E. Stuckey

At the heart of how citizens, governments, and the media interact is the communication process, a process that is undergoing tremendous changes as we embrace a new millennium. Never has there been a time when confronting the complexity of these evolving relationships been so important to the maintenance of civil society. This series seeks books that advance the understanding of this process from multiple perspectives and as it occurs in both institutionalized and non-institutionalized political settings. While works that provide new perspectives on traditional political communication questions are welcome, the series also encourages the submission of manuscripts that take an innovative approach to political communication, which seek to broaden the frontiers of study to incorporate critical and cultural dimensions of study as well as scientific and theoretical frontiers.

For more information or to submit material for consideration, contact:

    editorial@peterlang.com

To order other books in this series, please contact our Customer Service Department:

    peterlang@presswarehouse.com (within the U.S.)
    orders@peterlang.com (outside the U.S.)

Or browse online by series:

    WWW.PETERLANG.COM

www.ingramcontent.com/pod-product-compliance
Lightning Source LLC
Chambersburg PA
CBHW052020290426
44112CB00014B/2314